THE SHAAR PRESS

THE JUDAICA IMPRINT
FOR THOUGHTFUL PEOPLE

*A psychiatrist finds
a wealth of ideas
in the weekly
Torah reading*

THE
SHAAR
PRESS

Windows to the Soul

to the

Soul

בראשית – שמות
GENESIS – EXODUS

Rabbi Michael
Bernstein, M.D.

Published by **SHAAR PRESS**
Distributed by MESORAH PUBLICATIONS, LTD.
4401 Second Avenue / Brooklyn, N.Y 11232 / (718) 921-9000

Distributed in Israel by SIFRIATI / A. GITLER
10 Hashomer Street / Bnei Brak 51361

Distributed in Europe by LEHMANNS
Unit E, Viking Industrial Park, Rolling Mill Road / Jarrow, Tyne and Wear, NE32 3DP/ England

Distributed in Australia and New Zealand by GOLDS WORLD OF JUDAICA
3-13 William Street / Balaclava, Melbourne 3183 / Victoria Australia

Distributed in South Africa by KOLLEL BOOKSHOP
Shop 8A Norwood Hypermarket / Norwood 2196, Johannesburg, South Africa

ISBN: 1-57819-473-3 Hard Cover
ISBN: 1-57819-474-1 Paperback

Printed in the United States of America by Noble Book Press
Custom bound by Sefercraft, Inc. / 4401 Second Avenue / Brooklyn N.Y. 11232

This book is dedicated to the memory of my grandparents,

Morris and Dorothy Bernstein

and

Isadore and Eva Nash

Through their children they guided and inspired me.

For this I will be forever grateful.

.ת.נ.צ.ב.ה

Rabbi CHAIM P. SCHEINBERG

Rosh Hayeshiva "TORAH ORE"

and Morah Hora'ah of Kiryat Mattersdorf

הרב חיים פינחס שיינברג

ראש ישיבת "תורה אור"

ומורה הוראה דקרית מטרסדורף

<u>מכתב ברכה</u>

י"ח אייר, תש"ס

הנה שלחו לפני את ספרו של הר"ר מיכאל ברנשטיין נ"י רופא
מומחה בפסיכיאטריה. מחמת טרדותי הרבות ומאפס הפנאי
לא יכולת לעיין בדבריו, אבל נמסר לי על ידי אחד מתלמידי
החשובים שליט"א על גודל מסירותו של המחבר ללימוד
ושקידת התורה. וגם שמעתי שרבנים חשובים שליט"א שיבחו
את הספר שניכר מתוך דבריו גודל יגיעו ועמלו בהכנת
המקרא. על כן אמרתי, אף שאינני נותן הסכמות על ספרים
מטעמים כמוסים עימדי, מ"מ הנני מברכו שיהיה ספרו
לתועלת הרבים לקרבם לתורה ולתעודה, ובפרט לאחינו
שעודם רחוקים מדרך התורה, ויזכה המחבר להמשיך
להגדיל תורה ולהאדירה מתוך מנוחת הנפש והרחבת הדעת.

הכותב וחותם לכבוד התורה ולומדיה
חיים פנחס שיינברג

בס"ד

כבוד הרב המאור הגדול ר' מיכאל דר. ברגער שליט"א

I have perused many chapters of your sefer
and was impressed by its depth and originality
as well as the clarity with which your ideas
are presented.

Fortunate is the one who uses his innate and
developed talents in the service of G-d. You,
indeed, have the great merit of disseminating
Torah thoughts by using your originality and
your psychological perception to plumb the
depths of the Torah.

מבריך ומוקירו חותמך

דוד קאהן
רב דבית מדרש גבול יעבץ
כן תחיו הדבק

RABBI ZEV LEFF
Rav of Moshav Matityahu
Rosh Hayeshiva
Yeshiva Gedola Matisyahu
D.N. Modiin 71917 Israel
08-976-1138 Fax 08-916-5326

הרב זאב לף
מרא דאתרא מושב מתתיהו
ראש הישיבה ישיבה גדולה מתתיהו
ד.נ. מודיעין 71917
טל 1138-976-08 פקס. 5326 03976-08

Tammuz 29,5760

I have had the pleasure to read a portion of the manuscript of "Windows to the Soul" by Dr. Michael Bernstein נ"י. I found the material presented refreshing and interesting, informative, thought provoking, and inspiring.

Dr. Bernstein presents many new ideas in explaining various Torah topics, and although innovative I have found them to be well rooted in Torah sources and reflecting a true Torah perspective. I have found many lessons in Torah practice and thought that can be culled from these Divrei Torah. Additionally the author's professional experience as a child psychologist is woven into the Torah insights that truly present windows to the soul.

Although I had the opportunity to see the material only on Sefer Bereshis in its entirety and portions of Sefer Shmos, I am confident based on the integrity of the author and the solid consistency of the Divrei Torah I read ,that all the Sedras are dealt with in a like manner.

I highly recommend this Sefer as a source of serious Torah learning and as a resource for family discussion to enhance the Shabbos table,להגדיל תורה ולהאדירה

With Torah blessings,

[signature]

Rabbi Zev Leff
Moshav Matityahu

≈ *Table of Contents*

The Book of Genesis / Bereishis

Kingship / Ruth Fulfills the Promise / The Testimony of Seven Sheep / Plotting the Course of Life / After These Things / The Mountain of Oneness / The Providential Horn

Introduction

AUTHORSHIP IS AN OCCASION FOR SERIOUS INTROSPECTION and soul-searching. I offer up this humble book with trepidation and without illusions, fully aware that countless more learned Jews have, for whatever reason, not published; who then am I to tread where my superiors in learning and virtue have not? Nonetheless, I believe that in my own modest way I have something of value to contribute.

My embrace of intensive Jewish study began relatively late, after my second year in college, while I was traveling in Israel. A year later, I transferred to Yeshiva University where I attended the Talmudic lectures of the Rav, Rabbi Joseph B. Soloveitchik *zt"l*. Following graduation, before starting medical school, I was blessed with the opportunity to study for four years with Rabbi Israel Chait, one of Rabbi Soloveitchik's disciples. Like the Rav, Rabbi Chait is exquisitely sensitive to textual subtleties and nuance, and he is penetrating and relentless in pursuit of their meanings.

Over the years, I have accumulated a number of my own insights and interpretations, which have, I believe, a certain originality. In fact, I often wonder if my late start in Torah scholarship, when my intellectual faculties were more mature, is partially responsible for this originality.

While I feel confident that my questions and observations are valid, I readily admit that the solutions I offer are often quite speculative. If I have erred in any of these speculative interpretations and come into conflict with the teachings, philosophical principles and truths of the Torah, it was out of ignorance and not intent, and I ask to be corrected.

I readily acknowledge that I have not made an exhaustive search of the vast body of Biblical commentary, and it is reasonable to assume that some of the insights may already appear elsewhere. If so, I am grateful to God for letting me rediscover that which an earlier rabbi has already written. If I have seen or heard something and failed to acknowledge it, it was done without intention; may God and the author forgive me for this indiscretion.

Finally, it is my hope that my training as a psychiatrist allowed me to express, in an interesting fashion, concepts discerned from a careful examination of the Torah's text. As in the study of our sacred texts, my professional training also emphasized the importance of the nuance of language. Indeed, one of the "advances" psychoanalytic theory made for modern science was the rediscovery of the precision and depth of speech. In careful analysis of language, in its content, structure, slips and omissions, a vast iceberg of psychological significance can be detected beneath the verbal surface. Our rabbis from time immemorial, as several of the homiletics of this work illustrate, have practiced this type of analysis and may well have been its originators. This close attention to language, which I use in my clinical practice, underlies much of the Midrashic and Rabbinic literature.

A human being is a composite of emotions and rational thoughts. This is the field of interest of the Torah, and the field in which the psychiatrist operates. In many instances, my experience has been that my background sensitized me to important nuances buried in the Torah's subtleties.

The Torah prescribes our normative practices in order to mold the substrata of feelings and thoughts that form the building blocks of human existence. Dedication to Torah observance elevates us emotionally and intellectually and brings us to a higher level of existence. This, I believe, is the dimension of Jewish life and learning the *Baalei Mussar* emphasized; the psychotherapist is similarly but more superficially involved. Frequently, the nuances of the Torah illuminate the innermost aspects of the human personality and thereby give us windows to the soul.

This is a work of derush, homiletics, which is by nature occasionally speculative. Our rabbis have issued the disclaimer, *"Ein meishivin al haderush*; homiletic interpretations of Scripture are not be held to ordinary rules of proof."* Nonetheless, some *derush* insights are better than others.

A good *derush* consists of three components. The first is the question or observation, which may relate, for instance, to an apparent contradiction, superfluity of words or juxtaposition of verses. The second is the idea or concept that addresses the question, which must be in itself true; when a false concept is invoked to resolve a question, even if it fits nicely into the text, there is no dispensation of *ein meishivin al haderush.* Finally, the answer must appear to be a legitimate intent of the text. In the absence of this third criterion, we have sermonics or esiogesis, but not exegesis.

In this regard, I pray that my own endeavors offer, at a minimum, good questions, and that the concepts that underlie the solutions are correct. Whether they meet the third criterion of being reasonably inferred from the text is left to the reader to decide.

A final word about the style and purpose of this work. Numerous medieval rabbinic authorities have maintained that there is an obligation to know the Torah is true. God intended the Revelation at Sinai before an entire nation of over three million people to serve as convincing evidence of the Torah's veracity, as the Torah itself repeatedly declares. We also know the Torah is true through the experience of observing its precepts; its guidance runs true to the depths of our souls as imbued with the wisdom of its omniscient Author. Most of all, we recognize the Torah's truth in its study, wherein we encounter endless levels of meaning and wisdom in every idea, sentence, word and letter; it can only be divine.

By being faithful to the text, I have attempted to show its integrity and profundity, which reflect the infinite intelligence of the Almighty. The sophists are quick to discredit our holy inheritance when they see a question in the text; when they find seemingly unrelated passages in proximity, they unhesitatingly ascribe them to different periods and authors. In my writing, I have endeavored in many instances to show that the Creator, with perfect knowledge of human nature, intended in these instances to lead us to sublime understandings. Like the wise scientist who stands in awe at the infinite wisdom of God's creations, so are we taken aback as careful scrutiny of the text reveals a scintilla of the infinite genius of its omniscient Author.

Because of this desire, I have written in a style that makes this work accessible to the broadest range of my Jewish brethren. I have included as little Hebrew as is reasonable and offered some limited background information for some of the exegesis, although most readers will not need it. Although it is my hope that learned people will also find these insights interesting, I will serve the greater good if this book offers Jews distant from their heritage a tantalizing hint of the infinite grandeur and wisdom of the Torah, which is, after all, their inheritance as well.

Our Sages say there are seventy facets to the Torah. The Vilna Gaon once reported that he had dreamed of over a thousand interpretations to a single verse. It is my fervent prayer that I have grasped a small piece of God's infinite wisdom, which I share with you.

Michael Bernstein

Lawrence, New York
Tishrei 5761 (2000)

Acknowledgments

BIRCHAS HATORAH, THE DAILY BLESSING OVER THE MITZVAH of Torah study, has a feature nonexistent in other blessings over mitzvos. It includes a prayer for success and enjoyment. Why is this so? The answer, I believe, is that when we learn Torah we connect with God and receive knowledge and wisdom directly from Him. It is the only mitzvah whose successful performance depends not only on ourselves but also on a will other than our own. Therefore, we pray that we find the Torah sweet and desirable and that God deem us worthy receptacles of His wisdom. Fittingly, the blessing concludes by acknowledging God as the Teacher of the Jewish people.

I begin this book by expressing my gratitude from the depths of my soul to God, Who guides and graces my life with His boundless kindness, Who has given me the wisdom to seek Torah and the opportunity to study it. I pray I have been successful in conveying to the reader some of the exquisite pleasure I experienced in exploring and discovering His Torah.

Rabbi Akiva demonstrated that reverence for a rebbe (teacher) is a component of the obligation to be in awe of God. My rebbe, Rabbi Israel Chait שליט״א, has made this command easy to observe. For a quarter of a century, he has been my teacher in many ways. He has instilled in me an abiding love for Torah and an appreciation for its infinite wisdom, and he has taught me to think more clearly and deeply. I continue to benefit from his guidance.

I would like to thank Rabbi Reuven Mann, Rabbi Yehoshua Kalish and Mr. Ari Bergman for their friendship and instruction over the years. I am indebted to my friends Rabbi Shaya Sasson, Rabbi Shmuel Farber and Rabbi Chaim Krigsman for reading chapters and offering astute comments. I want to thank Rabbi Yaakov Yosef Reinman, whose editing has greatly enhanced the presentation and readability of this material. I am also grateful for his diligence, encouragement and friendship.

I wish to thank Rabbi David Weinberger, *Mara d'Asra* of Congregation Shaarei Tefillah, and Rabbi Nosson Scherman, of Mesorah Publications, for their kind support. I also wish to thank Dr. Joseph and Faye Geliebter, for their help in various ways, and Maddy Himy, my dedicated typist.

I gratefully acknowledge the following friends and institutions for their generous financial support: Louis and Laurie Barbanel, Leonard and Aliza Kestenbaum, Marvin and Roz Samuels, Congregation Zichron Shmuel Aaron and New Horizons Counseling Center.

I thank my parents, Mr. Robert and Mrs. Faye Bernstein, and my mother-in-law, Mrs. Ida Baum, for their lifelong love and support. Finally, last and most precious, I express my love and gratitude to my partner in life and in this enterprise, my wife Rose.

May God grant them all health and long life amongst the Jewish people.

בראשית
GENESIS

פרשת בראשית
Parashas Bereishis

i. *Jews Against Jealousy*

HY DOES THE TORAH BEGIN WITH THE STORY OF CRE-
ation? As essentially a book of law, shouldn't it have
begun with the first law given to the Jewish
people, the inauguration of the calendar months through the
sanctification of the new moon? This question is posed by Rashi
in the name of Rabbi Yitzchak, who goes on to explain that God,
as Creator and Master of all, is justifying His transfer of the
Promised Land from the pagan nations to the Jewish people.

But the Book of Genesis does not stop with the creation story.
It goes on to give a telescoped account of history that justifies
the selection of the Jewish people as the sole recipients of the
Torah. In this light, we can see a clear pattern and a sharp contrast between the beginning of the Book and its conclusion,
which illuminates the justice in God's selection.

After the expulsion from the Garden of Eden, human nature is transformed, and human history as we know it begins. The first human became mortal, and immediately, we witness the tragic story of Cain, driven by jealousy, killing his only brother Abel; the first brothers, the first jealousy, the first fratricide.

Mankind continues to decline, and the need arises for the emergence of Abraham, God's selected agent, to forge a nation that will redeem mankind. Jealousy roils the relationships between Abraham's sons, Isaac and Ishmael, and Abraham's grandsons, Jacob and Esau.

The Book concludes with the story of Joseph and his brothers. The hatred spawned by jealousy, the dramatic confrontation and its climactic resolution are spread over the last four *parshios* in meticulous detail. We see a complete reversal from the fratricidal beginning of Genesis. Though Joseph's brothers come within a hairsbreadth of fratricide, they resist. Furthermore, they ultimately find the inner strength to acknowledge their transgression and repent. They expunge from their hearts the jealousy that led them to sell Joseph into slavery in the first place. When Benjamin, Jacob's new favorite son, is accused of theft and imprisoned, the brothers come to his defense even though the incriminating evidence against Benjamin could have justified his abandonment; with jealousy apparently no longer a factor in their behavior, they joined together to rescue him.

In summary, jealousy was mankind's first egregious flaw after the expulsion from the Garden of Eden. Cain, his offering rejected by God, was jealous of Abel, whose offering was accepted. Cain coveted Abel's favored position and killed him in order to usurp it. This dreadful sin propelled mankind toward further corruption and resulted in the need to create the Jewish nation, the destined redeemers of mankind. Fittingly, the final part of Genesis, which describes how the seeds of Jewish nationhood were planted in the hostile Egyptian soil, focuses on the capacity of Jacob's children to overcome jealousy. Jealousy and its resolution are important themes of Genesis. Why?

Let us take a closer look at the psychology of jealousy.

People are not usually jealous of birds, though most of us would love to fly. But if our neighbors all had helicopters in their backyards and we didn't, might we not have jealous twinges then?

Clearly, people do not become jealous because they themselves are lacking something (in this case the ability to fly). Rather, it is being excluded from what others have that brings on feelings of jealousy. This may be called the "why me?" syndrome. Why should I be treated less favorably than someone else is?

In a similar vein, people are far more inclined to question the Almighty if they themselves suffer misfortune than if it befalls someone else. In actuality, however, what difference does it make? Why are other people's calamities acceptable while our own bring our faith into question?

The answer lies in our misperception of our place in the grand scheme of the universe. In our self-centered, small-minded view, we are the center of the universe, and everything else revolves around us. We are, therefore, convinced that life's breaks should go our way, and that we are entitled to any benefit or privilege that others may enjoy. When good fortune benefits someone else, we may become resentful and jealous, often without even being consciously aware of these negative feelings.

In actuality, however, we are not the center of the universe. Indeed, the greatest of all men, Moses, understood this most clearly, as he said concerning himself and his brother Aaron, "*Nachnu mah,* We are nothing." This then is the key to overcoming jealousy. When we recognize the infinite greatness of God and our own relative insignificance, we gain an accurate perspective of the world, and all our questions and jealousies fall by the wayside. When we decentralize ourselves, jealousy disappears.

The Book of Exodus returns to the theme of brotherhood. Moses and Aaron embody the ideal, jealousy-free brotherly love (see *Rashi, Exodus* 4:14). They are at the opposite extreme of the brotherhood spectrum from Cain and Abel; they are worthy of leading the Jewish people.

The elimination of jealousy starts the process of redemption. The final four *parshios* of Genesis, which devote so much attention to the conflict among the brothers and its resolution, emphasize this point. The downfall of mankind is jealousy and its egocentric roots; the redemption of mankind addresses the selfsame issues. When the Jewish family overcame their internal jealousies, the redemption of mankind began.

To the degree that a person is burdened by his self-importance, he is limited in his appreciation of God; he is incapable of understanding the fundamental truth that *"ein od milvado*, nothing has any real existence beside Him." According to *Mesillas Yesharim*, the purpose of life is to derive pleasure from one's relationship to God. A person who suffers from jealousy is limited in his ability to relate to God and is consequently deprived of the ultimate benefit that God has bestowed on mankind, to have a relationship with Him.

Mankind's struggle with jealousy and its underlying egocentricity finds clear expression in the Ten Commandments, which instruct us successively concerning our thoughts, words, deeds, again words and finally feelings. They open with the obligation to know God, to reject idols, to refrain from uttering God's Name in vain, to observe the Sabbath. They then go on to the obligation to honor parents and the forbidden actions of murder, adultery and kidnaping. These are followed by forbidden speech, such as false oaths and bearing false witness. Finally, we arrive at prohibited feelings — jealousy, you shall not covet.

Running the gamut from knowing God to overcoming jealousy, the Ten Commandments reflect a process in which ideas and then behaviors are intended to improve the internal cognitive/emotional framework by which we relate to His world, such that jealousy is removed.

The correlation between recognizing God and true brotherhood is also implicit in the mitzvah of constructing the Tabernacle (*Exodus* 25:8), "And they shall make a Sanctuary for Me, and I shall dwell among them." Referring to God's taking up residence in the Tabernacle, the Torah uses the phrase "among them" (*besocham*) rather than "in it" (*besocho*). A dwelling place for God may only exist when people create bonds with each other, when they are humble and selfless, when they see God as the center of the universe and have no feelings of jealousy toward other people.

Just before the end of the Jewish year, we celebrate the festival of Purim. There is a providential symbolism in the holiday's timing at the end of the year; it foreshadows the events that will precede the end of history — the resolution of the struggle between the Jewish people and our archenemy Amalek in the Messianic area. The Talmud (*Chullin* 139b) finds a reference to Haman, the villain of the Purim story, in the first *parashah* of the Book of Genesis. In the light of the pattern we have been developing here, one aspect of the connection becomes clear.

Haman, the epitome of the God-denying Amalekite, had an enormous ego and was "consumed with a jealous rage." The Jewish people, however, were victorious over him by humbling themselves before God. The victory, then and now, is celebrated by sending gifts of food to friends and giving alms to the poor. These acts promote camaraderie among the Jewish people instead of self-absorption, bringing out true brotherhood and dispelling jealousy. Just as the conquest of jealousy was a key factor in the formation of the Jewish people, so will the brotherhood that takes its place be a key factor in our ultimate redemption.

The centrality of fraternity in the message of Purim is reinforced by a curious detail of the mitzvah of sending food gifts, called *mishlo'ach manos* in Megillas Esther. The word *mishlo'ach*, sending, is somewhat problematic. We know that it is generally preferable to perform a mitzvah directly rather than through a messenger. Here, however, the mitzvah seems to require a messenger; the gifts of food must be sent, not given. Some commentators, despite the implications of the language used in Megillas Esther, recognize no preference for using a messenger over giving the gifts directly. The authoritative ruling is that this mitzvah calls for the use of a messenger (*Orach Chaim* 785; *Mishnah Berurah* 18). Why is this so?

Furthermore, according to the commentators that recognize no preference, why indeed does Megillas Esther speak of "sending" rather than "giving"?

Before we answer these questions, let us consider the receipt of a gift from the perspective of the recipient. When that gift is delivered via messenger, it engenders a special feeling of closeness. There is a common saying that "out of sight, out of mind." When you see someone you think about him, but as soon as he leaves your field of vision, you may forget him completely. When a person receives a gift via messenger, he knows he is not "out of mind," that the sender thinks of him even from afar, that the brotherhood represented by the gift is genuine, profound and lasting.

Whether or not we must actually employ a messenger to deliver the gift of food, the language itself highlights these ideas. Jewish people are bound by common laws, values and destiny. Ideally, they are humble, close to God and free of jealousy. By these virtues, they will merit the ultimate redemption, and through them all of mankind will be redeemed.

ii. *Where Evil Hides*

UR SAGES (*CHULLIN* 139B) WONDER WHERE WE CAN FIND an allusion in the Torah to Haman, the archvillain of the Purim story, and they answer that there is a veiled suggestion right here in *Parashas Bereishis*. After Adam sins by eating from the Tree of Knowledge, the Almighty says to him, "Did you eat from this tree (*hamin ha'etz*) from which you were commanded not to eat?" (3:11). The word *hamin*, with different vowelization, can be pronounced haman, an oblique allusion to the villainous Haman.

Two questions immediately arise.

First, why does the Talmud seek a reference in the Torah to a villain who would not appear on the scene of history for another thousand years, the antagonist in a drama commemorated by a festival instituted during the Rabbinic period? True, there are many commentators who contend that there are hints in the Torah, no matter how slight, to every detail of history. Nonetheless, why does the Talmud make an issue of finding Haman, of all people?

Furthermore, is the connection between this specific verse and the villain Haman only a play on words, or is there a deeper message connecting the two?

Before addressing these questions, let us take a closer look at Megillas Esther. Haman's sons are practically invisible throughout the narrative, and yet, after Haman's downfall, his sons leap to sudden and rather odd prominence. For instance, when the narrative tells about their execution, their names appear in the format used for special poetical passages (*shirah*). Furthermore, the reader is required to utter their names in one continuous stream without pausing to take a breath. In the *Al HaNissim*, the brief summary of the events we insert into our prayers and *Birchas HaMazon* on Purim, we mention that Haman's *and his sons* were hanged from a tree. Why this disproportionate emphasis on the fate of Haman's sons?

When the Megillah first introduces Mordechai and Haman, we are told that Mordechai is descended from the tribe of Benjamin and Haman from King Agag of Amalek. One of the most illustrious historical figures of the tribe of Benjamin was King Saul, the first king of Israel. Both he and King Agag had lived hundreds of years earlier. King Saul had gone to war against Amalek with the specific divine command to annihilate them. This he proceeded to do, except that in an act of misguided mercy he spared the life of Agag, the Amalekite king. The next day, the prophet Samuel rebuked King Saul for his lapse of duty and personally executed Agag. It was too late. During that one night, according to the Midrash, Agag sired the child from whom Haman eventually descended.

Generations later, when Mordechai executed Haman along with all his sons, making sure no offspring were left from at least this branch of Amalek, he fulfilled the commandment his ancestor King Saul had ignored. This may be an additional facet of the phrase "*kiyemu vekiblu*, they fulfilled and accepted," which occurs at the end of the Megillah. The Talmud understands this to mean that they reaffirmed their earlier acceptance of the entire Torah by their acceptance of the added laws of Purim. Perhaps this statement can also encompass their acceptance upon themselves to follow up on King Saul's unfinished business to the best of their abilities. The inordinate prominence given Haman's sons is now well understood. Their deaths represented the destruction of Amalek, King Saul's unfinished mitzvah.

Now let us return to our original question regarding why the Talmud seeks a source for Haman. Purim is the festival that represents the struggle of good against evil, the overriding theme of all history. The Talmud knows that just as the forces of good, the Jewish people, are represented in the very first word of the Torah,[1] there must also be an allusion somewhere to that personification of evil that can reject the Almighty and assail His people.

Where in the Torah is the hiding place of this personification of evil called Haman? It lies in Adam's capacity for sin that became manifest when he rejected God's command and ate from the Tree of Knowledge. Haman and his people Amalek ultimately represent rejection of God, while the Jewish people represent faithful allegiance.

The same passage in the Talmud that finds an allusion to Haman in the Torah seeks one for Mordechai as well. The Talmud

---

1. According to the Midrash, the word "*Bereishis*" alludes to the Jewish people, who are called "*Reishis.*"

finds a connection in the verse that lists the ingredients of the *ketores*, an incense-like compound used in the Temple service. One of the ingredients is identified as *mor dror*. *Targum Onkelos* translates this word into Aramaic as *morei dachya*, a word that resembles the name Mordechai.

At first glance, this connection seems extremely tenuous. What is the correlation between Mordechai and the aromatic substance burned in the Temple service? And we may also ask once again, why does the Talmud need an allusion in the Torah to the protagonist of a drama — memorialized by a rabbinic festival — that would not take place for another thousand years?

Let us take a closer look at the *ketores*. Every day of the year, the *ketores* was burned on the Golden Altar within the *Kodesh*, the outer section of the Sanctuary. On Yom Kippur, however, there was a special *ketores* service that the Kohen Gadol performed in the *Kodesh Kodashim*, the Holy of Holies, the innermost sanctuary, which could be entered only by the Kohen Gadol and only on Yom Kippur.

The Talmud (*Yoma* 35a) explains that the *ketores* service of Yom Kippur atones for the sin of *lashon hara*, the slander and gossip spoken by individual Jews against each other. This statement highlights the extreme gravity of the sin of *lashon hara*. When the holiest person in the world entered the holiest place in the world at the holiest time of the year, the expiation of the sins of murder, theft, idolatry or the like were not foremost in his thoughts. He was primarily concerned with the sin of *lashon hara*.

Lashon hara arises from the personality defects of aggression, hatred and jealousy, which are among the most basic and deep-rooted human frailties. The central *ketores* service of Yom Kippur is, therefore, a fitting time and place for the real and symbolic expiation of this cardinal sin.

The symbolism is strong. The Kohen Gadol's entry into the innermost sanctum signals the need of each individual to penetrate to the deepest recesses of his own heart and personality to uproot the mean-spiritedness that causes him to speak *lashon hara*. Moreover, the fragrant *ketores* represents the antithesis of *lashon hara*. According to the Midrash, Adam engaged all his senses when he ate the forbidden fruit of the Tree of Knowledge — except for the sense of smell. The Talmud (*Berachos* 43b) states, "Which thing gives pleasure to the soul but not to the body? It is a good fragrance." Smell, then, is that sense which is pure, uncorrupted and incorruptible. It is also the most internalizing sense, since we draw our breaths into *our* inner sanctum, suggesting that we have the capacity to find a spiritual purity within our deepest recesses. Bringing *ketores* into the innermost sanctum of the Temple is an appropriate symbol of the expiation of the sin of *lashon hara*.

Mordechai was sensitive to the feelings of others, as we can infer from the statement at the conclusion of the Megillah that he "found favor with the multitude of his brethren, he sought the good of his people and *spoke words of peace* [italics added] to all his offspring." The Megillah singles out Mordechai for his avoidance of *lashon hara*. In this light, we can understand the underlying symbolism in the connection the Talmud discerns between Mordechai and the *mor dror*.

In the story of Purim, Mordechai was best qualified to guide the Jewish people to victory over Haman, because he exemplified the ideal of internal perfection as represented by the *ketores* service on Yom Kippur. In a like fashion, our final redemption will occur, not only on a national level, but also in a personal framework, as each individual will aspire and make progress toward the human perfection exhibited by Mordechai. Thus, it is wholly appropriate that the Talmud should seek and identify a source in the Torah for the person who embodied the human characteristics necessary to prevail over the historic forces of evil.

iii. *Three Times From Nothing*

N THE BEGINNING, THE LORD CREATED THE HEAVENS AND the earth. This is the first and one of the most famous of all the verses in the Torah. The word used here for created, *bara* (בָּרָא), occurs exclusively with regard to creative acts of God, since it means creating something from nothing (*creatio ex nihilo*). *Bara* appears only three times in the creation story. The first time it refers to the creation of the heavens and earth, as above; the second time, to the creation of animal life (1:21), "And the Lord created the great *taninim*";[2] finally, it recurs during the creation of the first man (1:27), "And the Lord created the man in His own image."

Why are these three creations singled out as being *ex nihilo*? And even if we find some singularity in the creation of heaven and earth and the creation of man, what is so significant about the creation of the *taninim*? Why does it call for the word *bara*?

The translation of the word *taninim* is problematic. It is commonly translated as whales. Our Sages tell us, however, that it refers to a pair of animals called *leviathans*. According to the Talmud (*Bava Basra* 74b), the *leviathan* was so large that it would have consumed the entire world were it allowed to reproduce. Therefore, one was immediately killed, salted away and put into storage to be served to the righteous in the World to Come.

This teaching of the Talmud associates the *taninim* with the ultimate divine reward that awaits the righteous in the World to Come. The Talmud's intent is not to imply that the righteous will

---

2. The verse continues, "and all living things which the water caused to swarm forth, according to their species." For our purposes, we will assume that the verb *bara* relates only to the *taninim*, while "swarm" applies to the other creatures. It is instructive to note that *bara* is not used in connection with the formation of water creatures previously on the fifth day, nor with any of the animal life of the sixth day.

be served king-size *leviathan* steaks with all the fixings; rather, it is somehow symbolic of spiritual reward, the eternal life of the soul in a continual relationship with God. The use of the term "*bara*" in regard to the *taninim* serves as a subtle hint to the deeper significance of its creation. (The Torah refers to purely spiritual rewards, such as the Messianic era, the resurrection of the dead and the exquisite spiritual pleasures of the World to Come, in these kinds of oblique allusions, because we are expected to fulfill the Torah's commandments for their own sake.)

Rabbi Moshe Chaim Luzzatto, in *Derech Hashem*, points out that the metaphysical world, which effects God's providence in the world, functions according to its own set of divinely ordained laws. This underlying operating system, undetectable to mankind, actually governs the smooth functioning of nature.

In this light, we can discern a progressive pattern to the *bara* form of creation. First, we have the creation of the heaven and the earth. The physical world is created *ex nihilo*, something from nothing. All the subsequent stages of creation merely shape and reshape the original created matter and energy, and therefore, they do not warrant the term *bara*. Second, the Torah tells us about the creation of the metaphysical world, symbolized by the *taninim*, the *leviathans* that represent reward in the World to Come. Although this world is not material, it still needed to be created, and that creation was once again *ex nihilo*.

Finally, we arrive at the creation of the first man, a transcendent creature that straddles both created worlds; a higher form of being that has a soul; that enjoys free will, which releases him from the inevitability of natural law; a creature formed in the image of the Lord. A reshaping of prior creations will not suffice, and mankind must be created *ex nihilo*.

iv. Forbidden Fruit

HAT WERE THESE FRUITS OF THE TREE OF KNOWLEDGE that God forbade Adam to eat? One might have thought they were some sort of exotic rarity whose mysterious taste and texture tempted Adam's curiosity. But that was not the case.

The Talmud (*Sanhedrin* 70a) cites four possible identities for the forbidden fruit — wheat, dates, grapes, *esrog* (citron) — all of them widely available agricultural products. Adam could easily have eaten these fruits if he had obtained them from different sources. He was only forbidden to taste the ones that grew on the Tree of Knowledge.

It would seem that by allowing these fruits to be eaten as a general rule yet singling out those of a particular tree as the forbidden fruit, the Almighty was sending a message to Adam. What was this message?

Perhaps we can connect each of these fruits with an important concept.

The grape, through the wine it produces, represents unbridled emotion, as the Sages say (*Eruvin* 65a), "When wine enters, secrets emerge." (Interestingly, the letters of wine (יַיִן) and secret (סוֹד) both have the numerical value of 70.) The prohibition against eating from the Tree of Knowledge directed Adam to restrain his passions and unbridled emotions.

Wheat represents the sustaining and nutritive aspects of the material world. According to this view, Adam was being commanded to limit and govern his involvement in materialism.

The date affords pure palliative pleasure. The Torah repeatedly praises the land of Israel for its nutritious milk and the honey of its dates — a land of sustenance and pleasure. The Rambam, in *Sefer Kedushah*, lists only laws concerning sexual relations and proscribed foods, indicating that personal holiness depends on restraint in these two areas of conduct. These two drives have been identified by modern psychology as the essential id forces that drive the animalistic component of man (the *nefesh habahami* in the language of the Sages). Adam, already in the Garden of Eden, is instructed to limit his enjoyment of these pleasures.

Learning to control these appetites was an important element in Adam's early development. The first frustration a newborn encounters is a delay in having his hunger immediately satisfied. This frustration, which did not occur in the womb, is essential for his natural progression and the realization that he and his mother are not one.

This concept is echoed in the early development of the Jewish nation. Among the first commandments the Jewish people were given, even before they left Egypt, were prohibitions against eating leaven (*chametz*) and the obligation to eat matzah.[3] The Talmud (*Berachos* 17a) directly connects the leaven to the *yetzer hara*, the evil inclination. The Jewish nation in its infancy is differentiated from the seventy nations by being obliged to limit its enjoyment of those pleasures that mankind shares with the animals.

Finally, the *esrog* is described in the Midrash as the one fruit that fulfilled God's command that the tree itself should have the same taste as its fruit (1:11). At first glance, we are perplexed by this Midrash. How can a tree be anything other than what God intended it to be? According to Kabbalistic thought, the answer lies in the esoteric principle of *tzimtzum*, whereby God retracted the manifestation of His will or Presence, so to speak, to allow the material world to exist. This absence or rather concealment of God's will leaves room for deviation. The *esrog*, however, remains an almost vestigial remnant of God's unconcealed intent in creation. Its insides, represented by the tree itself, are like the fruit on its outside (*tocho kebaro*).

---

3. Interestingly, in *Parashas Ki Sisa*, which reiterates the prohibition of *chametz* in the Temple as well as the obligation of the Passover sacrifice, the prohibition against meat cooked in milk is also mentioned. Rav S. R. Hirsch finds in the command of separating milk and meat an allusion that the Jewish people, who are compared to a kid, should not mingle with the nations from which they emerged, represented by mother's milk.

According to this explanation, the prohibition against eating the *esrog* that grew on the Tree of Knowledge underscored the idea that mankind differs from the *esrog*. In the emotional and behavioral world, people must still aspire and toil to make their physical bodies a suitable receptacle for their souls. They must still strive to make themselves a pure reflection of the divine will.

Unlike the *esrog*, mankind has not yet achieved the goal of matching his cognitive/emotional makeup to the potential of his pure soul.[4] Before he committed his tragic sin, Adam was given the heroic task of struggling to achieve this goal.

It emerges then, that there is a double entendre to the term "the Tree of Knowledge." Not only does the tree represent knowledge inappropriate for mankind to possess, but it also, by its very prohibitions, conveys knowledge to people when they fully understand its teaching.

v. The Test Adam Passed

GIVING NAMES TO ALL THE CREATURES OF THE WORLD WAS the first assignment God gave Adam. It was, of course, an important responsibility in its own right, but it also seems to have been simultaneously a subtle test, as is indicated by the verses (2:19-20): "And God the Lord formed out of the ground all the beasts of the field and all the birds of the sky, and He brought [each] to the man to see what he would name it, and

---

4. The Mishnah (*Succah* 46a) states that at the conclusion of Succos, people would snatch and eat the children's *esrogim*. One of the central themes of Succos is the expression of the idealized relationship between the Jewish people and the Almighty. Children before the age of bar mitzvah lack knowledge (in a legal sense) and are, therefore, without sin. Perhaps one of the intents underlying this practice was to express the people's desire to regain the spiritual level of Adam before he sinned by eating from the Tree of Knowledge, when he was closer to having his *tocho* (inner self) like his *bar* (outer self), as exemplified by the once forbidden *esrog*.

whatever he called each living creature, that became its name. And the man assigned names to all the cattle, and to the birds of the sky, and to all the beasts of the field."

If we look closely at the text, one expression practically leaps out at us from the page. God does not bring the creatures to Adam "to name them." He brings the creatures "to see what he would name them." Adam is apparently being put to the test, and God is waiting "to see" what he will name them. This language is anthropomorphic. Moreover, God's knowledge is not dependent on the actions of people; but the verse does convey the idea that there was a test in progress.

What exactly did God want "to see" with regard to Adam's naming of the creatures? What deeper challenge might Adam have faced here?

If we take a closer look at the verses, other anomalies emerge. When God brings the creatures to Adam, they are grouped in two categories, beasts of the field and birds of the sky. But afterwards, when Adam assigns them names, he subdivides the category of beasts into domesticated cattle and wild beasts.

There is a further oddity to Adam's subdivision. Adam assigns names "to all the cattle, and to the birds of the sky, and to all the beasts of the field." The two types of animals, wild and domesticated, are separated from each other by the mention of birds. Moreover, the inclusive word "all" applies to every creature God brought to Adam. But when Adam assigns them names, the inclusive word "all" appears only with the cattle and the beasts, not the birds.

The second difficulty can be resolved by a look at the placement of the cantillation marks, which include the domesticated animals and birds in one musical clause. Therefore, the "all" of the cattle spans the birds as well. But why indeed did Adam group the creatures as he did? If there was to be any sorting of animal groups, as reflected in the cantillation marks, it would seem more logical to group domesticated animals with wild ones, all of them being mammals, than with birds. Why did Adam move away from this natural grouping?

In the divine service, only birds and domesticated animals are eligible to be brought as sacrifices. No wild beasts (*chayos*) are permitted on the altar. In this light, perhaps we can say that God brought Adam all the creatures in two large groups, mammals and birds, and then he waited "to see" if Adam would rearrange them according to the way they appear in nature or if he would focus instead on their relative spiritual roles in the divine service.

By grouping birds with the cattle, Adam responded successfully. He passed his test.

vi. *Crafty and Naked*

THE SNAKE IS DESCRIBED AS CRAFTIER THAN ALL OTHER creatures, and the word used to portray his craftiness is *arum*. Adam and Eve are described as being without clothes, and the word used to portray their nakedness is *arumim*, essentially the same word but in its plural form. Similarities in Biblical Hebrew are always significant, especially when such close homonyms appear within a few verses of each other. We would expect a certain commonality of meaning. Yet strangely, we encounter almost the exact opposite here; naked is something revealed, whereas crafty connotes concealment.

A closer examination of craftiness, however, reveals a strong correlation with nakedness. A crafty person is someone who takes advantage of another person's instinctive trust. What are the prerequisites of trust? In general, people are inclined to trust someone they know, someone whose motivations they can identify, someone from whom they expect no harm or malice. Conversely, when dealing with someone they do not know, people are more circumspect and wary of unexpected problems. A crafty person presents himself to his intended victim as a known quantity, a transparent person whose motivations, thoughts and plans are easily discernible. His deception succeeds because he falsely represents himself as transparent, figuratively naked, with nothing to hide. The unsuspecting victim responds with trust and leaves himself open to exploitation. Craftiness is the ability to project the illusion of nakedness.

vii. *Hiding Among the Trees*

AVING EATEN THE FORBIDDEN FRUIT, ADAM AND EVE "HID from Hashem the Lord in the midst of the trees of the garden" (3:8). What is the Torah's point in telling us precisely where they were hiding? Is anything to be learned from the location of their hiding place among the trees?

Perhaps the Torah is giving us here a paradigm for all hiding from God. How does a person presume to hide from God? "In the midst of the trees of the garden" serves as a metaphor for the materialistic world in which a person can delude himself into believing that God is not present. When a person adds unnecessarily to his home or wardrobe or toils mightily to build a business empire, he obscures the Presence of God. When he is preoccupied among the trees of the garden, especially when successful, he begins to believe that he is truly hidden from God.

viii. The Descent From Truth

NE OF THE BASIC PRINCIPLES IN FORENSIC PSYCHIATRY, the field concerned with legal and criminal matters, is that people find it difficult to lie with a straight face. There are subtle "tells" or signs that are giveaways that the subject is lying. For instance, a liar's response is likely to be evasive, it may offer too much information, or it may challenge the questioner. Invariably, the liar, feeling guilty, will not respond to a direct question with a simple yes or no. These principles are on display here (3:9-12).

God calls out to Adam and says to him, "Where are you?"

"I heard You in the garden," Adam replies, "and I was afraid because I am naked, so I hid."

"Who told you that you are naked?" God asks. "Have you eaten of the tree from which I commanded you not to eat?"

"The woman You placed beside me," Adam replied, "she gave me of the tree, and I ate."

God asks Adam two questions during this exchange — "Where are you" and "Did you eat from the tree?" Notice that Adam fails to respond with a simple, direct answer to either one. He is evasive, and he offers too much information. He is clearly not being fully truthful.

As we read about Cain killing his brother Abel, we notice an even further descent from the truth (4:9).

God says to Cain, "Where is your brother Abel?"

And Cain replies, "Am I my brother's keeper?"

Here we find the third characteristic "tell" of a liar. Instead of giving a simple and truthful answer to the question, or even an evasive one, Cain challenged the premise of the interrogator in asking the question. Am I my brother's keeper that you should even ask me such a question?

The Rambam, in *Guide for the Perplexed*, states that before

Adam ate from the Tree of Knowledge, mankind operated in a world of truth and falsehood. As a result of Adam's sin, however, mankind entered the more oblique moral universe of good and evil.

The Jewish people are the redeemers of mankind. Fittingly, the patriarch Jacob, the *bechir she'b'avos*, the ultimate patriarch, excelled in the virtue of *emes*, truth. It is our mission to use this virtue to reverse the descent into the world of good and evil and restore the world of truth.

ix. *The First Lawyer*

OT ONLY WAS ADAM THE FIRST MAN, HE WAS ALSO THE first lawyer. After he ate the forbidden fruit of the Tree of Knowledge, God confronted him and asked him if he had indeed violated the only prohibition he had been given. Cagily, Adam defended himself (3:12), "The woman You gave me, she gave it to me." Our Sages were not impressed with Adam's defense, characterizing him as ungrateful (*kafui tov*) for God's gift of a mate.

But let us consider more fully Adam's reasoning. God had introduced Eve to Adam to address his solitude. Yet the first thing we hear about this last creature of creation is that she induces her mate to sin. Where is the generosity in such a gift? Doesn't Adam appear to have some justification in his argument?

Let us listen to God's response (3:17), "Because you listened to the voice (*lekol*) of your wife ..." The seemingly superfluous words "the voice of" imply that Adam listened to something more than Eve's simple argument in favor of eating the forbidden fruit. How does "listening to the voice of your wife" differ from "listening to your wife"?

Later on, we find similar phrasing in another instance of heeding wifely advice. Abraham bristles at Sarah's suggestion that Ishmael be banished from their home because of his potential negative influence on Isaac, but God tells Abraham (21:12), "Whatever Sarah tells you, heed her voice (*bekolah*)." In this instance, we have come full circle. While God admonishes Adam for listening to Eve's voice, He instructs Abraham to listen to Sarah's voice.

There is an important difference in these two expressions of voice. Adam is criticized for listening "to her voice (*lekol*)" whereas Abraham is told literally to heed "in her voice (*bekol*)." Perhaps then we can say that "voice" refers to the personality that motivates the words. Listening "to the voice," *lekol*, would mean therefore unquestioned acceptance of the personality behind the words. Listening "in the voice," *bekol*, would mean only a limited responsiveness to that personality. The Malbim points out this distinction in phrasing, but he interprets it differently.

God gave Adam a wife to help both of them ascend toward Godliness, each struggling to attain this end according to his or her individual nature. It is a man's nature to seek his wife's approval throughout the course of life. This mirrors the ultimate approval (*ritzui*) the soul seeks from God, a transcendent quest in which a wife, being endowed with *binah yeseirah*, an extra capacity for intuitive insight, can be very helpful. Her *binah yeseirah* is only operative, however, when she overcomes her own distracting impulses (*yetzer hara*). It is only to this higher potential in a woman's personality to which a man must pay heed.

This was God's rejoinder to Adam. Adam had listened "to her voice" indiscriminately, accepting all her suggestions. He wanted her approval in all circumstances and followed her blindly. He allowed what should have been his own independently responsible personality to dissolve in their oneness. This is wrong. As God told Abraham, he must listen *bekol*, in her voice. He must exercise discrimination and discernment, following her only when she is leading toward higher religious attainment. It is the marital dyad of Abraham and Sarah that will redeem mankind from the consequences of the first couple's failings.

Parenthetically, we see in the repeated use of the word *kol*, which weaves itself through the Torah's first stories, an important literary device the Torah frequently employs to underscore its meanings. We first encounter *kol* when Adam and Eve hide from the *kol* of God in the Garden after they sin. Next we learn of Adam's error of listening to the *kol* of his wife. Finally, Cain kills Abel and the *kol* of his blood cries out from the earth. As we follow the thread of *kol*, we see that the Torah is setting up an equation. Because Adam listens to Eve's *kol*, he sins and hides from God's *kol*. This results in the divinely promised introduction of death as the *kol* of Abel's blood cries out from his grave.

x. Ceaseless Toil

AFTER ADAM SINNED, HE WAS BANISHED FROM THE GARDEN of Eden, and his life of ease came to an end. From that time on (3:17), he would work the land, and "with toil shall you eat [the produce of the ground] all the days of your life."

Let us consider for a moment these words, "all the days of your life." They seem superfluous. Why would we have thought that the punishment is limited to only part of Adam's life? If the change in his status were only temporary, there would certainly have been some mention of it. What then are we taught by the words "all the days of your life"?

There is a tendency among people toward excess; they devote inordinate amounts of time to physical fitness regimes or the pursuit of financial security. It is as if they believe that very large amounts of money and top physical condition will insulate them against the curse of worry or toil.

Not so, declares the Torah. Worry and toil are constant features of the human condition. They accompany a person from the beginning to the end "all the days of his life." It is futile and counterproductive to attempt escape. Rather, a person should strive to lead a spiritually productive life within the inescapable parameters of the human condition — the inherent insecurity and toil of physical existence.

xi. *The Road to Eden*

EXPULSION FROM THE GARDEN OF EDEN WAS NOT ENOUGH. God also put up barriers to Adam's return, as we read (3:23-24), "And God the Lord banished [Adam] from the Garden of Eden to cultivate the soil from which he was taken, and having driven out Adam, He stationed at the east of the Garden of Eden the cherubs and the flame of the revolving sword to guard the way to the Tree of Life."

These mysterious verses have absorbed the attention of numerous Midrashim and commentaries. For our purposes, we will focus here on the barriers themselves and their purpose. Why were barriers necessary? Why didn't God simply destroy or incapacitate the Tree of Life? What benefit was there for mankind in erecting barriers instead? Furthermore, why was there a need for two cherubs? Why wasn't one sufficient?

A fundamental aspect of a person's mindset is the awareness that he is perishable. This fear of annihilation drives many of his activities in life. At an even deeper level, even our immaterial souls are contingent on the continuous will of the Creator. This leads to a type of metaphysical anxiety, the successful resolution of which is the clinging to the will of God, which endows the soul's existence with eternity.

Metaphorically, this desire expresses itself in mankind's yearning to return to the Garden of Eden, to the ideal of its original pristine existence, in which death did not exist.

With this in mind, let us now examine the two elements guarding the return path separately.

The "the flame of the revolving sword" appears in the Hebrew as *lahat hacherev hamis'hapeches*. The word *cherev*, derived from the root word for destruction, portrays a sword, which is an instrument of death and destruction. According to the Talmud (*Sanhedrin* 67b), the word *lahat*, flame, represents flickering illusions, as in the sorcerers' tricks in Exodus (7:22). The word *mis'hapeches*, revolving, can be more precisely translated as turning over.

Putting the pieces together, we may read: God has set for mankind a path to the permanent or eternal existence represented by Eden, a path that entails death (*cherev*). But death is really an illusion (*lahat*), for in reality it only turns a person over (*mis'hapeches*) into the true existence of his pure soul. Earthly life is a mirage, a vestibule prior to the more real life of the soul. What must he do to remain on the path to eternity?

Here we turn to the second guardian of the path, the cherubs. In the entire Torah, we find cherubs only in one other place. Two golden cherubs sat atop the lid of the Holy Ark in the Holy of Holies, and the voice of God emanated from between them. The cherubs represent divine instruction in its purest form, as best seen in the Torah. It is through that instruction that mankind can attain eternity, by knowing and clinging to God's will.[5]

In brief, mankind, driven by the desire for eternal existence, seeks to return to Eden. The transformation effected through physical death and devotion to the will of God allow us to achieve that end.

---

5. Some of these points are discussed in the Malbim's commentary.

פרשת נח
Parashas Noah

i. Why Are We Here?

WHY DID NOAH FIND FAVOR IN GOD'S EYES SO THAT HE AND his family were saved from the Great Flood? The Torah informs us (6:9) that "he was a completely righteous man in his generation." The Torah does not simply pronounce him completely righteous; it adds the qualification "in his generation."

The Talmud (*Sanhedrin* 109a) records an argument between Rav and Shmuel regarding these words. One view infers that by the standards of Abraham's generation Noah would not have appeared as righteous. The other view is that the shortcomings of Noah's generation adversely affected him; he would have been even greater had he lived in Abraham's generation.

Both of these views seem to agree that Noah was in some way lacking. Their point of disagreement is with regard to his potential. Did he have the potential for greater righteousness under more favorable circumstances?

This question has significant implications for us today.

According to the view that Noah's merit was only relative to his generation, it would appear that the world was saved only because it was God's will that His creation not be totally destroyed. Noah's righteousness itself would not have been enough to merit his salvation and that of his family. God saved him, because He wanted mankind to continue. He selected Noah as the best of an inferior lot. If so, society today only exists because of the *Middas HaRachamim*, the Attribute of Mercy.

According to the other view, mankind survived because Noah was genuinely righteous and deserved to be saved. If not for his merit, the world would have been destroyed; the great human experiment would have ceased. If so, society today has a right to exist even by the standards of the *Middas HaDin*, the Attribute of Strict Justice. Noah earned it for us.

ii. *Noah's State of Mind*

OAH SPENT A FULL YEAR IN THE RELATIVELY PRISTINE, hermetically sealed world of the ark. He adjusted to it and fulfilled his duties as God had instructed him. But then the year came to an end, and it was time to return to the outside world. What went through Noah's mind during those final days? Did he feel a sense of excitement at the prospect of rebuilding the flood-wrecked earth or did he feel daunted by the enormity of what lay ahead? And when he finally did emerge from the ark, why did he plant a vineyard (9:20) when he should have planted staple crops?

A close reading of the verses that describe Noah's sending of the birds from the ark give us some clues regarding his state of mind.

The Torah records four instances of Noah sending birds from the ark. The first time it was a raven, the next three a dove. The four verses are as follows:

— And [Noah] sent out the raven, and it went to and fro until the waters dried upon the land (8:7).

— And he sent out the dove from alongside him to see if the waters had receded from the face of the earth (8:8).

— And another seven days passed, and again he sent out the dove from the ark (8:10).

— Another seven days passed, and he sent out the dove, and it no longer returned to him (8:11).

As we analyze these verses, we find subtle indications of Noah's progressive detachment from the animals around which his world had revolved for an entire year.

The Torah tells us why Noah sent out the dove, but it gives us no reason for his having previously sent out the raven. It has been suggested that he sent out the raven because it is a scavenger that feeds on human carrion. Perhaps Noah wanted to ascertain what had become of the people who had remained outside the ark. He was making his first tentative steps toward his new life.

This would be in keeping with Noah's apparent strong emotional involvement with his antediluvian society. Incredulous at what is about to happen, he is reluctant to separate from his compatriots and enter the ark until the rising waters forced him to (7:7). After the Flood, even when he sees the land is dry, he remains inside the ark, unwilling to witness the devastation, until God commands him to leave (8:16). The sending of the raven may have reflected Noah's continued interest in those he hesitantly left behind.

Noah then sends out the dove to determine if the "the waters had receded from the face of the earth." The first time the dove is sent out "from alongside him," the second time "from the ark." The third time, we are told only that "the dove was sent." The dispatch of the dove is becoming more and more impersonal. Noah is detaching himself from his wards.

We see this same progressive detachment in the description of the dove's return. The first time (8:9), Noah "reached out his arm to take it and bring it to himself to the ark." The second time (8:10), however, we are told rather impersonally that "the dove returned to him." His level of attachment is progressively diminishing.

When Noah finally leaves the ark, he gives thanks to God for his salvation. He has fulfilled his obligations to the animals, but his emotional attachment to them has not endured. He is, however, still distraught over the demise of the society he once knew. Clearly not invigorated by the prospect of building a new world, he plants what he hopes will be a remedial vineyard before he does anything else. Unable to redirect his focus from his sense of loss, he turns to wine as a type of balm to soothe his hurt and his loneliness. Indeed, the Midrash teaches that Noah debased himself by planting a vineyard before anything else. Mankind would have to wait for Abraham to appear and restart the process of vigorously restoring the world.

iii. To Drive Away the Raven

OR WHAT PURPOSE DID NOAH SEND THE RAVEN OUT OF the ark? The Torah only informs us (8:7) that Noah "sent out the raven, and it went to and fro until the waters dried upon the land." Later on, the dove is sent out to determine if the waters had receded, but the Torah never tells us why the raven was sent out.

According to the Talmud (*Sanhedrin* 108b), the raven hovered over the ark and hurled two accusations at Noah. It alleged that Noah had sent him away in order to seduce the female raven. It also accused Noah of attempting to destroy his species. Otherwise, the raven contended, why hadn't Noah chosen one of the kosher birds, of which there were seven pairs in the ark? Why risk the raven of which there was only one pair?

According to the Talmud, Noah proved he had no designs on the raven's mate by saying, "If I am forbidden to have relations with my own wife as long the world is beset by the Flood, certainly I can have none with your mate."

This argument effectively refuted the raven's first charge. But what about the second charge? There is no mention in the Talmud of any refutation, which suggests that it was valid. Apparently, the raven was right. Noah had indeed sent it out in order to prevent the propagation of its species. But why? What reason might Noah have had for wanting to rid the world of ravens?

In order to discover Noah's motivation, let us examine the raven. God forbade intimate relations during the year that all living creatures were confined to the ark.[1] Only three creatures violated this command: the dog, the raven and Ham, Noah's third son.

The raven was guilty of the sin of illicit relations in the ark, a grave infraction indicative of a fundamental indifference to God's will. Moreover, his irrepressible lust was reminiscent of the world's first sin, which according to the Midrash was motivated by the serpent's lustful desire for Eve. The Midrash here anticipates modern psychology in identifying this drive as among the most powerful, if not the most powerful, force of the animalistic side of human nature, which accounts for the capacity for sin and the consequent ability to exercise free will.[2]

What are the singular or distinguishing features of the raven? It is a scavenger that feeds on the carcasses of dead animals. This

---

1. *Bereishis Rabbah* 31:12, 34:8. The Midrash finds an allusion to this oral tradition in that God commanded the men and women of Noah's family to enter the ark separately. Furthermore, He only commanded them and the rest of the creatures to "be fruitful and multiply" after they left the ark. By inference, relations were forbidden as long as the world was being destroyed.

2. Following the destruction of the First Temple, the Sages prayed for the destruction of the *yetzer hara* of idolatry to which they attributed the great national calamity. At the same time, they also attempted to destroy the *yetzer hara* of illicit relations, but they had to withdraw their request when all procreation came to a halt.

again connects the raven to the original sin of Adam, whose byproduct was human mortality. It also connects the raven to the greatest source of impurity (*tumah*), which is death.

The Talmud (*Shabbos* 155b) finds a second aspect of the raven's nature in the verse (*Psalms* 147:9) "[God] feeds the young ravens when they call out." The raven, explains the Talmud, has no compassion for its offspring and neglects to feed them. Mercifully, God sets the laws of nature so that worms are attracted to the raven's droppings and its young feed on them.

The raven emerges before us as a prototypal instinctual creature driven by lust, without mercy for its young, feasting on the spoils of death, unpredictable and unreliable.[3] The dove, on the other hand, serves as character foil to the raven. It is so inordinately attached to its nest that it cannot survive the death of its mate. As such, in contrast to the instinctually driven raven, the dove could be trusted to fulfill its mission on the outside and then return to the ark to its mate.

Noah understood that in the aftermath of the Flood he would be called upon to rebuild civilization. He would become the second Adam, the father of humankind. With this mission in mind, he saw in the raven an evil vestige of the corruption and the disregard of God's will that characterized the defunct world obliterated by the Flood. In order to ensure the purity of his brave new world, Noah believed he had to eliminate the raven.[4]

There is actually an allusion to the negative characteristics of the raven in its Hebrew name, *orev*, which is etymologically related to the Hebrew word for mixing, *arev*. According to the Sages, the sin of eating from the Tree of Knowledge resulted in the displacement of truth and clarity by doubt and confusion; truth and falsehood became intermixed. The Talmud (*Gittin* 54a)

---

3. It is interesting to note that the black raven in literature and other art forms throughout history conjures up images of dark, even demonic forces.

4. Like Adam, Noah was prohibited from killing creatures, thus he had to wait to release the raven until a time when it could survive outside of the Ark, long before the rest of the creatures' departure so that it would not find its mate.

reinforces this association by telling us that the raven, the *orev*, is an inveterate liar.[5] The raven is driven by his instinctual desires and will do anything necessary to satisfy them.

We find support for the characterization of the raven as a malignant presence in the world in the Talmud (*Moed Katan* 9a) in the context of a discussion of the importance of celebrating mitzvos one at a time. The Gemara points out that King Solomon celebrated the First Temple's inauguration a week before Succos, even though it would have been more convenient to delay the finishing touch of the construction until just before the festival so that the two celebrations could be combined. The Gemara concludes, mitzvos must be celebrated one at a time.

What was this "finishing touch of the Temple construction"?

The Gemara identifies it as the installation of the *ama kalia orev*, the arm-like "spikes that drove away the ravens." These sharpened spikes were placed on the Temple roof to keep away ravens that might otherwise have been attracted by the smell of the roasting flesh of the sacrifices.

The role of these spikes as the finishing touch of the construction of the Temple, the final blow of the hammer (*makeh b'patish*) so to speak, suggests an importance of function. It would seem, however, that the spikes were essentially superfluous, for even without them, no raven would have perched on the Temple, just as miraculously no flies were attracted to the sacrificial meat in the Temple; the spikes were placed there only because "we do not rely on miracles." Since miracles were commonplace in the First Temple, the spikes were placed on the roof only for form's sake and served no practical function. This reinforces the thought that the spikes as the "finishing touch" implied a more profound symbolism in their presence.

In the light of Noah's rejection of the raven, we begin to discern this symbolism. The Torah states that the purpose of the Temple was to effect a relationship between God and the Jewish people and thereby create a dwelling place for God among them.

---

5. Interestingly, in the story related in this Gemara, the dove (*yonah*) is present and tells the truth.

The Temple is a vehicle designed to elevate the Jewish people, and by extension all of mankind, to a plane of existence that replicates the sinless state of mankind clinging to God in the Garden of Eden. The instinctual raven, the paradigm of primitive urges and disregard of God's will, is the antithesis of this exalted state, and therefore, the *ama kalia orev*, the "spikes that drove away the ravens," are a fitting capstone to the Temple. Symbolically, the Temple is meant to drive away the corrupt forces associated with ravens.

This theme is echoed in the following *parashah*, *Lech Lecha*. God informs Abraham that he and his descendants will inherit the land of Israel, and Abraham asks (15:8), "Whereby shall I know that I am to inherit it?" God instructs Abraham to take eleven animals, nine of which he severs in half, thereby sealing the Covenant of the Parts (*Bris Bein HaBesarim*). The Midrash comments that the animal parts were the symbolic answer to Abraham's question. He would merit the land by virtue of the future sacrificial service in the Temple. In the midst of Abraham's prophetic vision (15:11), "birds of prey descended upon the carcasses and Abraham drove them away." Abraham's act of chasing away generic birds of prey from the sacrifices foreshadowed the symbolic *ama kalia orev*, the crown of the Temple structure that "drove away the ravens."

iv. *Husband and Wife*

ESPITE NOAH'S FAILURE TO RESTART MANKIND ON A proper footing after he disembarks from the ark, God does not refrain from giving him instructive hints about how to conduct himself with his family in the aftermath of the Flood.

Originally, God told Noah (5:18), "And you shall go into the ark, you, your sons, your wife and your daughters-in-law with you." Later on (6:7), we see Noah and his family entering the ark in that exact sequence — himself, his sons, his wife, his daughters-in-law.

A year later, after the flood waters have receded, God commands Noah to leave the ark (8:16), "Go out from the ark, you, your wife, your sons and your daughters-in-law." The sequence has changed. Why?

Rashi explains that conjugal relations were forbidden during the year of the Flood. When God commanded Noah and his family to enter the ark, husbands were separated from wives, as the sequence of the verse indicates. When they emerged from the ark one year later, conjugal relations were again permitted. Now, Noah's wife is mentioned right next to her husband.

While Noah was still in the ark, God commanded him (8:17), "Be fruitful and multiply." Therefore, the order specified for their emergence from the ark points to more than the reestablishment of conjugality between Noah and his wife and the resumption of procreation. There must be another meaning to it.

With the world in utter ruin, Noah was to be the second Adam, the new father of mankind. Similarly, his wife was to be its mother. They would become the common ancestors of all humanity. This was a serious responsibility, far greater than the responsibility borne by other parents. In rearranging the sequence of the exit, God subtly suggested to Noah that in order to be successful in his transcendent mission there should be a close partnership between him and his wife.

For whatever reason, Noah did not heed God's directive. He and his family exited as they had entered (8:18), "himself, his sons, his wife and his daughters-in-law." The consequences of his failure to face up to his new responsibility immediately surface in the episode of the vineyard.

Interestingly, modern psychology has observed that as drug use increases, meaningful reciprocal relationships decline. We may conjecture that God, the Perfect Therapist, anticipated that

Noah might withdraw when he saw the world devastated and denuded of its inhabitants. Noah sought relief in his vineyard, but God had already advised him to deal with his sense of loss by investing his emotional efforts in his family.

v. *The Failed Redeemer*

ITHIN A FEW GENERATIONS AFTER THE FLOOD, NOAH'S descendants once again become corrupt, as had the descendants of Adam prior to the Great Flood. How do we account for this second relatively rapid failure?

If we analyze the verses relating to the birth of Noah and to the divine decree of the Deluge, we discover an interesting commonality.

Noah's father Lemech was "182 years old, and he fathered a son" (5:28-29). Unlike all other antediluvian births, we are told only afterward that Lemech named his son. He called him Noah because "this one will cause us to reconsider our deeds and the agony of our handiwork from the land God has cursed" (זֶה יְנַחֲמֵנוּ מִמַּעֲשֵׂנוּ וּמֵעִצְּבוֹן יָדֵינוּ מִן הָאֲדָמָה אֲשֶׁר אֵרְרָהּ ה'). According to *Midrash Tanchuma*, we are first told he was a *ben*, a "son," because the word is cognate with *banah*, to "build." He was the one who would rebuild the world.

The explanation of his name features four significant verbs — reconsider, (יְנַחֲמֵנוּ), curse (אֵרְרָהּ), agony (עִצָּבוֹן) and make (מַעֲשֵׂנוּ). Two of these verbs resonate with the original expulsion from Eden (3:17), "Cursed is the ground because of you and with agony shall you eat from it throughout your entire lifetime" (אֲרוּרָה הָאֲדָמָה בַּעֲבוּרֶךָ בְּעִצָּבוֹן תֹּאכְלֶנָּה כֹּל יְמֵי חַיֶּיךָ). Three connect to the subsequent destruction in the Great Flood (6:6), "And God regretted that he made man on the land, and he agonized over it in his heart" (וַיִּנָּחֶם ה' כִּי עָשָׂה אֶת הָאָדָם בָּאָרֶץ וַיִּתְעַצֵּב אֶל לִבּוֹ).

These resonances suggest that Noah had the potential to redeem mankind from the "curse" and the "agony" decreed at the expulsion, and to elevate mankind to the point where it would not need to be destroyed by the Great Flood. We also find in *Midrash Tanchuma* that Noah was born circumcised, a further sign of potential greatness. *Midrash Tanchuma* also tells us that Noah invented the plow, a tool that greatly increases the bounty of the earth that had been cursed as a result of Adam's sin.

In the end, however, only Noah himself and his family were deemed worthy of survival. The true redemption of mankind would only begin much later, with the arrival of Abraham. Abraham had the ability to go out and bring people closer to God and to a moral way of life; Noah, however, withdrew from society and its contaminating influences. How do we understand this difference? Perhaps Noah sought to protect his own spiritual condition by withdrawing from society. Therefore, he was unable to influence his contemporaries and save them.

vi. *Individuals and Tribes*

UBTLE DIFFERENCES APPEAR IN THE WAY THE TORAH records the lineages of Noah's three sons, Shem, Ham and Japheth. Japheth's offspring are listed first. All of Japheth's seven sons are mentioned by name. Japheth's grandchildren by Gomer, his firstborn, and Yavan, his fourth son, are also mentioned by name. The last two of Yavan's children, however, are called Kittim and Dudanim, literally Kits and Dudans, a reference to tribes rather than to individuals, as we see from the translation of *Targum Yonasan ben Uziel* (10:4).

Ham's children are listed next, all by their proper names.

However, Ham's grandchildren by Mitzraim, his second son, are listed as tribes, such as Ludes and Anams, rather than as individuals. The only other of Ham's grandchildren listed are those by Canaan, his fourth and youngest son. They are listed even more impersonally. They are called Jebusites (Yevusi), Amorites (Emori), Girgashites (Girgashi) and so on (10:16).

Shem's lineage, although he is Noah's middle son, is not listed until the end. Without exception, his progeny are all mentioned by their individual names. There is no reference to any tribes or peoples.

Why is this so?

What do we know about Shem, Ham and Japheth, Noah's three sons?

Shem was the most righteous of the three. The Midrash credits him with founding an academy that taught the concepts of monotheism. It lasted for centuries and was attended by our patriarch Jacob.

On the other extreme are Ham and his son and alter ego Canaan who together uncover Noah's nakedness (9:22). What exactly did they do? Our Sages state that it was either castration or sodomy (*Rashi*, 9:24). It is interesting to note that modern psychologists identify two components of the basic libidinal drives corresponding to the drives identified by our Sages as *kinah* (jealousy) and *taavah* (lust).[6] It is precisely these, the two lowest components of the animal soul (*nefesh habahami*), which drove Ham and Canaan to commit such cruel acts against Noah.[7]

Now let us see how these differences apply to the names recorded for their children. Shem, from whom Abraham is descended, is the most perfected of the sons, and he relates to his

---

6. According to Jewish thought, the father of modern psychology did not comprehend the totality of the human being, since he failed to appreciate the spiritual component. He was, however, an excellent scientific observer of man's lower elements.

7. My teacher, Rabbi Israel Chait שליט״א, has noted that Ham's punishment fit his crime. He was unable to control his own passions, and consequently, Noah cursed him that he would have others control those passions for him, i.e., he and his descendants through Canaan would be slaves.

children and they to theirs in the most individualistic way. Each son is raised according to his singular nature as expressed by his specific name.

Japheth also relates to most of his offspring in an individualistic way; the Torah records these children with their individual names. Some of his offspring, however, lose individuality and are referred to as tribes rather than individuals.

Ham has most of his descendants through Canaan, the son who embodies his traits. These offspring are referred to in the most abstract fashion, the Jebusites, Amorites and so on, which indicates that they developed more rapidly into amalgamated peoples. Perhaps this tendency is reflected in Ham's name, which means hot. Of Noah's sons, he is the most emotional and impulsive in following his base drives. The cultures that he spawns are less refined and quick to sprout. Their father lacked the ability to raise them according to their individual needs and strengths; the Torah hints at this by identifying them as tribal nations rather than individuals.

vii. *In Search of Terah*

WHO EXACTLY WAS TERAH, THE FATHER OF OUR PATRIARCH Abraham? What sort of a person was he? We get a certain perspective from the Passover Haggadah, which is organized to open with our lowly beginnings (*g'nus*) and conclude with our grandeur and praise of God (*sh'vach*). The lowly beginning with which the Haggadah opens is our ancestor Terah — an idol worshiper. We also find in the Midrash that Terah was a manufacturer of idols, and that he delivered his son Abraham to King Nimrod of the Chaldeans to be thrown into the furnace for rejecting the pagan religion.[8] Quite an awful picture.

But if we examine all the sources, yet another aspect of this enigmatic ancestor emerges.

An indication can be found in the chronology of the Torah. After leaving Ur of the Chaldeans, Abraham and Terah traveled together to Haran, then Abraham continued on himself to the land of Canaan. The Torah mentions Terah's death in Haran before Abraham sets out for Canaan, giving the impression that he was already dead when Abraham left. In fact, this was not so. Terah was alive when Abraham left; he died many years later.

Why then, wonders the Midrash, are we given this misleading impression? Because, explains the Midrash, Abraham was only obeying God's command when he left Haran without his father. Nonetheless, in order to avoid the appearance of impropriety on the part of Abraham in failing to honor his father for the remaining years of his life, the chronology is obscured.

Now, if Terah were really so evil, why would it be considered improper for Abraham to leave him in Haran and go on by himself to Canaan? The Talmud (*Pesachim* 56a) tells us that the righteous King Hezekiah dragged the dead bones of King Achaz, his wicked father, all over Jerusalem. Apparently, this was perfectly proper. Why then might it have seemed an indiscretion for Abraham to leave Terah and go to Canaan?

Let us now take note of a few other illuminating details. According to the Torah, all of Terah's contemporaries had children at around the age of 30. Terah, however, did not have his first child until the age of 70 (11:26). This delay suggests maturity and gravity in his approach to child rearing.[9]

Terah named one of his sons Nahor, the first person in the Biblical record to name his son in honor of his father, whose

---

8. According to the Midrash (*Bereishis Rabbah* 38:13), Terah was a leading figure in local pagan practice and delivered his son to Nimrod because of his son's monotheistic beliefs.
9. The number seventy is frequently associated with wisdom, as in the seventy elders of the Sanhedrin, the seventy families of languages, and so on.

name was also Nahor. In doing so, Terah further displayed the quality of appreciation (*hakaras hatov*) in honoring his own father.

There is more. All the patriarchs — Abraham, Isaac and Jacob — married direct descendants of Terah, a granddaughter, great-granddaughter and two great-great-granddaughters respectively.

Furthermore, the Torah states (11:31) that Terah was headed towards Canaan, although he never made it there and eventually died in Haran. Why was he heading towards Canaan? What business did he have there? Terah's interest in going to Canaan after Abraham's triumphant emergence from the fire of Ur of the Chaldeans points to a certain spirituality. Perhaps he wanted to investigate the monotheism his son preached and was on his way to Canaan to seek out Noah's son Shem[10] who taught these concepts in his academy. For some undisclosed reason, however, Terah aborted his spiritual quest in Haran and remained there.

Finally, when Abraham dies, he is described as being "gathered unto his people." According to the Midrash, this implies that his father, Terah, repented, gaining immortality for his soul, and was among the people to whom Abraham was gathered.

All this evidence leads us to conclude that Terah was a great man of sorts, a man of considerable potential. Though he was steeped in idolatry, we may imagine that Terah, unlike his contemporaries, was engaged in an earnest though misguided search for spirituality. His willingness to deliver his child to the authorities for death portrays him as a courageous but benighted man of principle; his son Abraham would one day draw on this courage when asked to deliver his son Isaac to God as a sacrifice.

---

10. According to *Targum Yonasan ben Uziel* and the Talmud (*Nedarim* 32b), Shem was Malchizedek, who was, according to the Torah, involved with monotheistic practice.

And so we see Terah as a man of many qualities — courage, conviction, appreciation and maturity, and we realize that Abraham was not born into a vacuum. It is understandable, therefore, that all the patriarchs were insistent on marrying into the family of their progenitor Terah.

Abraham would not have left his father behind in Haran had he not received divine instruction to proceed to Canaan on his own, and therefore, the Torah obscures the true chronology.

פרשת לך לך
Parashas Lech Lecha

i. A Lot of Trouble

IT IS NOT QUITE CLEAR WHAT LOT INTENDED BY ACCOMPA-nying Abraham to Canaan. Perhaps there is a clue in the verses that describe their departure. God commands Abraham to leave for an unspecified destination where he will form a new nation. The Torah then states (12:4), "And Abraham went as God commanded him, and Lot went with him." The next verse seemingly repeats itself (12:5), "And Abraham took his wife Sarai and his nephew Lot and all their property ... to go towards the land of Canaan." Why the redundancy?

It seems that we are being shown Lot's role here from two different perspectives, his own and Abraham's. First, "Lot went with him." Lot is the subject of the verb, the one who actively goes because of his own motivations. In the second verse, however, Lot's role is passive. His uncle Abraham, according to his own agenda, takes him.

Let us first take a look at Abraham's perspective on Lot. That verse identifies Lot, unnecessarily, as his nephew, whereas the first verse does not. Abraham is thinking in terms of family continuity. Abraham had no children of his own, yet God had promised that he would become a great nation. Abraham identifies his nephew Lot as his successor, who might be considered as his own child; just as the founder of a nation is considered "the father of his country," so would Abraham be considered Lot's father in a manner of speaking. The fulfillment of God's promise would come through him.

Lot was also thinking in terms of becoming Abraham's successor. He wants to join Abraham in his new mission, as we see from the mention of God's command in the first verse, but his intentions are not quite the same as Abraham's. We are told that Lot went "with him," *ito* (אתו). "With him" can also be expressed by the word *imo* (עמו). The Vilna Gaon points out that, in the Torah, *ito* refers only to physical accompaniment while *imo* suggests a shared purpose (*Numbers* 22:2ff).[1] Lot only went *ito*, accompanying Abraham in a physical sense but not sharing fully in his commitment to God's mission. He was like a prince in waiting, ready to assume Abraham's power, status and possessions but not his ideals.

Lot's ultimate unworthiness is confirmed when Abraham asks him to go his separate way after their servants quarrel over grazing land (13:5). The Midrash, quoted by Rashi, explains the underlying cause of their dispute. As Abraham's heir and ultimate inheritor of the land, Lot felt justified in appropriating the land for his present needs. Abraham considered this presumptuous and unethical; and he distanced himself from Lot.

At that time, God had not yet informed Abraham that he would have his own son from whom the Jewish nation would originate. Abraham could not see any prospect for building a nation other than through Lot. Nonetheless, in his great integrity,

---

1. This distinction explains why the angel stopped Bilam even though he was given permission in his prophecy to accompany Balak's messengers. He had been told only that he could go *ito*, with him physically. Nonetheless, he went *imahem*, with shared purpose.

Abraham disassociated himself from the morally unfit Lot. A lesser man with visions of building a nation of God might have found a way to rationalize and compromise. Abraham did not. He distanced himself from Lot, and right afterward (13:14), God informed him that he would be the biological patriarch of a new nation. Apparently, God had postponed this prophetic promise until Abraham expelled Lot.

The Mishnah (*Avos* 5:4) states that Abraham faced ten tests and passed them all. There is some disagreement among the Sages as to what these tests specifically were, but no one mentions Abraham's readiness to part from Lot. Why not? It must have been a difficult thing to do, especially in the light of our discussion.

Perhaps we can say that this test was really a preview of Abraham's final and greatest test, when God calls upon him to slaughter his son Isaac, thereby abandoning his only perceivable vehicle for the establishment of a nation; the test of Lot is, therefore, subsumed in the test of Isaac.

ii. *The Silence Treatment*

HERE IS A STRIKING CONTRAST BETWEEN THE TORAH'S respective introductions of Noah and Abraham. The Torah uses the equivalent of blaring trumpets, "a pure soul, righteous in his generation," to explain Noah's selection by God. At the opposite extreme, the Torah gives no prior reason or information to justify Abraham's being called on by God. While numerous Midrashim detail Abraham's greatness and noble deeds from his earliest childhood, the Torah itself is silent.

Or is it?

It would appear that there are subtle hints that give us insight into why God chose Abraham.

Originally, we see that Abraham and his father intended to travel to Canaan but only got as far as Haran. Now God calls on Abraham to go to an unspecified land and Abraham proceeds to Canaan. One view of the Ramban is that Abraham was indeed given no instructions as to the destination of his journey.

Why did Abraham go there?

Canaan may have been identified even in distant Mesopotamia with monotheism; as we learn later, Malchizedek, who was really Shem the son of Noah, served there at the time as a priest to God. Once Abraham arrived at the country's border in Shechem, God confirmed (12:7) that He would give the land upon which he now stood to his offspring. Without any further divine instruction, Abraham continues on "to the mountain," which seems to have been his original destination.

Rabbeinu Bachya identifies "the mountain" as the Temple Mount, as it is identified in several places in the Torah. When Abraham arrives at his destination, he builds an altar and "calls out in the Name of God." The Talmud (*Sotah* 10a) understands this to mean that he caused others to call out in the Name of God. In other words, he resumed in earnest his lifelong mission of bringing people closer to the worship of the one God. Thus, in a subtle fashion, the Torah reveals Abraham's quest even prior to God's initial directive to him.

But the question is not entirely resolved. Why does the Torah reveal Abraham's credentials in such an oblique manner? Why doesn't the Torah tell them to us as openly as it tells us about Noah?

It is possible, however, that this very silence is instructive. Although most of us come to Torah observance through the chain of tradition passed from generation to generation from an entire nation of our ancestors who stood at Mount Sinai, perhaps God wants us to find Him independently as well, just as Abraham did. The Torah's silence leads us to wonder about the observations and thoughts that led Abraham to his convictions and perhaps to seek them on our own as well. This sort of quest helps us forge a more powerful bond with God and His revealed word, a bond that will protect us from the prejudices and pressures of the antagonistic cultures that surround us, just as it protected Abraham.

iii. *Virtue Is Its Own Reward*

OMING BACK FROM HIS VICTORY OVER THE FOUR KINGS, Abraham was apparently distraught. God comforted and reassured him, saying (15:1), "Do not fear, Abram. I will be a shield for you." What did Abraham fear? According to Rashi, Abraham was concerned that the divine protection afforded him in battle might have depleted his deposits of accumulated merit.

This interpretation raises a broad philosophical question. If Abraham deserved reward because of his perfection, why should God's past protection deplete his merit? Since God's resources are inexhaustible, why shouldn't He continue to protect Abraham in the future?

The Talmud (*Eruvin* 22b) discusses God's attribute of being long suffering, which is called *erech apayim* (אֶרֶךְ אַפַּיִם); the word *apayim* (אַפַּיִם) is the plural form of the word *af* (אַף). Why? The Talmud explains that God is not only long suffering in punishing the wicked but He also delays in rewarding the righteous in order to give them greater rewards in the next world. The question arises again: If God's supply of benevolence is infinite, why should one reward diminish the potential for another?

In conceptualizing reward and punishment, the simplistic view is to think of a big ledger into which our scores are entered. When we do a mitzvah we get a merit point, and when we sin we get a demerit. At the end of our lives, God opens our ledger and totals up the points in the merit and demerit columns. And this determines our reward.

A more sophisticated view of reward and punishment considers the effects of our deeds on our immortal, immaterial souls. Throughout our lives, our souls are in a state of flux. When a person does God's will, acting kindly, doing mitzvos, learning Torah and so forth, the spirituality of his soul is enhanced, and consequently, after the body is peeled away, the soul's connection to the Almighty is strong. Otherwise, the opposite is true. This is how reward and punishment are determined in the World to Come.

When a person does good deeds and lives a righteous life, however, the temporal successes he enjoys may actually be harmful. They may dilute his desire to do what is right for its own sake, thereby risking his eternal rewards. For example, if a person is honest in business and profits mightily by this virtue, he may come to see honesty as desirable because it promotes material success, not because God wants us to act with truth. It is a paradoxical truth that the greatest good we can do for ourselves is to attach our souls firmly to God by doing His will for its own sake — and not for ourselves. Material reward in this world, however, can distract us from the true ideal and weaken our attachment to God.

This may have been Abraham's fear. Abraham was afraid that the physical protection he had received might have insinuated itself into his subconscious as a substitute motivation for living a model spiritual life, thereby weakening his attachment to God. That is why, according to the Talmud, God delays distributing reward to the righteous. He wants them to derive the most possible enduring good for their souls from their actions. This occurs when they do them without ulterior motives, only for their inherent virtue.

iv. *Abram vs. Abraham*

HE TWO NAMES APPEAR TO BE SOMEWHAT SIMILAR, Abram and Abraham, yet the difference is very signif-icant. God decrees the name change (17:5) to reflect the as-yet-childless Abraham's role as the *av hamon goyim* — "father of multiple nations." In fact, so serious is the difference that the Talmud forbids (*Berachos* 13a) the use of the name Abram now that his name is Abraham.

There are two views in the Talmud regarding the nature of this prohibition. Bar Kapparah considers it a prohibition implicit in a positive statement, an *issur asei*, derived from the words "and your name shall be Abraham." Rabbi Eliezer considers it an out-right prohibition (*lo saasei*) derived from the words "your name will not be Abram." What is at the root of this dispute?

Perhaps we can say that these two opinions differ in their understanding of the internal change that precipitated the name change. Bar Kapparah sees Abraham's transformation as evolu-tionary, Abraham's personality and historic mission being an out-growth and development of Abram's personality. There is nothing inherently untruthful in referring to Abraham as Abram, except for the failure to acknowledge the new facets of his personality and historic role. This failure is an act of omission, of not fulfill-ing an *asei*.

Rabbi Eliezer, on the other hand, considers the change as rev-olutionary, a radical transformation to a totally different historic personality. Referring to Abraham as Abram is inherently false, and the transgression is one of committing a *lo saasei*.

Further along in that passage of the Talmud, we find an inter-esting anomaly. Not only Abraham received a new name. Sarah, whose original name was Sarai, also had a name change, but only Abraham was forbidden to refer to his wife by her old name of Sarai. No other Jews are forbidden to refer to her as Sarai. Why is there this discrepancy between Abraham and Sarah?

The reason for this distinction may relate to the Jewish concept of "the honor of the princess is modesty" (כָּל כְּבוּדָה בַת מֶלֶךְ פְּנִימָה) (*Psalms* 45:14). Modesty is a particularly important element in a woman's spiritual development. Sarah's transformation is dealt with in the privacy of her home, and has practical implications for her husband Abraham (see following discussion). It had only casual implications for other people, and therefore, there is no prohibition for anyone other than her husband. Abraham, on the other, hand, was a public figure; it is incumbent on all Jews to acknowledge the transformation in his role.

The Talmud (*Berachos* 27b) tells the story of Rabbi Elazar ben Azariah's selection as *Nasi*, President of the Academy. When asked if he wanted the position, he said he would consult with "the people of his home" before making a decision. The Talmud relates that he went home and asked his wife. Although Rabbi Elazar always intended to confer with his wife, he did not reveal this publicly. Although she was his full partner and confidante in private, Rabbi Elazar avoided exposing his wife to the public eye, because a woman's honor is in her modesty.

v. *The Letter Trade-In*

OD COMMEMORATED ABRAHAM'S PERSONAL TRANSFOR-mation by the addition of a letter to his name. Sarah's name was also modified, but by exchanging a letter rather than by adding one. Originally, her name was Sarai, ending with the letter *yud*. When her name was changed to Sarah, the final *yud* was exchanged for the letter *hei*.

The Yerushalmi tells us (*Sanhedrin* 9:6) that the letter *yud* complained to God for having been removed from Sarah's name.

God reassured the letter *yud* that it would one day reappear in the name of the great leader Joshua. Joshua's name had originally been Hosea. But when he set out for the Promised Land in the company of the Spies (*Numbers* 13:16), Moses wanted to give him extra protection against their corruption. Therefore, he added a *yud* to his name, thereby changing Hosea to Joshua.

Upon reflection, there is a discernible similarity and connection between Sarah and Joshua. Both played supporting roles, as devoted students or junior partners, in facilitating the divinely directed paths of great Jewish leaders. There was one difference. Sarah remained in the background, even when her name was Sarai. Joshua, however, was a more visible number two. Nonetheless, despite being in the spotlight, Joshua's task was to reflect the greatness of Moses, like the moon reflects sunlight, like a capable but self-effacing vice president. Both of these secondary positions call for humility. The humility of being number two expresses itself, however, in two different ways. One occurs in relative anonymity, as with Sarah, symbolized by the changed letter at the end of the name Sarai. The other occurs in tantalizing publicity, as with Joshua whose name was changed at its beginning. The Midrash suggests that this capacity for selfless service was Sarah's legacy to her descendant Joshua.

How did Sarah's character change after the letter *yud* in her name was replaced with the letter *hei*?

Let us take a closer look at these two letters. The Torah states (2:4), "These are the generations of the heavens and the earth when they were created" (אֵלֶּה תוֹלְדוֹת הַשָּׁמַיִם וְהָאָרֶץ בְּהִבָּרְאָם).

Why is there a small letter *hei* in the word *behibar'am* (בְּהִבָּרְאָם)?

The Talmud (*Menachos* 29b), cited by Rashi, explains that God created the physical universe with the letter *hei*. The word can thus be translated not only as "when they were created" but also as "He created them with a *hei*." Rashi also states that the letter *yud* refers to the spiritual realms,[2] while the letter *hei* is connected to the earthly domain, a thought echoed in many Midrashic and Kabbalistic sources.

Apparently, Sarah made a great sacrifice in giving up the *yud* in exchange for the *hei*, a further withdrawal into the background. Previously, Sarai had aided in Abraham's activity of bringing his message to the world at large, albeit in a modest fashion. With the name change, the main expression of Sarai's spiritual devotion was to be expressed in Sarah's physical and moral rearing of Isaac. The willing diminution of her public self, in which she had had a modest but visible role in helping Abraham, brought Sarah to an even higher spirituality. And by doing so, she established for all time that the chief practical outlet for a Jewish woman's desire to do God's will is by raising Jewish children. Modesty, selflessness and devotion became the hallmarks of a Jewish woman.

vi. *Eleven vs. Five*

OW MANY ANIMALS DID GOD INSTRUCT ABRAHAM TO offer at the Covenant of the Parts? God commands Abraham (15:9), "Take for Me heifers threefold (*meshuleshes*), goats threefold, rams threefold, a turtledove and a young dove." What exactly does "threefold" mean? The language is ambiguous.

Targum Onkelos, which Rashi follows, interprets the word to mean three animals, bringing the sum total of animals offered to eleven. *Targum Yonasan* understands the term as referring to the age of the animal. If so, Abraham brought one heifer, one goat and one ram, each of which was 3 years old, for a total of five animals.

---

2. Based on *Pesikta Rabbasi* 21.

The Covenant of the Parts effected a bond between God and Abraham that would lead to the creation of the Jewish nation. Our Sages view Abraham's offerings as a seminal act that foreshadowed the sacrificial service in the Temple and, more broadly, the Jewish mission to establish God's kingship on earth amidst mankind. According to *Targum Onkelos*, this covenant called for eleven animals, while according to *Targum Yonasan*, it called for five.

The Maharal cites numerous connections between the number eleven and the presence or removal of idolatry. For instance, there were eleven ingredients in the *ketores*, an aromatic incense-like substance that counteracted the evil effects of national idolatry or gross deviation from God's will. Another example is that the 365-day solar year exceeds the 354-day lunar year by eleven days. The sun, that highly visible source of heat, light and growth, was the most frequent object of idolatry in the pagan world.

Five is a number that in a profound way reflects God's creation. The Torah cryptically alludes to this (2:4), "These are the generations of the heavens and the earth when they were created." The word *behibar'am,* "when they were created," is spelled with a small letter *hei* (ה). Our Sages comment that God created the Universe with the letter *hei*. Kabbalistic literature, expanding on this thought, describes five realms of creation and five levels of the soul. The significance of the concept of five underlying the plan of creation finds expression in the Five Books of the Torah and even the five fingers, five toes, five senses and five vocal sounds.

By connecting these concepts associated with the numbers eleven and five to Abraham's offerings at the Covenant of the Parts, we may possibly discern a fascinating though cryptic allusion to a famous dispute between the Rambam and the Ramban.

In his *Guide for the Perplexed*, the Rambam explains that the Temple sacrifices serve to wean the Jewish people from idolatrous practice. The Rambam's view, if misinterpreted, might lead one to think that if the Temple were rebuilt today there would be no religious need for these offerings, since idolatry has been scientifically discredited. In fact, the Rambam means nothing of the sort. Idolatry consists of any belief system or faith in an "ism" or reality outside of God. In this regard, modern society is not much advanced from its ancient counterparts. Idolatry is as rampant as ever, only it has assumed a different form. The sacrificial service in the Temple served, and will someday serve again, as a means of removing all distracting impulses from the realization of God's oneness. This is consistent with the Rambam's oft-expressed view that we gain knowledge of God and his Oneness by stripping away or negating false notions.

The Ramban, in the beginning of his commentary on Leviticus, rejects the Rambam's view. He explains that the word *korban*, commonly translated as sacrifice, is related to the word *karev*, close. The Ramban understands the Temple service to express a positive activity by which a person can bring himself closer to God.

Perhaps the concepts associated with eleven and five reflect these two different conceptualizations of the function of the Temple's sacrificial service. The Rambam's view would expect that Abraham offered eleven animals, symbolic of the later sacrificial service which was a means of removing idolatrous practice and dispositions. On the other hand, bringing five animals better reflects the Ramban's concept that the animal sacrifices were a positive expression of the goal of achieving a closer relationship with the Creator.

Understood this way, perhaps the Torah's ambiguous recording of the number of animals God commanded Abraham to bring reflects the divine endorsement of both interpretations, as both are true and the will of God.

פרשת וירא
Parashas Vayeira

i. *Water on the Lungs*

BRAHAM IS 99 YEARS OLD. HE HAS JUST BEEN CIRCUM-cised, and he is in pain. It is also extremely hot. Abraham sits in his doorway, recuperating, and God visits him in a prophetic vision. As the prophecy is in progress, Abraham suddenly spots three dusty travelers, who are really heavenly angels in disguise. He immediately takes his leave of God and runs to invite them into his home (18:1). According to the Midrash, this episode is a supreme expression of Abraham's dedicated hospitality and God's kindness in visiting the sick.

Why, however, did God trouble Abraham with visitors while he was recuperating from surgery?

The Talmud (*Bava Metzia* 86b) addresses this question. God saw that Abraham was distraught that the sun-baked road was empty of travelers to whom he could offer his hospitality. Therefore, God sent angels in the guise of travelers to visit him.

This answer, however, generates its own difficulties. In that same passage in the Talmud, we learn that God had caused the day to be unusually hot in order to keep the roads clear of travelers who might importune the recuperating Abraham by availing themselves of his hospitality. Now, why would God have distressed Abraham by denying him opportunities to do acts of kindness?

Let us digress for a moment. Water on the lungs is a very serious medical problem, but is it life threatening? If water is found in the lungs of a slaughtered animal, does this mean that it had suffered from a fatal disease and was therefore rendered unkosher (*treifah*)? The Talmud (*Chullin* 47b) discusses this question and resolves it with a recorded precedent. It once happened that Rabbi Hananiah was sick, and Rabbi Nathan and all the leading rabbis of the generation visited him and asked this selfsame question. Rabbi Hananiah answered that the meat was kosher.

It is possible that this story means to do more than resolve the question of whether the meat was kosher; it instructs us on a deeper level. Could "Rabbi Nathan and all the leading rabbis of the generation" not have be able to resolve the halachic issue on their own? It seems likely that their question was designed to send Rabbi Hananiah a message.

Barring trauma, most terminal geriatric illnesses involve the heart, lungs or liver. When diseased, these organs frequently have the sequelae of accumulated liquid in the parenchymal spaces and alveoli of the lung. It is thus likely that the rabbis were asking Rabbi Hananiah about a symptom similar to one which he himself was experiencing. When he declared the animal kosher, he affirmed that this symptom did not necessarily signal a terminal condition in the animal and, in effect, reassured himself. Subtly, the rabbis sent him a message of hope.

The story of God visiting Abraham serves as the paradigm for the mitzvah of visiting the sick. By causing the day to be exceedingly hot and then sending him angels disguised as travelers, God demonstrated that the mitzvah in its noblest form is not performed by a mere mechanical presence at the bedside of the sick. It calls for an investigation of the emotional needs of the ailing person and the discovery of creative methods to bring him hope, encouragement and relief.

ii. The In and Out Policy

KINDNESS WAS ONE OF ABRAHAM'S OUTSTANDING VIRTUES. Three days after his circumcision, at the height of his recuperative discomfort, he runs to bring three dusty travelers into his home. He offers them a crust of bread, but in actuality, he serves them a feast for a king (18:5-8). He offers a little but does a lot.

The Midrash offers many illuminating details about Abraham's hospitality. Two of them are quite remarkable: We are taught that Abraham's house had open doors on all four sides, so that strangers arriving from any direction would feel comfortable about entering. In addition, Abraham always escorted his departing guests four cubits past his door, a distance of about seven feet. What do these two details tell us about Abraham?

His open door policy suggests that he was selfless and giving; he accepted people for who they were, no matter what baggage they carried and where they originated. Abraham thought that these three travelers were idol worshipers, yet in no way does he recoil from them. The open doors on all sides further suggest that Abraham sought out others in need before they even came to him. Finally, the open door left him open to scrutiny and reflected his confidence that his behavior was always exemplary, that all his actions were a *kiddush Hashem*, a sanctification of God's Name.

The policy of escorting his departing guests beyond his door reveals another dimension to Abraham's personality. It is only natural for a person to want to relax and enjoy the privacy of his home. When he has guests, even if he thoroughly enjoys their company, he will almost inevitably feel a certain sense of anticipation when the time comes for them to leave the sanctity of his home.

Abraham, however, did not display this attitude. When his guests left, he expressed his sense of loss without any hesitation. By escorting his guests for a distance of four *amos*, the legal boundary for personal space, he conveyed to them that he was in no hurry to separate from them and return to his fortress of solitude. The guests saw clearly that Abraham found it difficult to part from them, that he appreciated their visit and held them in high esteem, that he did not look down at them because of their religious beliefs and practices. This was the beauty of Abraham's approach to bringing people closer to God. This is how he sanctified God's Name.

Incidentally, Rashi reveals to us another interesting method that Abraham used to bring people closer to God. Rashi states that Abraham refused to accept people's thanks for the hospitality he showed them, insisting that they thank the Creator instead. There was profound wisdom to this behavior, since people have a natural desire to express their gratitude. At its deepest level, this desire stems from the aversion to eating *nahama dikisufa*, the bread of shame — the *Zohar's* term for a benefit one receives without reciprocation. By refusing the thanks of his guests, Abraham placed them in a predicament. They could choose not to thank anyone, and feel ungrateful. Or else, they could direct their thanks to God, as Abraham advised, and acknowledge the One to Whom all thanks are due. Moreover, failure to thank God would have implied that they had taken advantage of the kindness of a deluded man, not an emotionally appealing prospect.

iii. Direct Notification

THREE ANGELS VISITED ABRAHAM IN THE GUISE OF wayfarers. Why three? The Sages explain that there were three missions to be carried out, and since no one angel can undertake multiple missions, three angels were necessary. The three missions were the notification of the future birth of Isaac, the rescue of Lot and the overthrow of Sodom. Therefore, we find that only two angels proceeded to Sodom. The angel who brought the news of Isaac's birth did not accompany them, since he had already fulfilled his mission.

The Ramban (18:15) wonders why the third angel was at all necessary. God Himself had already informed Abraham earlier that he and Sarah would yet have a son and instructed them to name him Isaac. What new information did the angel add?

The angel came to inform Sarah, explains the Ramban. Abraham had never told her about his own prophecy, since he thought God would send a special messenger to Sarah to inform her directly.

We can understand this reasoning as follows: As the future mother of Israel, whose new name reflected her greater responsibility, it was necessary for Sarah to know about Isaac's impeding birth through her own revelation. By hearing the news from an angel, she would recognize the full import of her position as the designated mother of the Jewish people. Thus, regardless of whether or not Abraham informed her of his prophecy, God sent the third angel to inform her directly.

iv. A Little Bit of Water

ROM THE MOMENT THE THREE TRAVELERS ENTERED Abraham's house, they were swept up in the urgency and completeness of his hospitality, which the Torah depicts in great detail. The first thing he did was issue instructions that his guests be given "*me'at mayim,* a little water," to wash their feet (18:4). The Torah apparently sees fit to inform us that he only asked for a little bit of water. What are we meant to learn from this? And why indeed did Abraham specifically ask for only a little water in contrast to the large quantity of other food he personally supplied?

One interpretation may be that the small amount reflects another aspect of Abraham's kindness. It is clear from the language of the verse that Abraham asked someone else in his household to bring the water; he did not bring it himself. In order to strike a balance between his kind impulses toward his guests and his kind impulses toward the one he had sent for the water, he specified that only a little water be brought. The guests would have enough water to wash their feet, yet there would be no undue strain on the one who brought them the water.

The Talmud, however, takes issue with Abraham for sending someone else for the water rather than bringing it himself. The Talmud observes that Moses rather than God Himself provided water for the Jewish people in the desert and explains (*Bava Metzia* 86b), "For all those things Abraham did personally for the angels, God personally repaid His descendants. For all those things Abraham delegated to others, God delegated agents to repay His descendants." How are we to understand this lapse in Abraham's hospitality? Why didn't he get the water himself?

We find the answer in the *Midrash Rabbah,* which identifies the person sent for the water as Ishmael, Abraham's son by Hagar. The boy was 13 years old at the time, and Abraham wanted to condition him to do mitzvos. Abraham wanted Ishmael to understand that he was being sent for his own growth and edification, not to ease his father's burden. Therefore, he sent Ishmael to bring the guests "a little water," a relatively simple and easy task.

One problem remains. Based on this Midrash, Abraham's actions are so clearly justified that we no longer understand why the Talmud takes issue with him for sending someone else to bring the water. He was not shirking his responsibilities in any way. Rather, he was using the opportunity to initiate his son into the mitzvah of hospitality. Why then should Abraham's descendants hundreds of years later have to suffer a certain distance in their relationship with God because he delegated to Ishmael the task of bringing the water?

The answer may lie in the prophecy Abraham received just two days earlier. God informed him that he and Sarah would yet be blessed with a son from whom the Jewish people would descend. The divine balance had been reset, and Abraham's obligation to educate Ishmael no longer superseded his own personal expression of love of God in attending to the wayfarers. Thus the Talmud suggests it would have been better had Abraham brought the water himself. The proper object of Abraham's pedagogy should have been the unborn Isaac, the son from whom the Jewish people would be descended.

v. Two Kinds of Kindness

THE ANNOUNCEMENT OF THE IMPENDING BIRTH OF ISAAC echoes in the Book of Samuel where the prophet Elisha informs a childless couple that they will be blessed with a son. As we read in the *Haftarah*, the couple had extended themselves to provide lodging for the prophet whenever he was in their vicinity, and in gratitude, he gives them his blessing.

The Talmud (*Berachos* 27b) records a debate between two Amoraim, Rav and Shmuel, as to the nature of the lodging the couple provided for Elisha. One maintains it was a second-story garret, the other that they partitioned off a room in their house.

At first glance, we are puzzled by this discussion. What difference is there really between a garret and a partitioned room?

Perhaps we can say that the issue of their discussion was the merit of this couple that earned them the prophet's blessing. If they partitioned off a room in their house, their kindness took the form of giving generously of themselves, their home and their privacy to the wayfarer. If they gave him a room in a garret, their kindness took on the form of acknowledging the superior nature and righteousness of the prophet by setting him above themselves. This was the merit that earned them the blessing.

In fact, we may say that the two opinions are not in conflict; rather, they reflect two distinct aspects of the couple's virtue, for which they were rewarded. For giving generously of themselves, God rewarded them generously. For adding a room to their home, a child was added to their family.

vi. *Sodom Is Squeezed Out*

MANKIND'S HISTORY IS REPLETE WITH UNTOLD NUMBERS OF thoroughly corrupt cities, and yet only once in all of history does God single out one city, or rather one set off cities, for miraculous destruction. Only once does He rain down fire and brimstone from the heavens to obliterate a metropolis of evil. Sodom, Gomorrah and its three sister cities enjoy this dubious distinction. Why were these cities singled out for destruction?[1]

Previous to their destruction, these same cities play a central role in another drama involving Abraham and Lot (14:1-16). The five cities rebel against their Mesopotamian overlords, and a war ensues. The invading armies are victorious. They denude the five cities of all their wealth and carry off Lot as a hostage, but Abraham pursues and defeats them, frees Lot and restores the captured booty to the five cities.

There is an interesting difference between Western and Eastern cultures regarding the rescue of a person in mortal danger. In the West, if a person saves someone else's life, the rescued person is beholden to the rescuer for the rest of his life. In the East, however, the opposite holds true. The rescuer becomes obliged to the one he has rescued. Since he interfered with the natural course of destiny, he is now responsible for the changes in it.

This Eastern notion, although not fully analogous to Sodom's relationship with Abraham, may help us understand it. Abraham restored Sodom and its four sister cities to their former status, and therefore, in a sense, Abraham was the cause of their continued existence and, after a fashion, bore a responsibility for them. They would always be connected to and identified with Abraham in people's minds.

At the same time, these cities personified a value system and a social order that was the antithesis of God's plan for man and what Abraham represented. In order to institute a new dawn for mankind by the establishment of the Jewish people through Abraham, God first had to destroy the hotbeds of evil with whose existence Abraham had become associated as a result of saving Lot. Their continued existence would tarnish the noble and exalted nation destined to emerge from him.

This allows us to resolve another difficulty with regard to

---

1. *Targum Yonasan ben Uziel* states (18:24) that five cities were destroyed, the five that Abraham saved during the war against the four kings.

Sodom. We find that God engaged Abraham in a dialogue before proceeding to destroy these cities. Surely, God did not consult with Abraham with regard to all His doings. Why then, in this single instance in all of history, did God deem it proper to consult with someone about a planned destruction? In the light of our discussion, the answer becomes clear. Abraham had unintentionally caused their fate because of his association with them, and a prior consultation with him was in order. God's perfect justice demanded the dialogue.

Perhaps we can now resolve some simple but important questions regarding the interactions of Abraham, Lot, Sodom and the angels. Why does the destruction of Sodom occur simultaneously with the visitation of the angels to Abraham to inform him of the birth of Isaac? These events would appear to be independent of each other.

Furthermore, why do all three angels arrive at Abraham's home? The Talmud (*Bava Metzia* 86b) tells us that one of the angels came to heal Abraham and — later — to rescue Lot, and a second angel came to announce the impending birth of Isaac. The third angel, however, was only on his way to overturn Sodom. Why did this third angel come to Abraham's home?

At that juncture in history, with the conception of Isaac, the Jewish nation was about to make the transition from the theoretical to the actual. That transition mandated that the five corrupt cities Abraham had saved through his intervention, and were thereby identified with him, could no longer continue to exist.

With this thought, we can understand both the simultaneity of the missions of the angels to Abraham and Sodom, and the reason all the angels traveled together. It was all one large mission to implement the will of God that the nation of Abraham should begin to emerge.

vii. Lot Seeks Refuge

WITH THE DESTRUCTION OF SODOM IMMINENT, THE ANGELS urge Lot to flee "to the mountain" with his family (19:16). Fearing that "the evil will cling to me, and I shall die," Lot asks instead to go to a nearby city (Mitz'ar), which was to be named Tzo'ar soon afterward (19:19). The angel agrees to spare the city of Tzo'ar and urges Lot to go, because he can do nothing as long as Lot remains in Sodom (19:22). Although Lot and his family are not harmed in the destruction of Sodom, Lot leaves Tzo'ar and ascends to a cave "in the mountain." Two brazen acts of incest occur there on successive nights.

The Talmud explains (*Shabbos* 10b) that Lot's plea for amnesty for Tzo'ar was based on its relative youth and lower level of sinfulness (Mitz'ar may mean near or young). Several questions arise. If the angel can do nothing, why is it urgent that Lot leave? Lot could have stayed and protected Sodom. If Tzo'ar was indeed less corrupt, why was it marked for destruction in the first place? And if it did deserve to be destroyed, why would Lot's presence protect Tzo'ar?

A basic tenet of Jewish belief is that God allows man's free will the maximum possible reign in which to operate. Causality and predictability governed by the laws of nature facilitate this, while miracles inhibit man in choosing the good by his own free will. For instance, if the results of evil deeds would be miraculously negated, people would no longer consider evil as an option, and they would effectively lose their free will. Therefore, in order to maintain as high a level of free will in the world as possible, God minimizes miracles both in scope and in the number of observers. For example, before Elisha revived the dead child, he "closed the door." The clear implication is that he wanted to screen the miracle as much as possible from the public eye.[2]

---

2. *Oznaim LaTorah* gives this same interpretation.

When God determined to destroy Sodom along with its three sister cities Abraham had also saved, the nearby city, later to be called Tzo'ar, would have been destroyed as well. While its iniquity was not so great as to initiate its own divine decree, it was sufficiently evil that it not be spared the destruction wreaked on its neighbors.

Lot's presence there, due to God's will that Abraham's nephew should be saved, would allow for providential protection of that city. This was the logic behind the angels urging him to hurry there before sunrise. Lot's presence in Sodom would not have saved it. On the contrary, he would have perished along with it.

Upon seeing the realization of the prophecy of the angels with regard to Sodom, Lot was frightened and abandoned Tzo'ar, which was originally also intended for destruction. But instead of going "to the mountain," he goes to a cave "in the mountain."

God had intended not only to save Lot physically, but more importantly, spiritually. One of the commentators states that the angels waited for Lot to invite them to his home in Sodom so he would gain "merit" for doing the kindness of inviting in a stranger. This is amplified by the Midrash which understands the angels' initial advice to go "to the mountain" as instructions to return to Abraham who was living in that region and, by extension, to his philosophy and lifestyle. Later, after witnessing Sodom's destruction, Lot fled to the cave "in the mountain," seeking only physical salvation out of fear, not out of desire to return to the path of Abraham. His subsequent debased behavior, therefore, came as no surprise.

We can now resolve several puzzling questions about Tzo'ar. The Torah records that it was called Tzo'ar, because it was *mitzar*, young. Why is it important that we know this seemingly insignificant detail? Moreover, why did this determine the name of the city? Didn't it already have a name before the events at Sodom? Most puzzling, why wasn't Tzo'ar destroyed when it reached the age of its sister cities, even years later? The answer lies in the name Tzo'ar, which recorded for posterity that it only existed because it was young in relation to the other four cities; otherwise, it would have been destroyed along with them. This memorialization of the city's deserved destruction through its new name was enough to break its association with Abraham and thereby allow it to avert the decree.

viii. *The Dangerous Salt of Sodom*

OUR SAGES ESTABLISHED THE OBLIGATION OF WASHING our hands following a bread meal (*mayim acharonim*) to ensure that we do not come into contact with salt from Sodom (*melach sedomis*). The Talmud (*Chullin* 105b) states that this salt is dangerous and can lead to blindness. Abaye adds that the danger is so great that even one grain of Sodom salt in a *kor* of ordinary salt (a vast amount) can cause blindness.

This passage in the Talmud gives rise to some questions. First, we do not find anywhere in the world today such a powerful salt, nor do we hear of cases in which people who failed to wash their hands suffered any special ill effects. What then is the intent of Abaye's remarks?

Furthermore, the Talmud only requires washing the hands after bread meals. Why? If the effects of Sodom salt are so pernicious, we should be required to wash our hands well and often throughout the day when we come into contact with anything that may contain this salt.

Perhaps we can discern an additional intent in the requirement of washing after a bread meal.

Sodom was a society marked by outstanding selfishness. Their traits are tersely summarized in *Pirkei Avos* (5:13) as "what is yours is mine and what is mine is mine." Now, if we examine the act of eating, it is by its nature a supremely selfish act, since it gives pleasure and sustenance exclusively to our physical selves and brings benefit to no one else.

Knowing that a person's personality is affected by his actions, our Sages were concerned that we might be adversely affected by the necessary but self-indulgent act of eating. Little by little, such acts can steep us ever more deeply in self-involvement, leading us in the direction of the horrible sins of Sodom. Our Sages understood that just as the salt of Sodom poses a physical danger, so too does the self-indulgent culture of Sodom pose a spiritual one.

Aware of the peril, they instituted the obligation to wash our hands after we have completed a substantial bread meal. Not only does our hand washing remove any stray traces of Sodom salt that may endanger us; simultaneously, it reminds us to protect ourselves from the spiritual salt of Sodom, a caustic cause of spiritual blindness.

ix. *Lot and His Daughters*

 RUNK AND SENSELESS, LOT HAD INCESTUOUS ENCOUNTERS with his two daughters on successive nights; the first night with his older daughter and the next night with the younger. As we examine the verses carefully, we find subtle differences in the language used to describe their acts.

On the first night (19:33), "the older daughter came and lay with her father." The next night (19:35), "the younger one arose and lay with him." We find two distinctions. One, the older daughter "came," while the younger daughter "arose." Two, the older daughter lay "with her father," while the younger lay "with him." What does this tell us about these events?

In the Hebrew language, the verb "to come" is often associated with carnal activity. This would seem to indicate that for the older daughter this was a more important factor in her motivation, and that she was more brazen in general. That is why she lay "with her father." The younger one, however, is more demure. She arose rather than came, and she lay "with him," a vaguer, less personal expression.

These differing characteristics also come to the fore a little later on, when the daughters name their newborns. The brazen older daughter calls her son Moab, from my father, shamelessly broadcasting her incest to the world. The younger daughter's child, Ammon, has a more generic name reflecting nationhood. The younger daughter's motivation, it seems, was to establish a nation, not to reflect any personal carnal interest in her father.

Perhaps we can discern another aspect of the older daughter's motivation from the beginning of the story (19:31), where she tells her sister, "Our father is old, and there is no man in the land to come upon us, as is the way of all the land."

What exactly did the older daughter mean by the words "our father is old"? At first glance, one might think that she mistakenly believed that the entire world had been destroyed along with Sodom, leaving her father as the only male. Since he, too, was getting old, there was no time to waste. If so, however, the order of the phrase should have been reversed, stating first that there are no men in the land and only afterward that their father is old, which is only meaningful as an expression of urgency in the context of the first part of the phrase.

Written, though, as it is, a different interpretation suggests itself. In those days, as in many places in the world today, a good marriage was near impossible without a father and dowry. "Our father is old," she was saying, and incapable of ranging far afield to find us a proper mate, and "there is no man in the land" with whom he now can easily make a marriage for us. Therefore, it was pressing that they act immediately, for he might not live long enough to help them when a suitable mate came along. According to this explanation, the older daughter was not so much concerned with perpetuating civilization but rather with finding a good mate for herself.

The younger daughter, however, may have feared a more global catastrophe, and she was concerned about creating another people and repopulating the earth. The name she gave her child reflected the broader scope of her intent.

Finally, to add further understanding to the story of Lot, there is a quality of measure for measure in what happened to him. When the angels had come to save Lot in Sodom, he had offered up his two daughters to the rabble gathered outside his door in order to protect his guests.

x. The Fountainhead of Jewish Kingship

AT FIRST GLANCE, IT SEEMS INCONGRUOUS THAT THE INCEST-uous union of the drunken Lot and his eldest daughter should produce the seeds of the kings of Israel and ultimately the Messiah. Nonetheless, this is in fact the case. Our Sages point out Ruth the Moabite, King David's ancestress, was descended from that illicit union. We also know that the Davidic dynasty will give rise to the Messiah, the redeemer of the Jewish people and all mankind. Wherein lies the virtue of this unchaste daughter's brazen act such that mankind's most illustrious royal lineage and eventual savior should arise from it?

Let us look a little more closely at the antecedents of the royal

House of David. The illicit act between Lot and his daughter was the first of a succession of three important unions that led to David's birth. The second is between Tamar and Judah, where the widowed Tamar mates with her unsuspecting father-in-law and gives birth to Peretz, King David's ancestor. Finally, there is the relationship between Ruth and Boaz.

What is the common thread between these three unions? In all three instances, the women made heroic efforts for the sole purpose of bearing a child. What, however, does this extraordinary maternal drive have to do with the concept of Jewish royalty?

Perhaps we can find the answer to these questions at the very inception of mankind. The first commandment God gave Adam and Eve was (1:28), "Be fruitful and multiply, populate the earth and take control of it." Rabbi Joseph Soloveitchik, in *The Lonely Man of Faith*, explains that man acts in the image of the Lord when he takes control of his physical environment and develops it. When he too is a creator, man is more in the image of the Lord. He comes closer to Him. The verse connects the proliferation of men and women to their control of and dominion over the earth.

The commandment of "take control of it" forms the basis of Jewish kingship. The role of the Jewish king is to guide and direct the subjugation of the physical environment in a manner that reflects the image of the Lord.

From the beginning, the urge to "take control of it" and thereby act in the image of God as Creator and Master was strong. How did the serpent entice Eve? By telling her (3:5), "On the day that you eat the fruit of this tree, you will become like the Lord." The Midrash (*Bereishis Rabbah* 18-19; *Tosefta Sotah* 4) explains that "she would be able to build or create worlds." In this way, the serpent cunningly seduced the first woman into a fruitless union. Her creative drive, expressed in mastery, had been subverted.

Adam identified the misguided impulse that led his mate to sin. Immediately after the sin, he named her Eve (Chavah), "the mother of all life" (*chai*, life, being cognate with Chavah), in order to redirect her creative impulse to their first commandment,

"Populate the earth." The maternal drive does not end with procreation. Motherhood includes raising children and nurturing their intellectual and moral development. It was to this task that Adam directed Eve. He recognized the correct outlet for a woman's desire to build worlds.

Our Sages find an acronym in Adam's name to a summation of history. The first letter, *aleph*, refers to Adam; the second letter, *dalet*; refers to David; and the third letter, *mem*, refers to the Messiah. It is the role of the royal House of David, and in particular its final scion who will be the Messiah, to lead mankind to redress the original sin of Adam and Eve. These three unions that manifested the correctly directed creative drive — for maternity — fittingly gave rise to the fountainhead of Jewish kingship. Their acts were diametrically opposed to Eve's first sin, and as such, they were a correction. According to several Midrashim, based on strong indications in the text, each of these three unions lasted only one night, underscoring the seminal and universal significance of these three couplings.

On a deeper level, an examination of the barriers or impediments these three women overcame to forge their respective unions reveals that they correspond to the three manifestations of the *yetzer hara*, the evil inclination. As our Sages tells us, three things remove a man from the world — jealousy, desire and the pursuit of honor. These inclinations, according to our Sages, became ingrained in mankind when Adam and Eve first sinned. Mankind's final redemption will occur with the subjugation of the material side of man (his *yetzer hara*) by the divinely endowed spiritual one.

These three inclinations correspond to the lower three levels of the soul, as identified by the Maharal, in the following ascending order. Desire corresponds to the animalistic component of the soul (*nefesh*), jealousy to the emotional component (*ruach*) and the pursuit of honor to the intellectual component (*neshamah*). Lot's daughter, Tamar and Ruth overcame precisely these tendencies in this specific order to populate the earth.

Lot's daughter overcame desire (*taavah*) in order to fulfill her strong maternal drive. No relationship is more repulsive than an incestuous union between a daughter and her father, especially if he is in a drunken stupor. Nonetheless, Lot's daughter overcame her natural aversion.[3]

Tamar overcame jealousy (*kinah*), which the Vilna Gaon identifies with the aggressive impulse. She must have known from the beginning that her pregnancy would be discovered and that she ran the risk of execution. Nonetheless, she refused to slander Judah and identify him publicly as the father of her unborn child in order to exonerate herself. In her quest for a child, she was prepared to accept the ultimate violence against herself rather than commit an aggressive act against Judah.

Ruth overcame her sense of personal honor. She was a princess and a modest one at that, yet in order to forge a union with Boaz she stepped out of her character to "lie at his feet." Furthermore, Boaz was an old man at the time, and according to one Midrash, he actually died after his first conjugal visit. Most young women would not find value or esteem in a relationship with someone so aged, yet Ruth pursued this union. Boaz, in fact, praises Ruth for eschewing honor and increased self-esteem through a union with an old man (*Ruth* 3:10, see *Rashi* and other commentators). Thus, Ruth's heroic act redeemed in part the third component of the *yetzer hara*, honor (*kavod*).

Together, these women set the stage for the birth of David and the rectification of the first woman's sin. Their creative acts helped establish the fountainhead of Jewish kingship, from which the Messiah will emerge and lead mankind to its final redemption.

---

3. According to this approach, there is a positive connotation as well in the Torah's emphasis on Lot as his eldest daughter's father in the story of their incest.

xi. Ruth Fulfills the Promise

E SEE IN THE STORY OF LOT AND HIS DAUGHTERS HOW LOT progressively debases himself after separating from Abraham until he sinks to the depraved act of incest. Lot's failure is corrected generations later by Ruth, his descendant from that very act of incest. Unlike Lot, she clings to the offspring of Abraham and is unwilling to separate from Naomi. Moreover, contrary to her debauched ancestor, she is a model of chaste modesty in her encounter with Boaz. Why indeed, we have to wonder, was one of Lot's descendants given the opportunity to make amends?

Our Sages speak often about the forging of a partnership between God and the righteous. This is expressed in *Pirkei Avos* (2:4) as "make your will like His, and He will make His will like yours." This concept, that God commits Himself to the desires of the righteous, is extended by our Sages to include even conditional utterances of the righteous, which He upholds.[4]

It would appear that the righteous represent the fulfillment of God's plan in creation in that they choose, as an expression of their free will, to do the will of God. Once they have crystallized and expressed their desire it somehow creates a providential force. In this way, the righteous become partners with God in that their specific will is realized.

This capacity is somewhat akin to the power vested in the Sages to determine the structure of the observance of Chol Ha-Moed (the Intermediate Days of Passover and Succos), where the Torah indicates but does not specify the type of work which is prohibited. Both in the realm of the laws of the Torah itself, and in the providence which guides history, God is in partnership with the righteous, and He empowers them with the ability to have their wishes fulfilled.

---

4. The Talmud (*Makkos* 10a) makes this point in regard to King David and Achitofel.

Abraham had high hopes for Lot. He brought him along to Canaan and expressed a desire that Lot join him in his divine mission. The desires of the righteous are fulfilled, and although Lot himself squandered his opportunity, in his descendant Ruth, Abraham's will was realized.

xii. *The Testimony of Seven Sheep*

UCCESS BRINGS NEW FRIENDS, AND THUS, THE DIVINE providence showered upon Abraham resulted in a rapprochement with a Philistine chieftain named Abimelech (21:22ff). There had been a problem with the wells. Abraham would dig wells, and Abimelech's servants would steal them. But now Abimelech seeks a treaty of friendship with Abraham, and Abraham agrees.

The treaty is signed, and Abraham separates seven sheep for Abimelech. Abimelech asks about the purpose of the sheep, and Abraham responds (21:30), "Take seven sheep from my hand as a testimony for me that I have dug these wells."

The Torah leaves us to wonder how exactly these sheep would give testimony to Abraham's ownership of his wells. We may wonder If Abimelech's servants had stolen the wells once, what would prevent them from doing it again?

We find another riddle with the wells later on in the time of Isaac. The Torah in *Parashas Toldos* (26:14) describes how Isaac also ran into trouble with the Philistines over the digging of wells. First, the Philistines filled in the wells dug by Abraham, forcing Isaac to dig new wells. But the Philistines stole each new well

Isaac dug, until finally he was successful in producing an uncontested well. Wanting to deprive Isaac of his wells, the Philistines filled in the wells Abraham had dug and stole the one Isaac himself had dug. Why didn't they also steal the ones Abraham had dug? After all, it makes more sense to steal a well and use its water than to fill in and destroy this resource.

Perhaps we can say that in those days, as is also the case now, ranchers used to brand their sheep. This then was how the sheep were meant to serve as a testimony to Abraham's ownership of the wells. People would see sheep branded with Abraham's mark in Abimelech's flock, and they would wonder what they were doing there. Abimelech would be forced to explain that the sheep had been given to him at the signing of the well treaty, and in this way, the agreement would be publicized. Once the wells were established in the public realm as belonging to Abraham, it would be difficult for anyone subsequently to claim ownership.

Many years later, trouble developed between Abraham's son Isaac and the Philistines over the wells. The commentators as well as several Midrashim discuss many things to which these wells alluded. On the simple level, however, we can see them as a means of reaching out to people by offering them free water and drawing them close to God.

The Philistines wanted to combat Isaac's growing influence on the populace, and they felt they could accomplish this by cutting off his water supply. It would have been easiest and most advantageous just to claim the wells as their own. This would not have worked, however, with the wells Abraham had dug, since the testimony of the seven sheep had firmly established their true ownership in the public mind. They had no choice but to fill them in. The wells dug by Isaac, on the other hand, were fair game. The Philistines did not have to go to the trouble of filling them in. All they had to do was take possession and claim them as their own.

xiii. *Plotting the Course of Life*

OR MOST PEOPLE, THE WHIMS OF THEIR EMOTIONS AND the circumstances of their environment buffet them throughout their lives. They ricochet off events and emotional experiences without the compass of virtue and the direction of considered values to steady and guide them. In contrast, great people survey their lives in advance, like a voyage about to be undertaken, and they plot for themselves the best course.

The Torah tells us (21:34), "And Abraham sojourned in the land of the Philistines for many days." The *Seder Olam*, quoted by Rashi, understands this to mean that he lived in Beersheba for twenty-six years. This is inferred from the words "many days," which must be instructive. They indicate that Abraham spent more years in Beersheba than he had in Hebron. He arrived in Hebron at age 75 and left at age 99, for a total of twenty-five years. Therefore, we can assume that he spent twenty-six years in Beersheba. Rashi continues, "And he immediately returned to Hebron."

What exactly does Rashi mean by telling us "he immediately returned to Hebron"? What does Rashi seek to convey by noting Abraham's urgency to return to Hebron?

The implication is that the length of Abraham's stay in Beersheba, when it surpassed the time spent in Hebron, stimulated his return to Hebron. This raises more questions. If it was important for Abraham to be in Hebron, why didn't he go there sooner? Why wait so long and then rush back?

Apparently, Abraham was reluctant to leave Beersheba, because there was a value in his remaining. This value, however, was superseded by his desire to spend the majority of his life residing in Hebron. Thus, he had to leave as soon as his years in Beersheba surpassed those spent in Hebron.

Beersheba, as maps of the ancient world indicate, was an important crossroads on the travel routes between North Africa and the civilized eastern world. Located in a desert area, Beersheba offered Abraham the singular opportunity to attract people to God and spread monotheism and the ethical behavior it entailed. Arriving parched and famished, travelers especially appreciated the water offered from the wells Abraham had dug and the food and lodging he generously provided. In this fashion, Abraham could deflect people's natural gratitude towards him to the Source of all benevolence, God.

But Hebron held a deeper significance for Abraham. The word Hebron is related to the root word *chaver*, which means "join." At Hebron, where he would be buried, Abraham joined his earthly temporal self to his eternal one. It was similarly chosen by Adam and Eve. Abraham felt his life should be defined by where he spent the bulk of it. Therefore, when the years at Beersheba accumulated to the point where they surpassed his years in Hebron, he knew it was time to leave. By returning to Hebron, Abraham demonstrated that the overriding theme of his life was the connection of his physical existence to his eternal one. In advance, Abraham had charted out the definition and direction of his life's work, and he had plotted his course accordingly. This is the way of the wise and pious.

xiv. *After These Things*

THE STORY OF THE *AKEIDAH*, THE BINDING OF ISAAC, BEGINS with the words, "And it was after these things that God tested Abraham" (22:1). The question immediately arises: After which things? What is the connection between the *Akeidah* and the events that preceded it?

The Hebrew words that appear in this verse are *achar hade-*

varim ha'eileh, which in this context are usually translated as "after these things." Rashi, however, quotes the Aggadah (*Bereishis Rabbah* 55:4; *Sanhedrin* 89b; *Targum Yonasan*) which is based on their alternate translation as "after these words." The Aggadah examines the *Akeidah* both from Abraham's perspective and Isaac's. The reference to "these words" is either to Satan's words to God questioning Abraham's commitment, or to Ishmael's taunting words to Isaac questioning his devotion to God. Neither of the conversations appear in the Torah.

Perhaps we can also find meaning in taking the phrase at face value and translating it as "after these things." Our Sages say, "*Ain mikra yotzei midei p'shuto*, The plain meaning of the verse is also significant." What does the plain meaning of the verse seem to be saying? Immediately preceding the *Akeidah*, we read about the covenant between Abraham and Abimelech to coexist in the land. How does this connect to the *Akeidah*?

It would appear that this covenant marked the completion of the promise God made to Abraham when he sent him on his divine mission. Abraham had become wealthy and respected in his environment. He and Sarah had been blessed with a son. And he had just secured a peace with Abimelech which would, he believed, give him and his family an uninterrupted presence in the land of Israel. The stage was set for the chosen nation to blossom and flourish through his son Isaac.

At this point, we are faced with an important question. To what extent, if any, did the glory and importance of having a crucial role in history motivate Abraham?

The *Akeidah* answered this question. The Torah tells us that "after these things," after all the pieces are in place for the grand fulfillment of the promise, God instructed Abraham to go to the land of Moriah and sacrifice his son in the tenth and last of his *nisyonos*, his tests. Abraham went without hesitation, and when it was all over, God declared (22:12), "Now I know you have awe of God and you have not withheld your son, your only one, from Me."

The *Akeidah* demonstrated that Abraham would give it all up if God so directed him. And it sheds light on his perspective from the very beginning. The words with which God instructs Abraham to go to the *Akeidah* echo the words with which He sent Abraham off to the Land of Canaan: "*Lech lecha,* Go for yourself." When he set out from Ur, he was told to leave "your birthplace, your land and your family." Before the *Akeidah*, he is similarly instructed to give up "your son, your beloved one and your only one."

When the angel stays Abraham's hand before Isaac is slaughtered, we become aware of Abraham's motivating forces in all the previous years. It is as the angel of God states, "Do not do anything to [Isaac], for now I know that you are in awe of God." Now, *after all these things,* it becomes clear that awe, the realization of one's own insignificance before God's unfathomable greatness, drove Abraham. Without understanding God's purpose, Abraham was prepared to do all He asked of him without hesitation. As demonstrated by the *Akeidah*, all Abraham's acts were solely to fulfill the Awesome One's will.

As Abraham and Isaac proceed to the *Akeidah*, they engage in conversation. The Torah records this dialogue (22:7), "And Isaac said to his father Abraham, and he said, 'My father!' And [Abraham] said, 'Behold, I am here, my son.' And [Isaac] said, 'Here are the fire and the wood, but where is the sheep for an offering?'"

This brief conversation raises several questions. What is the meaning of Isaac calling out "my father" before he asks his question concerning the sheep for the offering? What is the meaning of Abraham's first reply? And what purpose is served by the Torah recording this brief conversation?

Perhaps it can be said that Isaac suspected that God's instructions to Abraham were indeed to slaughter his son. Since Abraham, his revered father, had chosen not to tell him, Isaac did not broach the subject directly. Nonetheless, he wanted reassurance that, in all he was about to do, Abraham still retained the devotion of a father to his son.

Therefore, he began simply, "My father!"

Abraham responded to the implicit question, "I am here, my son."

Yes, his heart was still filled with the natural love of a father, with natural reluctance to see harm befall his beloved son. Abraham's love for his son was superseded only by his love for God. Abraham knew that if God, in His infinite wisdom, decreed that Isaac's physical existence was to be ended prematurely, this was also for the good.

xv. *The Mountain of Oneness*

BRAHAM DID NOT KNOW HIS DESTINATION WHEN HE SET out to the *Akeidah*. All God had told him (22:2) was to take his son Isaac to the land of Moriah and bring him as an offering "upon one of the mountains that I will indicate to you."

The expression "one of the mountains" seems somewhat unusual. Why didn't He say simply "the mountain"? What additional information are we meant to derive from the word "one"?

According to our Sages, the drama of the *Akeidah* was played out on the mountaintop upon which the Holy Temple would later stand. This was the place where God, who is One (*Echad*), would most manifest His Presence to the Jewish people and the whole world. Perhaps then, the use of the word "one" is to intimate that upon this mountain the clear vision of the Oneness of God would shine forth to humanity.

Moreover, the Midrash tells us that during creation the entire world was derived and expanded from one foundation stone called the *even shesiah*, which lies beneath the Holy of Holies on the Temple Mount. This may be another allusion in the word "one." It is the "one" mountain, from whose pinnacle stone all of the earth is established.

xvi. *The Providential Horn*

PON HEARING THE ANGEL CALL OUT TO HIM TO STAY HIS hand from sacrificing his son, Abraham looked around to see what he could sacrifice on the altar he had prepared for God. "And he saw, and behold there was a ram instead, caught in the bramble by its horns" (22:13). Abraham took the ram and offered it up in his son's stead.

Why couldn't the Torah have told us simply that he found a ram? Why was it necessary to add the seemingly superfluous detail that the ram was trapped in the bramble by its horns? What is so special about the ram's horn?

Rashi, quoting the Mishnah in *Avos* (5:6), states that the ram offered in lieu of Isaac had been prepared for this purpose during the sixth day of creation. Why was it necessary to prepare a replacement ram at the dawn of creation? Surely, there were plenty of rams in the world at the time of the *Akeidah*. The message the Midrash conveys is that the intent in all of creation, from the very beginning, was for mankind to achieve perfect obedience to God. The ram connects the *Akeidah*, which was the expression of that ultimate goal, with the original creation of the world.

On Rosh Hashanah, the day of judgment and remembrance, the story of the *Akeidah* is read in the synagogue. On that day, when we take stock of our lives and examine its direction, we reflect on the transcendent purpose of life, which is absolute compliance with the will of God. And we sound the shofar, the ram's horn, to recall the *Akeidah*.

Why is the ram's horn the particular symbol used to remind us of the *Akeidah*? After all, the ram only appeared in its aftermath. It is there to remind us of the divine providence that guides all our lives. It was no coincidence that the ram was entangled there. God had engineered its presence so that it should be there, available at the moment Abraham refrained from sacrificing Isaac. Therefore, it is important that we be told of the instrument of its entanglement, so that we will associate the horn with divine providence for all generations.

When we sound the shofar on Rosh Hashanah, we think of God's providence, and the level Abraham achieved when there was no reality for him other than to fulfill God's will with perfect faith.

פרשת חיי שרה
Parashas Chayei Sarah

i. *A Time to Depart*

MMEDIATELY AFTER WE READ ABOUT THE *AKEIDAH*, WE learn of Sarah's death (23:2). Why? Rashi tells us, in the name of *Midrash Tanchuma*, that when Sarah heard that Isaac had nearly been slaughtered "her soul burst from her and she died."

What exactly does this mean? According to some commentators this means very simply that her shock at the frightening news of what had almost happened to her son was so great that her heart gave out and she died. Others commentators take the exact opposite view. Taking note of the idiomatic expression used for "nearly slaughtered," *kim'at shelo nish'chat*, which translates literally as "he almost wasn't slaughtered," they suggest that Sarah's profound disappointment that Isaac wasn't taken as a sacrifice to God caused her death.

Perhaps we can also suggest a slightly different interpretation. Sarah's overriding purpose in her life was to raise Isaac, the patriarch who would form the central link in the *Avos* between Abraham who was the initiator and Jacob from whom the nation of Israel commences. When God showed that He considered Isaac worthy of being a perfect sacrifice (*olah temimah*), and when Isaac showed he was ready to offer himself up with a perfect heart, Sarah realized she had accomplished her purpose in life. She experienced such a spiritual expansion that "her soul burst from her and she died."

Thus, Sarah did not die from mental anguish. She had fulfilled her life's duties. There was nothing more she needed to give to Isaac. Abraham's work, however, was not complete. He still had to arrange the marriage of Isaac and teach the concepts of the Torah to his grandson Jacob. This work would take many more years.

The language of the Midrash lends some credence to this approach. It would appear that she did not die from any physical complication but rather that "her soul burst from her and she died." Apparently, her soul was no longer able to maintain its tenuous connection to her physical body. Her life was not terminated. It was completed.

We also find support for this approach in the first verse of the *parashah* (23:1), "And Sarah's life was one hundred years and twenty years and seven years, the years of Sarah's life." Rashi, in the name of *Bereishis Rabbah*, notes that the use of this unusual expanded language rather than a concise "one hundred and twenty-seven years" is instructive. It teaches that into her hundreds she was as free of sin as a 20-year-old (who has just reached the age of responsibility), and she had the pristine beauty of a 7-year-old.

In the view of our Sages, a person's death has an element of atonement for the sins of his life. But Sarah, according to the Midrash, was free of sin. Why then did Sarah die? She is not listed among those who died only for the sin of Adam. Perhaps it was because she did not die from sin or physical fatigue. She had fulfilled her life's work, and her exalted soul sought to return to its Creator.

ii. *Double or Nothing*

BURIAL GROUNDS DID NOT COME CHEAP IN ANCIENT Canaan, or at least that was how Abraham wanted it. The Cave of the Machpelah, where he wanted to bury Sarah, was on the lands of a Hittite named Ephron, and he offered to buy it (23:7-9). He asked the Hittites to approach Ephron and request that he "grant me his Cave of the Machpelah, on the edge of his field; let him grant it to me for its full price, as a burial ground in your midst." The initial offer was for the Cave itself and nothing else.

And yet, at the conclusion of the sale we read (23:20), "Thus the field with the Cave that was in it were confirmed as Abraham's as a burial ground from the Hittite people." All of a sudden, he has bought not only a Cave but also a field. And the amount he pays for it is the exorbitant sum of 400 silver shekels.

How and why did this purchase metamorphose into a larger transaction?

Ephron, it seems, was quite a crafty and greedy fellow. He wants to extract as much money as possible from Abraham, yet he must keep up appearances in front of his people. Abraham had asked to purchase the Cave, and the protocols of nobility call for Ephron to offer it as a gift instead. But he does not want to. So what does he do?

He offers to give Abraham not only the Cave but the field as well. In doing so, he indicates that the two form one indivisible package in his mind, and the offer of the Cave must include the field as well. He knows Abraham will not accept a burial ground for Sarah as a gift, and that he will insist on paying. He wants him to pay for the entire package, not just the Cave.

Ephron is right. Abraham declines the gift but accepts Ephron's coupling of the Cave and the field. He insists on paying for both the Cave and the field (23:13). Ephron comes back with the inflated price of 400 shekels (23:15). Had he sold him only a cave, he would have been embarrassed to ask a steep price for a simple cave in front of his townspeople. But now that he was selling Abraham a field as well, it had become a substantial purchase, and he could name a grossly inflated price.

A person selling a bag of apples is restricted in the price he can ask. But if he is selling an apartment building he has much more leeway. The more substantial the purchase the vaguer the price guidelines. By selling the Cave together with the field, Ephron put himself in a position where he could name his own price.

Abraham readily accedes to Ephron's exorbitant price without a hint of protest. In fact, according to the Midrash, Abraham overpaid voluntarily by using the highest quality currency (*oveir lasocheir*) even though the deal did not call for it.

It would seem that Abraham saw two benefits in purchasing the Cave for a ridiculously high price. One, he created a hubbub (*kol*) about the sale, i.e., people would be telling their neighbors, "Did you hear what Ephron got for his field?" By doing this, Abraham achieved the largest possible public awareness that the Cave and the field belonged to him and his descendants. The second benefit was that a high price was a testimonial to Sarah's greatness. Abraham did not wish to have it appear that he bought her plot at bargain basement prices. The price of 400 shekels was a public expression of his highest regard for Sarah, his beloved, departed wife.

iii. *The Divine Matchmaker*

 IXTY-SIX VERSES OF THIS *PARASHAH* ARE EMPLOYED TO describe the arranged marriage between Isaac and Rebecca. The Torah gives numerous details regarding the events, and these in turn give rise to numerous questions.

As the story unfolds, Abraham sends off his faithful servant Eliezer with clear instructions (24:3-4): "And I bind you with an oath of God the Lord of the Heavens and the Lord of the Earth that you will not take a woman for my son from the daughters of Canaan amongst whom I dwell. Rather, go to my land and my birthplace and take a woman for my son, for Isaac."

Logically, one would have thought, Abraham should first tell Eliezer that he wants him to find a wife for Isaac, and then to add the reservation that he is not to bring back a Canaanite wife. For some reason, however, Abraham does the exact reverse. First, he tells him not to look among the Canaanite women, and only then does he tell him to find a wife for Isaac.

Furthermore, it would appear from the verses that the oath did not bind Eliezer to seek a wife for Isaac. Rather it bound him not to bring back a Canaanite woman. Why was this so?

As the dialogue continues, Eliezer asks (24:5), "Perhaps the woman will not want to follow me to this land; shall I return Isaac to the land from which you have come forth?"

And Abraham responds (24:6-8), "Be careful, lest you return my son there ... But if the woman does not want to follow you, then you shall be released from this oath of mine."

Is this what we would have expected Abraham to answer? Shouldn't he have told Eliezer that if the woman did not want to follow him he should continue his search elsewhere? Surely, there existed somewhere a good woman who would want to marry Isaac and move to Canaan. Shouldn't Abraham have told Eliezer to search for her? Moreover, what is the point of mentioning the release from his oath? If his mission will have come to an end, his oath would obviously be over as well.

So Eliezer goes to Haran, and there he discovers Rebecca. She seems to be the answer to his prayers, and Eliezer tells her brother Laban about his mission. But he makes a change in the wording. Abraham had told him (24:4) to go "to my land and my birthplace." Eliezer, however, tells Laban (24:38) that Abraham had instructed him to go "to my father's house, to my family." Why is the meaning of Eliezer's subtle change?

Earlier (22:20), immediately after the *Akeidah*, we are presented with a listing of the descendants of Abraham's brother Nachor, Rebecca's grandfather. The section begins with the words "And it happened after these things." Clearly, there is a connection between Nachor's family tree and the *Akeidah*. Rashi explains that after Isaac's reprieve God wanted Isaac to marry, and He arranged for Abraham to learn of Rebecca's existence. If so, what was Abraham's purpose in sending Eliezer out blindly to find a wife for Isaac when he already knew about Rebecca?

All these questions seem to point us in a certain direction. It would appear that Abraham sought to have God act directly as the intermediary, the Divine Matchmaker so to speak, for Isaac and his preordained wife. Knowing that the offspring of this union would complete the foundation of the Jewish people, Abraham felt that it needed to be sanctified by God's direct and overt involvement. With this in mind, he sent Eliezer on his mission with only the most general instructions. He did not tell Eliezer about Rebecca, relying instead on providence to effect the actual selection.

Therefore, when Eliezer asks Abraham what to do if the woman refuses to come, Abraham responds (24:7-8), "God, the Lord of the Heavens, who took me from my father's house, and from the land of my birth, and spoke about me and swore to me, saying, 'I will give this land to your offspring,' He will send His angel before you, and you will take a wife for my son from there. But if the woman does not want to follow you, then you shall be released from this oath of mine."

Providence, Abraham tells Eliezer, will be directing his steps. But providence does not need to search; it get it right the first time. If the woman refuses, Eliezer is obviously not the agent of providence in this matter, and there is no point in his continuing the mission.

Abraham knew that in order for Eliezer to be a faithful agent of providence, he first needed to remove from Eliezer any slight or unconscious ambivalence that might have impeded him from being fully devoted to his mission. According to the Midrash (*Bereishis Rabbah* 59:9), Eliezer had a daughter whom he wanted Isaac to marry. Abraham's first words to Eliezer made it perfectly clear to Eliezer that Isaac would never marry a Canaanite, thereby effectively eliminating Eliezer's family, which was of Canaanite descent. Now Abraham could send Eliezer on his mission free of ambivalence, a worthy agent of providence.

Eliezer understood the implications of Abraham's instructions. He knew providence was guiding him because of the importance of his mission. Even though Abraham had told him to go "to my land and my birthplace," Eliezer told Laban that Abraham had sent him to "my father's house, to my family," where he would find a woman of exalted lineage, possibly even Rebecca of whose existence he had already been informed. Presumably, Eliezer did so to show Laban that Abraham held his family in high esteem.

Now we can better understand the method Eliezer used to discover Rebecca. Eliezer knew he was to be an agent of providence. Consequently, he contrived a situation that would form a proper setting for providential events. Fully aware that the outstanding trait that characterized Abraham and Sarah, the hallmark of their home, was *chessed*, kindness, Eliezer arranged a test of *chessed* for the girl who would come along. What more appropriate way of identifying Isaac's future wife than by a demonstration of *chessed*? And thus Isaac's providential match came through an elegant poetic justice engineered by the Divine Matchmaker Himself.

iv. Two Vision of Kindness

LIEZER, ABRAHAM'S FAITHFUL SERVANT, SET UP A TEST TO determine who would be Isaac's bride (24:14): "And the girl to whom I will say, 'Please tip your jug that I may drink,' and she will say, 'Drink! And I will also give your camels to drink,' she is the one …"

As it turned out, however, Rebecca's response was slightly but significantly different (24:19): "And she began to give him to drink, and she said, 'I will draw [water] for your camels as well until they have finished drinking. '"

Eliezer had only asked for enough water to break their thirst from the long journey, but Rebecca offered to give them enough water until he and his camels had finished drinking. Ten camels can drink an enormous amount of water until they are full; it must have been no easy task, to say the least, for a young girl to draw so much water from a well. There really was no immediate need for such an effort on her part. Camels can go over a week without water. After giving them a little water to slake their thirst, Eliezer could have finished watering them a day or two later when he was rested. Nonetheless, Rebecca insisted on giving the camels their fill of water. Why?

The human impulse to do *chessed* with others can derive from two sources. Some people identify with other people. They may even feel a natural kinship for all of mankind. Even further, a person may feel so integrated with other people that he considers himself as an individual to be part of the greater whole of mankind. When such a person sees another in distress, he feels impelled to lend a helping hand. After all, the person in distress is part of his own team. Allegorically, he is like a foot that endures discomfort so that the mouth and stomach may enjoy the food at the end of a long trip, since they are all part of one body. In our High Holiday liturgy, we express our prayer and expectation that all mankind will form a single entity of brotherhood in unified worship of God (*agudah achas*). It is this feeling of identification that leads us to be kind to others. Motivated by identification, we extend ourselves to others who may not be as capable as we are, since we are all in the same boat, so to speak.

There is also another source for the impulse to do *chessed* with others. In the final chapter of the *Moreh Nevuchim* (*Guide for the Perplexed*), the Rambam describes the characteristics of a person who attains the highest level of refinement through his knowledge of God. Such a person seeks to perform acts of kindness, justice and righteousness in emulation of God's ways. It is a cornerstone of Judaism that God created the universe as an act of kindness (*olam chessed yibaneh*), and that kindness underpins God's continuous will toward His creation. An exalted individual stands, so to speak, in God's jetstream of kindness, as he emulates His ways.

Eliezer's vision of *chessed* was more mundane. He considered it sufficient for Rebecca to share his burden out of a sense of identification with another human being; he only expected a little bit of water, enough to quench the immediate thirst of his camels and relieve him of their immediate burden after a long and arduous journey. There was no reason for her to keep watering the animals until they were full. A day or two later, a stronger, well-rested Eliezer would easily be able to finish the watering.

Rebecca's *chessed*, however, went beyond identification with other people. She loved doing kindness for its own sake, because that is God's way. The Torah states (24:20) that she "ran to water the camels" and that she "ran to refill her jug." She ran, because she loved what she was doing.

Eliezer had not anticipated such an elevated embodiment of *chessed*.

In response to Rebecca's generosity, the Torah reports (24:21-22), "The man was astonished by her, wondering whether God had made his path successful or not ... When the camels had drunk their fill, the man took [jewelry and gave it to her]."

Throughout, Eliezer is identified as Abraham's "servant" or

just "the servant." In these two verses, however, he is called "the man." Afterwards, he is called "the servant" once again. Why?

Eliezer's response is also puzzling. First, he is described as astonished and unsure if he has succeeded. Nonetheless, he impetuously gives jewelry to Rebecca before he determines her lineage. How could a man as great as Eliezer behave so rashly? (See *Rashi,* who explains that he was confident that she was the right one. Perhaps we can offer an additional insight.)

The Midrash (*Bereishis Rabbah* 59:9) states that Eliezer had a daughter whom he wanted to give to Isaac as a wife. A cryptic hint to this is found in the two spellings of the word "perhaps" in the story. When Abraham instructs Eliezer to seek a wife for Isaac, Eliezer responds (24:5), "Perhaps (אוּלַי) the woman will not want to follow me to this land." Later, however, when Eliezer recounts to Laban his previous conversation with Abraham (v. 39), the word "perhaps" appears as אֻלַי, with the same pronunciation, *ulai,* but spelled without the extra *vav.* The word אלי, using different vowels, can be read as *eilai,* which means "to me." Our Sages find in this change of spelling an allusion to Eliezer's desire that his daughter marry Isaac.

The Kotzker Rebbe commented that the two spellings of the word reflect the dual aspects of the mind. The first spelling, with the *vav* (אוּלַי), reflected Eliezer's conscious intent, which was to execute his master's will faithfully. The second spelling (אֻלַי) reveals the subconscious part of Eliezer's mind in conflict with his conscious mind, since he wanted his own daughter to marry Isaac.

Based on the idea of the subconscious intent, perhaps we can discern yet another nuance of interpretation in the change in spelling. Subconsciously, Eliezer was expressing a desire that the mission would fail because of his self-interest, "to me." Perhaps he was so astonished and affected by Rebecca's incredible generosity, kindness and beauty[1] that he subconsciously wished he could have her for himself. This subconscious thought led him to

---

1. The Torah (24:16) describes her as very beautiful.

hand her the gifts impulsively, in a spontaneous response to her kindness. At this point, therefore, he was acting as his own "man," albeit subconsciously, rather than as Abraham's servant. But the moment passed, and Eliezer faithfully carried out Abraham's mission, and so the Torah once again refers to him as the servant of Abraham.

Perhaps we can offer yet another explanation for Eliezer's seemingly impulsive act of giving Rebecca the jewelry even though a moment earlier, as the Torah tells us, he was unsure if she was Isaac's intended.

There is a very important piece of information given between the time Rebecca offers to give the camels their fill of water and the gift of the jewelry. We are told that Rebecca actually did as she had said.

When Eliezer heard Rebecca offer to help all the camels drink their fill, he was "astonished." But it is one thing to make a promise and quite another to fulfill it. That is why he was unsure if his prayers had been answered. He needed to know if she would keep her promise when she became increasingly fatigued by the heavy burden she had set for herself. He needed to know if she was more than just talk, if she would be faithful to her word no matter how difficult it was. This was, of course, not one of Eliezer's original criteria. Nonetheless, once she made her extravagant promise, it was important to see if she had the integrity to keep it.

When Eliezer saw Rebecca give all the camels to drink until they wanted no more, he understood that Rebecca was not only incredibly kind but also a woman of her word. And so he gave the jewelry to Rebecca, for she had fully demonstrated that she met the highest standard of virtue that Eliezer had set for Isaac's future mate.

פרשת תולדות
Parashas Toldos

i. Rebecca Abstains

EBREW WORDS CHARACTERIZE THE INNER ESSENCE OF the named entity. Rabbi Shamshon Raphael Hirsch observes that the Hebrew word for name, *shem* (שֵׁם), using a different vowel sign, can be pronounced *sham*, meaning there. Just as the word "there" designates one location to the exclusion of all others, so does a Hebrew name identify and define an entity in an exclusive fashion. Our Sages say, "*Kishmo kein hu*, He is just like his name."

It stands to reason that name-giving is a grave responsibility. Who bore this responsibility for our forefathers? We do not know who gave Abraham and Sarah their initial names. However, we do know that God Himself designated the final names by which we know them. God also ordained Isaac's name.

What happened in the next generation? With regard to the first of Isaac's sons, the Torah tells us (25:25), "They called him Esau"; according to many commentators, "they" refers to people in general. The Midrash (*Tanchuma Shemos* 4) specifies that it was

Isaac, Rebecca and Esau himself who gave this name. With regard to the second son, there is only a single originator of the name (25:26), "He called him Jacob." The simple meaning is that "he" refers to Isaac; different Midrashim identify the "he" as either God or Isaac.

Let us now jump forward another generation. Who named Jacob's children? We find that Jacob's wives Rachel and Leah named eleven of the twelve children. The only exception was Levi (29:34), "He called him Levi." The *Midrash Rabbah* comments that it was God who declared his name to be Levi.

We notice that all the names were given either by God or by the mothers, except for Jacob's name which, according to one Midrashic view, was given by Isaac. Why didn't Rebecca give Jacob his name or at least participate in the process?

Specifically with regard to the naming of Jacob, Rebecca's silence is surprising. It was Rebecca who had been prophetically informed that she was pregnant with twins of opposite natures; the Midrash amplifies this by relating that one was attracted to idolatry and the other to divine worship. Later on, it is once again Rebecca who is sensitive to Jacob's superior nature and ensures through subterfuge that he gains Isaac's blessings. Why wasn't she involved in Jacob's naming? This question is especially strong according to the Midrashic view that follows the most simple reading of the text and sees her as involved in naming Esau but not in naming Jacob.

Finally, as a more general question, why indeed was the role of the mothers greater than the role of the fathers in naming our illustrious ancestors?

It is a principle of Jewish family life that it is the father's responsibility to teach the laws and ideas of the Torah to his children. The development and integration of ideas into the fabric of human personality, however, is accomplished primarily by the mother's nurturing and guidance.

Furthermore, our Sages say that women are endowed with a *binah yeseirah*, a greater capacity to make distinctions, a trait that facilitates the fulfillment of potential. Jacob's work would be carried on by his twelve children, but this transference was still in an amorphous state of potential. It was the task of the mothers to separate the specific roles of each of the children. Rachel and Leah understood how to define the roles and identify them by their names. The exception was Levi whose eventual holiness and dedication to the divine service was already indicated by God's prophetic communication.

Returning to Rebecca, when she saw her first son, mature with hair, "done," as implied by the name Esau, she understood that this was the son attached to earthly desires. She could easily agree with her husband on the name Esau. When she saw her second son, she knew he would be Isaac's spiritual successor. As such, she did not feel that the name Jacob fully described that destiny. Jacob means to hold back; it also means crooked. She did not think that this name reflected her son's essence, and therefore, she did not participate with her husband in the naming.

Rebecca could not know that the name reflected the epic struggle of Jacob and his descendants throughout history to "hold back" the forces represented by the earthly Esau. Only God could know this. Ultimately, God gave Jacob the name of Israel, meaning straight of God, which fully reflected his essence.

ii. He Honored His Father

N THE WRITINGS OF THE SAGES AND JEWISH LORE, ESAU IS the epitome of an evil person; he is called Esau the Wicked. But the Esau that emerges from the narrative and the elucidations of our Sages is quite a complex person.

Apparently, there is more than one side to this evil man.

On the one hand, we find that the Midrash considers Esau the paradigm of a person who fulfills the commandment to honor one's father. The Torah mentions that Isaac loved Esau but makes no mention of Isaac's love for his son Jacob (25:28). Although Isaac undoubtedly loved both his children, it seems Esau occupied a special spot in his heart. Furthermore, Isaac originally intended to bestow his blessings for material success on Esau. This lends further support to the view that Esau had redeeming qualities, including fulfilling the obligation to honor his father.

On the other hand, we find a plethora of negatives in Esau's behavior, beliefs and relationship with his father. He sold the rights of the firstborn to the divine service for a bowl of porridge. He married local Canaanite girls to the displeasure of both his parents. When bringing food to his father, he speaks harshly and without reference to God, in contrast to Jacob, who uses the word "please" and makes reference to God when he speaks to his father. Esau is a feral hunter, while Jacob remains in his tent and pursues spiritual goals. Finally, as we are told by the Midrash (*Bereishis Rabbah* 63:10), he misrepresents himself to his father as very religious by asking, for example, how to tithe salt.

Let us consider the mitzvah of honoring one's parents. The Talmud (*Kiddushin* 31a) explains that its correct performance depends on causing *nachas ruach*, emotional pleasure, to one's parents (see *Rashi*). No other mitzvah in the Torah depends on another person's emotional state for its fulfillment. The Talmud considers this mitzvah so difficult that Rabbi Yochanan consoled himself on the passing of his parents that at least he would no longer have to deal with the onerous requirement of this mitzvah.

Esau was a ruddy, earthy and gruff man, but he wanted very much to please his father. He even masqueraded before Isaac as the very religious son he would have wanted him to be, all in order to please his father. Because of his efforts, Isaac was under the impression that Esau had a real ability to be "a man of the field" and at the same time aspire to spiritual goals, to elevate the mundane. Therefore, despite all his limitations, Esau actually did honor his father on a very high level, because he conveyed the sincere message that he would do anything to please his father. Reflexively, Isaac felt honored by Esau, as indeed he was.

iii. *When Esau Saw Red*

NWITTINGLY, ESAU GAVE US A RARE INSIGHT INTO HIS INNER thoughts when he sold his birthright to Jacob. Esau returned famished from a day of hunting, and found Jacob cooking up a pot of lentils. Then (25:30), "And Esau said to Jacob, 'Please feed me from that, the red red [*ha'adom ha'adom*] stuff, for I am weary.' Therefore, he was called Edom." The name Edom is reminiscent of the red [*adom*] porridge.

Esau's language borders on the bizarre. Why does he express himself so emphatically and repeatedly about a food's redness without even identifying it as food? Moreover, why is Esau's identity memorialized for history by the name Edom, a term connoting redness?

The conscious mind is the tip of an iceberg. Beneath it lies a vast domain of thoughts and feelings of which we are usually not aware — dreams, slips of the tongue and the like are windows into or small expressions of this inner realm. Psychotic individuals also give us glimpses into this world of the unconscious.

Ideas in the unconscious are strung together by emotional linkages rather than by language. This is called primary process thinking. Dreams are a good example. They emerge disguised from the unconscious, not sequenced by a logical pattern but by inner emotions and drives. Similarly, a psychotic person's speech is often disorganized in both content and form. He will often speak about primary drives, including the religious, sexual and aggressive. His speech may take the form of jumbled sentences, with detours to rhyme words, or he may repeat a word if it appeals to some unconscious force. The organizing conscious sense of self has evaporated, and the emotions have taken over. The cognitive abilities of an infant, prior to mastering speech, function similarly to that of the unconscious.

An extremely mild form of primary process thinking occurs with a slip of the tongue. In a momentary leak of the unconscious, a person will make a statement that emanates not from the organized logic of his conscious mind but from the sea of emotions in his unconscious.

Perhaps this will give us some insight into Esau's odd language on the day of the sale of the birthright. Esau was a materialistic man, yet he still had a certain primitive, superficial religiosity that expressed itself most in religious posturing rather than deep religious convictions. As mentioned above, the Midrash indicates that he would inquire about the method of giving tithes on foods, such as salt, for which it was not required.

What was the source of Esau's primitive religiosity? It would seem reasonable to connect it with his illustrious grandfather Abraham. Esau had seen how his grandfather had gone from a despised solitary individual to an important, successful and respected chieftain. Abraham enjoyed tremendous material success, and all, in Esau's view, because of his new religion. Esau hoped to attain similar material security and success with his own religiosity. True spirituality, clinging to God, was not part of Esau's religious interest.

Furthermore, Esau may have believed that Abraham's righteousness would earn him not only enormous wealth but also a reprieve from the decree of death. He would overcome the damage done by Adam's sin by pledging allegiance to the true God. To gain an extension of earthly benefits, Esau was prepared to place restraints on his pursuit of them. This is what spurred Esau to pursue his crude religiosity. Somehow, he harbored an irrational hope that by going through the motions of religious observance he might gain wealth and immortality.

On that fateful day of the sale of the birthright, however, a shattering event took place. According to the Midrash, Abraham died earlier on that very day. The Talmud tells us (*Bava Metzia* 87a) that until the time of Jacob people did not go through a period of infirmity prior to death. They just died suddenly. The death of Abraham came as a terrible shock to Esau, and his shaky theological edifice came crashing down.

All his life, Esau had somewhat suppressed his primal physical drives in order to gain God's favor. And now, in one shocking moment, he was reminded that Abraham's religion had not brought him immortality. He had not become like Adam before the sin, who would not have died, nor had he even become like the people in the antediluvian world who lived for many centuries. Religion secured none of these bonuses. Esau was suddenly faced with the prospect of his own mortality, and he was devastated.

Let us listen closely to Esau's words when he rejects the birthright and sells it (25:3), "Behold, I am going to die, why do I need the birthright?" Why did he think he was going to die? Would a few hours of hunger and thirst kill a seasoned hunter such as Esau? Perhaps he referred to his reawakened and now inescapable awareness that he himself would die one day. This is what triggered his profound depression and his rejection of his birthright. His religiosity was too primitive to embrace the concept of immortality beyond the context of the material world; to him death meant that his very existence would come to an end, a profoundly disturbing thought.

With Esau's whole worldview destroyed, a torrent of suppressed animalistic and instinctive drives were released from his unconscious. Esau is described as returning from the fields *ayef* (עָיֵף), which translates as weary. The more appropriate word famished is not employed. The Midrash comments on the word *ayef* that Esau spent the day in licentious wantonness, murder and idolatry; according to *Targum Yonasan*, he also denied the immortality of the soul. But his furious regression into the drives of his coarse animalistic nature did not satisfy him. They only led to greater lust and then greater dissatisfaction until Esau wearied of his rampage and stumbled home.

Then he saw Jacob's red porridge.

Psychoanalytic literature describes how certain items take on a deeper meaning to the unconscious; our dreams are replete with them. In Hebrew, the word "red" (*adom*) shares the same root letters with that of blood (*dam*). Blood, and the color red by extension, is to the unconscious mind a symbol of life itself. The Torah plainly refers to blood as the life force in man (*dam hu hanefesh*). When Esau in his shocked state saw the red lentil porridge, he could only refer to it in the way his unconscious craved it, namely as emblematic of life.

The red porridge struck a resonant note in his inflamed unconscious, and all he could see was the redness, the life quality, of the food.

His repetitive use of the word red has the quality of primary process thinking. Depleted of his fantasy that he could attain security with false religiosity (one of appeasing God for favors), he rejected all spirituality and leaped into the world of physical passions. This is what the red porridge meant to him, and this is why he wanted it so desperately.

It is the nature of those who attach themselves to the realm of the physical that the more security they try to find in it the more their underlying fear of mortality is aroused. This quality finds its fullest expression in Esau's grandson Amalek. The nation he formed represents the antithesis of Jewish belief and has been the nemesis of the Jewish people throughout history. Their antipathy toward us stems from their embrace of the physical as the only reality. Beneath this external posture lurks the fear that there is an absolute spiritual reality. To protect themselves against this unspoken fear, they violently oppose the Divine and the Jewish people who are its representatives.

This reactionary hatred by Esau is expressed at the conclusion of the sale (25:34), "Jacob gave Esau bread and lentil stew, and he ate and drank and got up and left, and Esau scorned the birthright."

When did Esau scorn the birthright, when he sold it for the "red red stuff" or when he "got up and left"? It would seem that he should have expressed his scorn for the birthright at the point of sale, yet the Torah tells us otherwise. Why? Because at the time of the sale, Esau was not yet governed by scorn. Face to face with his own mortality, he was shocked and disoriented. And when he turned away from spirituality and embraced absolute materialism, he began to hate all things divine. The smoldering detestation grew as a defense mechanism against the sneaking suspicion that he might have given up something of incalculable value. After the passions of the moment, Esau defensively scorned the birthright to the divine service.

And thus, Esau's name became fixed as Edom, because he had traded away a world of divine service to blindly cling to the world of physicality as represented by the redness of the lentil porridge.

In this light, we may understand another expression in the story. Both when Jacob asks Esau to sell him the birthright, and when he makes him swear on the sale, he uses the word *kayom*, "as this day." The simple meaning is that the transaction was to occur on that day. However, it seems unnecessary, as without that expression, there would have been little reason to think it would occur at any other time. Rashi and the Ramban raise this question and offer interpretations. Perhaps we can also say that Jacob was aware of Esau's inner torment and emphasized the nature of the day, the day of Abraham's death, the day which would be his *yahrzeit*. This day would always remind Esau of the temporal nature of his existence and of the fact that even Abraham's brand of religiosity gave no final protection against mortality.

iv. The Gripes of Greed

HE TORAH TELLS US (26:13) THAT GOD BLESSED ISAAC AND he became very wealthy. His great wealth aroused jealousy among his neighbors, especially the Philistines who filled in the wells Abraham, Isaac's father, had dug. Finally, Abimelech, king of the Philistines, tells Isaac (26:16), "Go from among us, for you have become much mightier than we are" (לֵךְ מֵעִמָּנוּ כִּי עָצַמְתָּ מִמֶּנּוּ מְאֹד). And Isaac goes.

The common translation of *a'tzamta mimenu me'od* as "you have become much mightier than us" raises a puzzling question. If Isaac had indeed become much mightier than Abimelech, how then could the weaker Abimelech force the stronger Isaac to uproot himself and move away?

In actuality, the words *a'tzamta mimenu* can also be translated as "you have grown mighty or strong *from* us." In other words, Abimelech was complaining that Isaac had attained his wealth at Abimelech's expense. Indeed, it is typical for wicked people, in their egocentricity and avarice, to feel that everything is coming to them. Whatever Isaac had acquired, Abimelech contended, would otherwise have gone to him. He wanted Isaac gone.

Let us now look at the last word in the verse — *me'od*, very much. Once again, this is an attitude characteristic of the wicked. In their self-importance, they magnify their grievances. Abimelech could not tolerate any of Isaac's success; he saw all of it as too much. Abimelech's behavior is understandable. Despite all his griping, Abimelech remained more powerful than Isaac, and when he demanded that Isaac leave, he had no choice but to comply.

v. *A License to Deceive*

WHY DID REBECCA THINK SHE HAD A RIGHT TO DECEIVE HER husband Isaac so that he would give Jacob the blessings intended for Esau? In fact, Jacob himself posed this question to his mother, and she replied rather cryptically that she would take the moral responsibility for the subterfuge (27:13). What inspired her to do this?

Earlier (25:22-23), we read that Rebecca had a difficult pregnancy and sought out spiritual advice as to its significance. Through prophecy, she learned she was to have twins from whom two nations would arise and that "the older will serve the younger."

As it was, Rebecca never informed Isaac of this prophecy she had received. The Ramban gives two possible reasons for this. Either it was because of her modesty or because she assumed that her husband, who was an even greater prophet, would also receive the same prophecy directly.

Through the years, however, it must have become clear to Rebecca that Isaac was unaware of the different and conflicting natures of the brothers. She must have realized that her husband was not privy to the prophecy she had received. She probably wondered why and concluded that it was God's plan that only she should know. Perhaps it was best for the proper upbringing of the children that Isaac have no preconceived notions about how they would turn out.

When the time came for Isaac to give his blessings she knew these would play a critical role in the fulfillment of the prophecy she had received. Then (27:16), "Rebecca took the desirable clothing of her son Esau, the older one, which was with her at home, and she dressed her son Jacob, the younger one." The Torah stresses here that Esau was the older son and Jacob the younger. Why? We are fully aware of this basic point of information. Perhaps it refers to the prophecy that "the older will serve the younger." Rebecca knew that only she was aware of this prophecy and not her husband. Consequently, she realized it was her responsibility to engineer a situation in which her younger son would receive the blessings to fulfill the prophecy. The mention of "younger" and "older" alludes to Rebecca's perceived license to deceive Isaac and thwart his plan.

vi. *Esau's Narrow Miss*

JACOB MUST HAVE THOUGHT HE HAD PLENTY OF TIME TO impersonate his brother Esau and take the blessings, but actually he did not (27:30). "And it happened that just as Jacob left the presence of his father Isaac that his brother Esau returned from his hunt." The expression Jacob had "just left" (יָצָא יָצָא) indicates that Jacob got out just in the nick of time.

Why does the Torah emphasize this narrow margin of success for Jacob? Certainly, this serves to underscore God's providence in making sure that Jacob got the blessing. But on closer examination, the question still remains.

When Jacob accepted his mother's plan of the deception, he understood his brother had gone hunting to provide the food his father had requested. Undoubtedly, he also assumed he would be able to get in to his father to receive the blessing and get out before his brother returned. This notion was supported by Isaac's statement to Jacob when he arrived (27:20), "How is it that you found food to return so quickly?" From this it would appear that it should not have taken any special act of providence for Jacob to obtain the blessing and be long gone by the time Esau returned.

It follows that the narrowness of Jacob's escape was the result of a divine providence that actually hastened Esau's return rather than delayed it. Apparently, God wanted Esau to return and discover that he had narrowly missed preventing Jacob from making off with his blessings. What benefit could there have been in such intervention?

Let us consider. What difference would it make to Esau if he comes a moment too late or an hour too late, as Jacob and Rebecca seemed to have expected? How would it affect Esau's mental state? The answer lies in one word: frustration. When Esau discovered that he had been bested by a hairsbreadth, his inevitable anger was coupled with the not inevitable new element of frustration.

Frustration is an unpleasant emotion. Human emotions are not logical but fluid. It is natural for unpleasant feelings, such as frustration, to spill over and exacerbate anger or trigger it in another area. For example, a frustrating day at work may cause a person to be inappropriately quick-tempered at home. Esau was understandably angry when he discovered that Jacob had taken the blessings, but his frustration at the narrowness of Jacob's escape sent him into an irrational murderous rage. It was the frustration coupled with the anger that pushed Esau over the edge. He then vowed to kill Jacob. Rebecca overheard and gained Isaac's support in sending Jacob away (27:41). This providentially directed chain of events led to Jacob's marriage and the birth of the Jewish nation.

On an even deeper level, perhaps the close call served to grease the path of history, so to speak. Esau's seething rage, which is barely containable, is the paradigm for the attitude of Edom (most European peoples) toward the Jewish people throughout history. Esau will forevermore serve as God's ready rod to chastise us when we fail to follow our ordained mission faithfully. This eagerness was set in motion by that seminal event when frustration was added to the already explosive mix of rejection and anger.

i. *Fallen Angels*

NE OF THE MOST MEMORABLE SCENES IN THE BOOK OF Genesis is Jacob's dream. Fleeing the wrath of his brother Esau, Jacob is on his way north to his mother's family in Haran. Along the way, he goes to sleep in the open and has a spectacular dream. The Torah tells us (28:12), "And he dreamed, and behold, a ladder stood on the earth, and its top reached to the heavens, and behold, angels of the Lord were ascending and descending on it."

These celestial images presently metamorphose into prophecy, and God promises to bless his offspring and give them the land of Israel. But what was the meaning of the images of the angels? Were they messages in the form of metaphors or did they have some sort of reality?

Targum Yonasan sees these images as real events that took place on the metaphysical plane and translates the verse accordingly, "And [Jacob] dreamed, and behold, a ladder stood on the earth, and its top reached the heavens. And behold, there were two angels that had gone to Sodom and were expelled from their place [in Heaven] because they revealed secrets of the Master of the Universe. And they wandered in exile until Jacob left his father's house. They accompanied him with love until Beis-El. On that day, they went up to the heavens above, and they declared, 'You [angels], see Jacob the righteous whose image is fixed on [God's] Throne of Glory, the one you have always yearned to see.' And thus, the other holy angels of God came down to look at [Jacob]."

We can trace these two angels back to Sodom and discover a hint of the misdeed for which they were banished from Heaven. The Torah relates (19:13) that the angels sent to destroy Sodom and save Lot warned him to flee "for we will be destroying this place." Later (19:22), one of them tells Lot, "I can do nothing." The Midrash (*Bereishis Rabbah* 50), quoted by Rashi, explains that the angel was forced to make the humiliating admission that "I can do nothing" because he and his companion angel had presumptuously claimed personal credit for destroying Sodom. They should have said, "God will destroy this place."

These were the two angels ascending the ladder in Jacob's dream. They were the very ones who had deviated from God's will when they encountered Lot 123 years earlier and were still banished from Heaven.

Numerous questions immediately come to mind, both with regard to the Midrash describing their transgression in Sodom and *Targum Yonasan's* description of the interchange among the heavenly angels. First of all, angels are understood to be different from humans in that they have no free will and no capacity to sin. If so, how could it be that these angels sinned? What aspect of their mission might have prompted their failure? And if they had indeed sinned, how would their looking at Jacob gain them entry back into Heaven, as implied by *Targum Yonasan*?

Moreover, Jacob was already 63 years old at that time, and yet, the angels had never previously entered his dreams nor enlisted his help in any way to get them back into Heaven. What led them to contact Jacob now? Finally, what is the significance of Jacob's image appearing on God's Throne of Glory? And why were the other angels so eager to see the real Jacob?

There is another famous episode involving fallen angels in the Torah (6:2), "[During the generation just prior to the Great Flood,] the sons of gods saw that the daughters of men were fair, and they took them." The Midrash (*Bereishis Rabbah* 20) identifies the sons of gods as angels who had intermingled with humans and become corrupt.

What is the commonality between these two episodes of fallen angels? It is that they both were exposed to human societies so degenerate that even angels were affected. Ordinarily, free will exists only in humans who are forced to choose between the polar influences of the spiritual soul and the material body. Angels, not having that conflict, have no free will. Apparently, however, even angels can be drawn to the physical if they find themselves in extremely licentious societies, such as the antediluvian generation and the city of Sodom. In these circumstances, they may gain the free will to choose between good and evil. The angels that sinned in Sodom chose to do other than God's will and were ejected from Heaven.

The question remains: How did the fallen angels gain entry back into Heaven through their encounter with Jacob?

The Book of Genesis, for the most part, tells the story of the three patriarchs. In general, when the successor appears on the stage of history the predecessor ceases to be visible, even though he continues to live for many years. Abraham arranges a marriage for Isaac, and then he is heard of no more, even though he lived until his grandsons were 15 years old. Similarly, Isaac disappears from the pages of the Torah when Jacob leaves Beersheba, even though he lived another fifty-seven years, past the time of the sale of Joseph to Egypt. There is a lot of overlap in their lives but very little overlap in the stories as they appear in the Torah. Why? Because at these junctures, they have already finished their work laying the ground for the future nation, and the mantle of leadership has passed to the next generation.

When Jacob left Beersheba after sixty-three years in his father's house, he had developed intellectually and morally to the point where he became the preeminent patriarch (*bechir she'b'avos*) of the Jewish nation. At that point, he reached such a level of human perfection that his image was mirrored on the Heavenly Throne. The epoch of Jacob had begun. This was the time when the angels, through a transcendent encounter with Jacob, could be readmitted to Heaven.

There is yet another reason why the angels encountered Jacob at this particular time in this particular place. The Ramchal, in *Derech Hashem* and *Daas Tevunos*, explains that just as there is a system of natural law that governs events, there is also an underlying metaphysical system of providence that interacts with and overrides natural law. It is based on a hierarchy of values. For instance, two people are waiting for a bus. One is the greatest rabbi of the generation, the other an ignorant boor. Let us assume that the timeliness or tardiness of the bus will affect them in opposite ways. The hierarchical system of providence, therefore, mandates the outcome more appropriate for the great rabbi.

By this rule, God's will that the Jewish nation be established and achieve its ultimate goals is the supreme value — and all of providence is directed to this end. Therefore, the providence directing Jacob's life reached ascendancy when Jacob left Beersheba and assumed his full role as the third patriarch. It is precisely at that time that Jacob attracted the attention of the fallen angels, and they sought him out to help them reenter Heaven.

In seeing Jacob, the angels saw the reverse of their own error. Our Sages refer to Jacob as the preeminent patriarch. The tension between the earthly draws of physical man and the spiritual aspirations of the soul had been resolved in Jacob with the complete submission and servitude of the physical to the spiritual. When Jacob describes his firstborn Reuven as "the first of my strength" (*reishis oni*), our Sages comment that Jacob never had an involuntary nocturnal emission in his life. This is but one reflection of Jacob's extraordinary character. Every bit of his potential was harnessed in the service of God. Nothing was squandered. This capacity represented the reverse of the angels' experience when exposed to Sodom and its earthly licentious culture. In some fashion they distanced themselves through this exposure from the will of God. Jacob's example of elevating material existence rather than being corrupted by it allowed them to correct their error. It allowed them to reenter Heaven.

This is what the fallen angels reported to the other angels in Heaven. Up until then, perfect spirituality had existed only among the angels in Heaven, while the lower realm was the scene of conflict between the material and the spiritual. But Jacob's perfect devotion to God out of his own free will represented the ultimate realization of God's plan for creation. Consequently, it is he who is represented on the Heavenly Throne. The fallen angels alerted their colleagues that God's goal was realized in Jacob. Heaven could now be found on earth, and so the other angels descended to behold God's ultimate glory.

ii. *The Neck of the World*

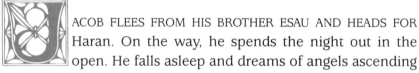

ACOB FLEES FROM HIS BROTHER ESAU AND HEADS FOR Haran. On the way, he spends the night out in the open. He falls asleep and dreams of angels ascending and descending a ladder planted on the earth and reaching to the heavens. As the vision continues, God speaks to Jacob and describes to him the destiny of his offspring. Upon awakening, Jacob remarks (28:17-19), "'How awesome is the place! It is none other than the Lord's house and this is the gateway to heaven.' ... And he named the place Beis-El, although Luz had been the city's original name."

Our Sages identify "the place" called Luz and afterward Beis-

El as Mount Moriah, the site where the *Akeidah* took place and where the Holy Temple would eventually be built. It is interesting that the Torah finds the fact that Beis-El was originally named Luz noteworthy. Of what importance is it to know the original name of a place?

Luz is an interesting word. Our Sages have identified a bone by this name at the top of the neck, on which the skull rests. According to tradition, the *luz* bone does not deteriorate in the grave along with the rest of the body. It will form the nucleus from which our bodies will be reconstituted when the dead are resurrected during the Messianic era.

What else do we know about the *luz* bone? According to the *Mishnah Berurah* (300:2), this bone gets its nourishment exclusively from the food we eat at the post-Shabbos meal (*melaveh malkah*). The Talmud states (*Berachos* 28b) that the original eighteen blessings of the *Shemoneh Esrei* correspond to the eighteen vertebrae of the back, which bows before the Creator. The supplementary nineteenth blessing, in which we pray for the demise of apostates and other enemies, corresponds to a small bone of the neck. The *Aruch* identifies this small bone as the *luz* bone.

What is the common thread between all the attributes of this little bone called *luz*? In all of them, the *luz* serves as the bridge between the spiritual and the physical, the higher and the lower, the holy and the profane.

The *luz* connects the head, the domain of intellectual and spiritual functions, with the body, the domain of physical functions. For that reason, the *luz* will serve as the link between the returning soul and the regenerated body when the dead are resurrected. The post-Shabbos *melaveh malkah* meal also serves as the link between the pure spiritual worlds of Shabbos and the mundane week that follows it. It is from this meal that the *luz* bone draws its sustenance. Perhaps the connection between the *luz* bone and the prayer for the demise of apostates can similarly be explained. The continued association of apostates with the Jewish people acts as a barrier, an anti-link, between the people and their Creator, and their demise reestablishes this link.

In this place called Luz, a place suited to linkage between the physical and the spiritual, Jacob has a vision of a ladder that reached from the earth into the heavens, connecting mankind to God in heaven. This place would also one day be the site of the Holy Temple, which served as the bridge between the material and spiritual worlds. After the vision, Jacob sanctifies the place further by giving it a name that mentions God, but nonetheless, the name Luz is still significant as a key to its true character.

The word *luz* (לוז) itself is odd. There is no other Hebrew word to which it is associated. Let us analyze this strange word a little further and see what deeper meanings are revealed.

The name of the letter *lamed* (ל) means to teach. Kabbalistic literature identifies this teaching specifically as divine instruction brought down to mankind, just as the *lamed's* top descends from above the line.

The name of the letter *zayin* (ז) has two meanings. It can mean a weapon of war, representing the aggressive drive to domimate others. It can also refer to physical sustenance or nutrition, representing the appetitive drive. These drives are united by the broader concept of the most physical or animalistic aspect of man's existence.

The name of the letter *vav* (ו) means hook; it is used as the conjunctions "and" and "or" in Hebrew.

With this in mind, we can penetrate to the deeper meaning of *luz*. Luz is that place or thing where the spiritual (*lamed*) is connected (*vav*) to the physical (*zayin*). It is our function and purpose as individuals, as a nation and ultimately as mankind to create a place in the physical realm where God may be present. As the Torah tells us (*Exodus* 25:8), "And they shall build for me a dwelling place, and I will dwell among them."

This gives us a deeper insight into the reason we are told that "Luz had been the city's original name." From time immemorial, this name reflected the singular, exalted holiness of the place and the role it would play in human history.

With this understanding of the neck as the symbolic connection between the upper and lower realms, perhaps we can discern a new facet of meaning in a famous Talmudic passage. Later on we read about the dramatic meeting between Joseph and his brother Benjamin, who had been 9 years old when Joseph was sold into slavery. Twenty-two years later, they were reunited (45:14). "Then [Joseph] fell upon his brother Benjamin's neck and wept; and Benjamin wept upon his neck."

The Talmud comments (*Megillah* 17b) that prophecy prompted their tears. Joseph cried because he foresaw the destruction of the First and Second Temples, which would be in Benjamin's territory. Benjamin cried because he foresaw the destruction of the Tabernacle of Shiloh, which would be in Joseph's territory.

Where is the allusion in the verse to these prophecies? According to our discussion, it lies in the word "neck." The Tabernacle and the Temples were the necks of the world, so to speak, the points of connection between Heaven and earth, between spirituality and the mundane. Joseph and Benjamin cried over each other's "necks."

Perhaps, according to this Aggadah, the prophecies of Benjamin and Joseph arose at that moment of joy when they were reunited, because they sensed that their joy could not be complete. The forces of jealousy that led to their separation were not fully resolved. They saw prophetically that these smoldering conflicts would cause future divisiveness and separations, as those that led to the destruction of the Tabernacle and the Temples and the exile of the people.

iii. *A Watched Pot Does Not Boil*

ROM THE MOMENT HE FIRST SEES RACHEL, JACOB IS ENRAP-tured. Laban, Rachel's father, took full advantage of Jacob, demanding seven years of servitude in exchange for her hand in marriage. The Torah tells us (29:20) that these years "were in his eyes as but a few days, in his love for her."

Actually, this is a somewhat surprising expression. It is well known that "a watched pot does not boil." So, too, does time pass slowly for a person who must wait for his desire to be fulfilled. Why then did these years fly by for Jacob like "a few days"?

We can conclude that the Torah is not speaking of frustrated earthly passions. It was Rachel's immense spiritual value that inspired Jacob's love. To Jacob, seven years of service seemed but a small consequence for the great spiritual good he would gain with her as a wife.

iv. *But Rachel Was Barren*

ACOB HAD TWO WIVES, LEAH AND RACHEL, AND HE LOVED them both, apparently unequally, however: "And [Jacob] loved Rachel as well, more than Leah (29:30)." Yet in the very next verse (29:31), we encounter a seemingly con-tradictory statement, "And God saw that Leah was hated, and he opened her womb, but Rachel was barren." How does the divine Narrator declare in one verse that Jacob loved Leah and in the very next that Leah was hated? Moreover, is it possible that our holy patriarch Jacob hated his wife?

Of course not. The word hate used here bespeaks Leah's

subjective experience. Women have a profound emotional need for complete commitment from their spouses. Leah saw that Jacob did not love her as much as he loved her sister Rachel, with whom she shared a marriage, and therefore, she felt "hated." We find that Eve had a similar attitude. The Midrash tells us (*Bereishis Rabbah* 19:5) that after Eve ate from the Tree of Knowledge of Good and Evil she gave Adam to eat from it as well. The Midrash explains that, once Eve knew she would die, she could not tolerate the thought of Adam outliving her and taking another wife.

Let us now turn to another puzzling aspect of the second verse. Leah was the first of Jacob's wives to give birth, and the Torah connects her pregnancy to her being "hated." Why, however, does the Torah mention Rachel's barrenness in this context? What is the connection between her infertility and Leah's sense of inferiority with respect to their husband?

A later encounter between Rachel and Leah may shed some light on this question. When Leah already had four sons of her own and an additional two sons through her handmaid Zilpah, Rachel was still barren. It happens one day that Reuven, Leah's firstborn son, is returning from the fields with *dudaim*, mandrakes, for his mother. Rachel asks her sister for them, and Leah replies (30:15), "Isn't it enough that you have taken my husband; now you also want to take my son's *dudaim*?" Rachel then "purchases" the *dudaim* by giving her night with Jacob to Leah.

Leah's remark to Rachel is exceedingly odd. Where is there any previous indication that Rachel had taken Jacob from Leah? Furthermore, according to the Midrash, Jacob would have discovered that Laban had substituted Leah for Rachel on his wedding night, because he and Rachel had agreed on prearranged signs to prevent just such a deception. Rachel, not wanting her sister to be embarrassed, had revealed the signs to her and allowed the marriage to go through. By an act of unimaginable kindness, Rachel had put herself in a position to lose Jacob. As it was, she allowed her sister to share the husband who should have been exclusively hers. How then could Leah ignore her sister's selflessness and accuse her of taking her husband when the exact opposite had occurred?

Let us consider for a moment. Why exactly did Rachel want these *dudaim*? Why were they so important that she was ready to exchange a night with Jacob for them?

According to Sforno, among other commentators, the *dudaim* were a medicinal aid to conception. According to one view quoted by the Ramban, they were a type of aphrodisiac, which was probably also intended to facilitate conception. Rachel had apparently concluded that her situation called for some more practical efforts (*hishtadlus*) on her part. Until then, she had relied exclusively on her trust in God and her prayers in order to help her conceive. Now, when she saw the *dudaim*, it occurred to her that perhaps she should also use chemical agents to help her achieve that end.

Rachel's request for an agent that would add to her relationship with Jacob unleashed in Leah a flood of suppressed feelings. Leah complained bitterly that, in effect, she had always been second fiddle in the home. When she complained that "you have taken my husband," she was actually saying that "you have failed to let me be a full co-wife."

When Rachel heard Leah's previously unexpressed complaint against her, she realized that this might very well be the cause of her childlessness, and she strove to rectify it. She offered to allow Jacob to sleep that night in Leah's tent, thereby signifying that she would not stand in the way of Leah's achieving an equal status in the home. This was the deeper significance of the exchange.

Now we can understand why Rachel's barrenness is connected to Leah's being "hated." As long as Leah felt that her status in Jacob's household was inferior, Rachel was withheld from having children. Only when Rachel discovered Leah's grievance, and redressed it, was she finally ready to give birth to Joseph.

As for Leah, it took a measure of selflessness on her part to give Rachel the *dudaim* and thereby enhance Rachel's relationship with Jacob. For her virtue, she was rewarded with two more children.

Why was Rachel required to achieve such an extremely high level of personal excellence before she could bear Joseph?

Perhaps it was to give her the ability to prepare Joseph, her first-born, for the leadership role he was destined to play in the development of the Jewish nation. Leaders, because of their superior position, can easily evoke undercurrents of jealousy and resentment. Providence directed that Joseph's mother forgo her own superior position for the sake of familial harmony and a true sorority with her sister. Her son would follow her example.

When Joseph is born, Rachel says (30:23), "God has gathered in my shame." Ultimately, that was Joseph's role, to gather the brothers physically and spiritually into a loving fraternity prior to their descent into Egypt.

v. *The Right Time to Leave*

AFTER TWENTY YEARS OF SERVICE IN THE HOME OF HIS father-in-law, Laban, Jacob's welcome wears out. Despite Laban's efforts to keep him subservient and restricted, Jacob prospers and becomes wealthy. Laban's sons voice their suspicions that Jacob had enriched himself at Laban's expense, and Jacob notices that Laban begins to look askance at him.

Just at this time, God instructs Jacob to leave Laban's house and return to Canaan. Jacob tells his wives Rachel and Leah about the deterioration of his relationship with their father, and he confides in them his recent prophecy. Rachel and Leah agree to leave, and the family flees (31:1ff).

Many questions immediately come to mind: Why does God tell Jacob to return home just when his relationship with Laban sours? Why should Laban's new manifest attitude play a role in the timing of the divine plan for Jacob's return? And why is it dependent on Jacob noticing it? Furthermore, why did Jacob preface his recounting of the divine order to leave with a description of this deteriorating relationship?

Let us consider for a moment what would have gone through Jacob's mind had he been commanded to leave without first perceiving Laban's jealousy and resentment. Laban had given Jacob his daughters in marriage. He had provided a safe environment for Jacob and his family for twenty years, and he had given him the opportunity and means to attain great wealth. By all rights, Jacob should have felt *hakaras hatov*, gratitude, toward Laban. He should have been prepared to stay. And yet, God tells him to leave.

Jacob could easily have drawn the wrong conclusion had God commanded him to leave under such circumstances. He might have thought that *hakaras hatov* was not a sufficiently important consideration when weighed against building the Jewish nation. Therefore, God told Jacob to return only after he saw through Laban's benevolent façade and saw his jealousy and resentment at all his son-in-law's accomplishments. Jacob was not bound by gratitude to remain with such an ill-willed father-in-law.

Jacob had the same considerations in mind when he broached the subject of leaving with his wives. Now that he understood that God had delayed the prophecy until he could see clearly that leaving was not an act of ingratitude, he wanted to make sure his wives enjoyed the same clarity. He did not want them to perceive any ingratitude in their abandonment of Laban, and so he reviewed the entire chain of events with them. Rachel and Leah respond that their father was never concerned about their welfare and that they are prepared to leave. They, too, realize that everything their father had done was self-serving. They, too, are ready to see Jacob's prophecy fulfilled.

Many years later, Moses would follow this same model when he leaves the house of his father-in-law Jethro and returns to Egypt. After God informs him of his mission at the burning bush, Moses first returns to ask Jethro's permission (*Shemos* 4:18). Only after Moses fulfilled the requirements of proper *hakaras hatov* to Jethro, who really deserved his gratitude, does God actually command him to leave.

פרשת וישלח
Parashas Vayishlach

i. Three Paths to Prayer

S THE CONFRONTATION WITH ESAU DREW NEAR, JACOB DID everything he could to prevail. As Rashi notes, he attempted to appease Esau with gifts, he divided his camp into two parts in anticipation of an armed struggle and he prayed to God. Let us take a closer look at the strategy of prayer.

The Talmud (*Berachos* 28b) discusses the *Shemoneh Esrei*, the eighteen-benediction prayer known as the *Amidah*. Rabbi Hillel the son of Shmuel bar Nachmani associates it with the eighteen mentions of God's Name in Psalm 29. Rabbi Joseph states that the blessings relate to the eighteen mentions of God's Name in the *Shema*. Rabbi Tanchum, in the name of Rabbi Yehoshua ben Levi, says that the eighteen blessings are analogous to the eighteen vertebrae of the spine.

The first two opinions cited appear to be wrestling with the issue of the *Shemoneh Esrei* prayer's fundamental theme. According to one opinion, it is associated with praise and acknowledgment of God's deeds, the general theme of Psalms.

According to the other, it relates to the obligation to recognize His kingship and sovereignty, the most basic concept in the *Shema*. How would we define the third opinion?

The Talmud quotes Rabbi Yehoshua Ben Levi as saying further that each of the four times a person bows down during the *Amidah* he must bend low enough for all the vertebrae of his back to protrude. Ulla adds that he must bend low enough to see a coin called an *issar* opposite his heart. What does this mean? Rashi explains that he must double over until a fold of flesh the size of an *issar* coin forms on his chest.

This is an odd way to express the need to bend the upper body until it is horizontal to the ground. Perhaps Ulla is sending us a message in his choice of words. The term *issar* refers to a coin, but the same letters with different vowels read as *assur*, forbidden or bound. These two concepts are closely related to the daily prayer.

First of all, we have the issue of money. Our Sages understood the powerful allure of money, which in its liquidity and abstractness can capture a person's fantasies. With this in mind, our Sages interpreted the first verse of the first paragraph of *Shema*, which concludes with the command to love God "with all your *me'od*," as meaning "with all your money."

Second, *issur* means restriction. It is the nature of people to rebel against the notion that anyone or any being is superior to them, because this would oblige them to act in certain ways or refrain from certain activities they find desirable. These restraints are called *issurim*, rules that bind.

Embedded in these two meanings is a reference to the two primary elements of the *yetzer hara*, the evil inclination. The desire for money represents excess physical desires, called *taavah*. The urge to rebel against restrictions represents pride or a sense of superiority, called *gaavah*. These are the forces against which a person conducts his *milchemes hachaim*, the internal battles of his daily life, until his last breath.

By using the word *issar* to express the extent of a person's bow, Ulla may be suggesting that a person must subjugate the two inclinations of greed and rebellion, which are impediments to prayer and divine service.

In this light, we may understand the third opinion of the Talmud, quoted in the name of Rabbi Yehoshua ben Levi. As opposed to the first two opinions which contend that prayer is an expression of either praise or reverence, his view is that a person's very imperfections oblige him to humble himself before his Creator — the eighteen benedictions of *Shemoneh Esrei* are analogous to the eighteen vertebrae of the erect spine, which must humble itself before God.

A nineteenth blessing, instituted later, pertains to the downfall of apostates. Each of the opinions in the Talmud mentioned above finds an additional source for this nineteenth blessing.

While it is interesting that the Sages of the Talmud seek a scriptural allusion to the *Shemoneh Esrei*, which was a rabbinical enactment, it is more remarkable that they do so even for the nineteenth blessing, which was added to the prayer's original corpus centuries later.

Yet they find a hint to this added blessing either in an additional oblique mention of God's Name in Psalms and the *Shema*, or in a nineteenth vertebra.

It is fitting that these references are somewhat veiled, since the prayer for the demise of the apostates is a grudging concession to necessity. For example, the word *echad*, one, in the first verse of the *Shema* ("Hear O Israel, God is our Lord, God is one") is the allusion to the nineteenth blessing according to Rabbi Yehoshua Ben Levi. It is God's ultimate will that mankind form one group united in His worship, a goal that overrides our reluctance to pray for the demise of fellow Jews who thwart that aim.

Nonetheless, the Sages were reluctant to call for the demise of other Jews. Although the nineteenth blessing was always a theoretical possibility, the Sages refrained until that moment in Jewish history when the damage caused by the apostates and slanderers (*minim* and *malshinim*) reached intolerable proportions. This is analogous to the fourth and final blessing of the *Birchas HaMazon*, which was instituted at the nadir of Jewish history when the current 2,000-year exile began. That blessing, which expresses our confidence in God's providence, had to await the moment when things seemed most bleak, and yet God's providential hand showed itself.

The three opinions cited in the Talmud diverge only with regard to identifying the most essential element in the *Shemoneh Esrei*. As for being important aspects of prayer, all the opinions are true. Prayer includes praise and acknowledgment, recognition of God's sovereignty and the subjugation of one's distracting impulses.

Let us now read Jacob's prayer when he prepared to meet Esau (32:10-11). "And Jacob said, 'Lord of my forefather Abraham, Lord of my father Isaac, God Who said to me, "Return to your land and to your birthplace, and I will be good to you," I am humbled by all the kindness and the truth You have done with Your servant.' "

"Lord of my forefather Abraham" is an expression of reverence. "God Who said to me, 'Return to your land' " is praise for God's kindness. And "I am humbled by all the kindness" is the subjugation of the self. Jacob's prayer featured all three important themes.

ii. *The Unanswered Question*

WHEN ESAU ENCOUNTERED JACOB FOR THE FIRST TIME IN thirty-four years,[1] "He lifted his eyes and saw the women and the children, and he said, 'Who are these to you?' " (33:5). What was Jacob's response? "They are the children God granted your servant." The children are clearly mentioned, but not the women.

---

1. According to the Midrash, Jacob spent fourteen years in the academy of Shem and Ever, and over twenty years with his father-in-law Laban.

Jacob's answer was typical of the righteous and displays Jewish values in general. His not calling attention to his wives was an expression of the modesty and chastity which is characteristic of the Jewish home.

iii. Why Shechem Was Annihilated

HE STORY OF THE ABDUCTION OF DINAH AND THE destruction of the city of Shechem raises puzzling questions. Shechem, the son of the town's founder, is smitten by Dinah, Jacob's only daughter. He assaults her and detains her against her will. Jacob's family, which is dedicated to developing a holy nation, is shocked and outraged.

Shechem and his father, Chamor, approach Jacob's sons and make a generous offer for Dinah. Jacob's family will choose maidens from the town as mates, and they will offer their own daughters to the townsfolk as brides. The brothers respond positively but with the guileful stipulation that all the men of Shechem must circumcise themselves. They explain that this will allow them to form one people. The episode comes to a grisly end (34:25), "And it came to pass on the third day, when they were in pain, that two of Jacob's sons, Shimon and Levi, Dinah's bothers, each took his sword and they came upon the city confidently and killed every male."

The Ramban, among others, wonders why only Shimon and Levi acted against Shechem. All the brothers responded positively to Chamor's offer by adding the condition of circumcision. Why weren't they involved in the attack on Shechem?

Moreover, as many commentators ask, how could an entire

town be held liable to capital punishment for the act of one individual?

The Ramban suggests that the brothers originally planned to place the town in a weakened condition, allowing the brothers to enter and rescue their sister without putting themselves at risk. Shimon and Levi, however, acted precipitously on their own to defend their sister's honor.

Perhaps we can suggest a somewhat different approach. When Shechem and Chamor returned to their town, they misrepresented the arrangement they had already made with Jacob's sons. They had agreed that Jacob's family would take the daughters of Shechem and give their own to the townsfolk. The selections would be by the brothers. But that was not what Shechem and Chamor told the townspeople. They said that the Shechemites would choose from among Jacob's daughters, getting the cream of the crop so to speak, and they would decide which daughters to give up, allowing them to get rid of their less desirable maidens. Additionally, Chamor and Shechem stressed that the Shechemites would share in Jacob's great wealth, something that had never been discussed; it was only as an afterthought that they mentioned mandatory circumcision.

Why did they change the terms of the agreement? Presumably, Shechem and Chamor understood that the counteroffer made by Jacob's sons, which included circumcision, would be unacceptable to their people. Knowing this, they falsified the terms and stated them in a more favorable form.

Had Jacob's sons anticipated this change? And if not, had they believed that the townspeople would accept their less favorable proposal including as it did the provision of circumcision?

It can reasonably be argued that Jacob's sons also fully expected the Shechemites to turn down the offer. In fact, this was the crux of their plan to gain Dinah's release. They understood that Shechem and Chamor's very generous initial offer revealed that they acknowledged the legitimacy of Jacob's family's claim to have Dinah returned, and felt guilty over the incident. The brothers decided they would gain her release by attaching a condition that would appear eminently reasonable to Shechem and Chamor, but would never be accepted by the townsfolk of Shechem. Once the offer was turned down, Shechem would feel obliged to release Dinah.

Dinah's brothers had not anticipated, however, that Shechem and Chamor would lie to their own people. Once the Shechemites all circumcised themselves, the situation went from bad to worse. Not only had they failed to secure the release of their sister, they now had a whole town of pagans who identified themselves as a part of the nation of Abraham and shared in his covenant.

The attack on Shechem was, therefore, not part of the original plan, and it did not involve any of the other brothers. Only the zealous Shimon and Levi seized the initiative and responded to the new situation. They attacked and utterly destroyed the city of Shechem, freeing their sister and preventing the possibility of any pagans claiming a portion in the covenant of Abraham. Shimon and Levi killed the Shechemites not only because of the abuse of Dinah, but also because the residents distorted and threatened the covenant of Abraham.

iv. *Measure for Measure*

UR SAGES CALCULATE THE NUMBER OF YEARS JACOB WAS separated from his beloved son Joseph as twenty-two. Joseph's brothers sold him into slavery when he was 17 years old, and he was reunited with his father when he was 39 years old. They further find in the number twenty-two an appropriate rebuke, measure for measure (*middah keneged middah*) for the twenty-two years Jacob failed to fulfill the commandment of honoring his parents (see *Rashi,* 28:9). Jacob spent these twenty-two years almost entirely with Laban, getting married and building his family and possessions.

A question immediately arises. Why did the Sages find fault with Jacob for his separation from his parents? He had fled for his life, urged on by his own parents. What else could he have done? How can these years be considered a lapse in the fulfillment of his obligation to honor his parents?

The Torah tells us (33:17) that after Jacob headed back to the land of his birth he stopped at Succos, where he built a home and a temporary structure for his livestock. The Talmud teaches (*Megillah* 17a) that he stayed there for eighteen months.

Jacob undoubtedly had reason to stay in Succos. Nonetheless, the Midrash that considers him partially at fault for the twenty-two-year separation may be focusing on this stopover in Succos. He may have chosen to name the place Succos to show that the layover was only temporary and that he was eager to return to his parents; a *succah* by definition is a temporary dwelling. However, such a long hiatus in his journey indicates less than absolutely perfect zeal to return to his parents and honor them. God holds the righteous to a strict standard (*medakdek kechut hasaarah*) in order to bring them to absolute perfection. Jacob's delay implied that throughout his involuntary separation from his family he might have been less than perfectly sensitive to their suffering. To help him perfect that sensitivity, God decreed that he himself undergo a similar separation.

In actuality, Jacob was separated from his family for thirty-six years. In addition to the twenty-two years spent with Laban, he also spent fourteen years in the yeshivah of Shem and Eiver. The Talmud tells us (*Megillah* 17a) that Jacob was not punished for these fourteen years because learning Torah supersedes honoring parents. We may also add that learning Torah was in reality the greatest honor he could have bestowed on his parents; there was no lapse during these fourteen years.

פרשת וישב

i. Joseph Rises Twice

OSEPH HAS TWO DREAMS. IN THE FIRST, HE DREAMS ABOUT sheaves of wheat, and he tells his brothers (37:7), "And behold, my sheaf arose and it even stood erect, and behold, your sheaves gathered around and bowed down to my sheaf."

Two things happened with Joseph's sheaf — it arose and it stood erect. This seems to allude to two distinct stages, one in which the sheaf arose but was still somewhat wobbly, and the second when the sheaf found its balance and was able to stand erect. What is the significance of these two stages?

A short while later, Joseph has another dream, and he relates this one as well to his brothers (37:9), "Behold, have had another dream, and behold, the sun, the moon and eleven stars were bowing down to me." Unlike the first dream, this time there is no uncertainty, no hesitation, no need to find balance. Why is this so?

The Beis HaLevi comments that the first dream, which related to things of the earth, suggested that Joseph would have some sort of physical dominion over his brothers. The second dream, of heavenly bodies, predicted Joseph's eventual spiritual elevation and leadership.

This distinction between the first and second dreams may hold the answer to our questions. True to the prediction of the dream, Jacob had designated Joseph to be a leader in his family in the physical realm. But it was a leadership that teetered. His brothers did not want him, and they deposed him. Years later, however, Joseph's leadership in the physical realm reasserted itself in a very real way when he became viceroy of Egypt.

In the spiritual realm, however, Joseph attained leadership only once — after the reunion in Egypt. In the beginning, he never became their spiritual leader, although Jacob would have wanted him to be. Since the brothers did not acknowledge his spiritual superiority, Joseph was by definition not a leader. There can be no spiritual leader without followers. The dream mentions only one rising in the spiritual realm.

Alternatively, if we were to contend that Joseph did indeed become the spiritual leader of his brothers while still in Hebron, we can offer another explanation for there being only one rising in the spiritual realm. Shortly after he arrived in Egypt, Joseph was put in charge of the entire estate of an important royal minister (39:5). In that position, he would have had ample opportunity to send a message to his father that he was still alive. Joseph declined; he felt the divine hand directing him toward his destiny. He willingly endured twenty-two years of separation and self-imposed silence in order to fulfill God's will for his family. Even in exile, Joseph displayed uninterrupted spiritual leadership.

ii. The Favorite Son

HY DID THE BROTHERS HATE JOSEPH? THE TORAH GIVES two justifications for their hatred (37:2), "And these are the experiences of Jacob, Joseph was 17 years old ... and he was a youth ... and Joseph would report [his brothers'] evil doings to their father, and he was a youth ..." Rashi quotes the Midrash (*Bereishis Rabbah* 84:7) that Joseph was prone to youthful behavior, devoting too much time to his personal grooming, an indication of a trace of immaturity and self-absorption. By our own standards, we might find no fault with Joseph's behavior despite the Torah's exaggerated depiction of his flaws; we might attribute it to youthful exuberance. But in the context of Joseph's overarching righteousness it was considered a flaw.

Here we would seem to have sufficient cause for fraternal hatred. Joseph carried tales about his brothers to his father and he showed himself to have an immature and self-absorbed personality. But this is not why they hated Joseph. The Torah provides a different reason (37:3-4), "And Israel loved Joseph from among all his sons, for he was his *ben zekunim* ... And the brothers saw that their father loved him from among all his brothers, and they hated him." It was envy of their father's love. Joseph's deeds and personality would help them rationalize their actions against him, but their inner motivation was hatred born of jealousy.

But were they justified in their jealousy? Did Jacob really love Joseph more than his other children?

The Torah indicates that the brothers were mistaken in their perception. Jacob loved Joseph, the Torah tells us, because he was his *ben zekunim*. Ordinarily, these words would be translated as "the child of his old age." But in this context, it is a problematic translation. First of all, Joseph was not the youngest. Benjamin was, and therefore, Benjamin should have been considered the *ben zekunim*. Furthermore, the age span from Reuben the oldest of Jacob's children to Joseph was only six years, during which all the children besides Benjamin were born. Surely, Jacob had not become old during these six years.

Perhaps for these reasons, *Targum Onkelos* offers a different translation of *ben zekunim*. Since *zaken* in Hebrew can mean either old or wise, he translates *ben zekunim* as *bar chakim*, a son who perpetuates his father's wisdom. Jacob's "love" for Joseph was not the personal love of a father for his child but a special affinity for the son who would carry on his spiritual work. In fact, when the Torah speaks about Joseph's personality flaws and characteristics, his father is identified as Jacob, but when the Torah tells us Jacob "loved" Joseph he is identified as Israel, which relates to his role as a patriarch of the Jewish people. In that role, as the *Targum* indicates, Jacob perceived special qualities and potential in Joseph that drew them together.

Joseph's brothers, however, were either unable to see or to accept the distinction their father had made, and they hated Joseph in their jealousy over their father's love.

iii. Jacob Monitors the Situation

OLATILE WOULD BE A MILD WORD FOR THE SITUATION IN Jacob's household. The brothers resented Joseph because they perceived him as their father's favorite. Joseph, for his part, poured oil on the flames by relating his grandiose dreams to the rest of the family. After he retells the second of his dreams (37:11), "His brothers were jealous of him, and his father monitored the matter."

Why does the Torah make a point of telling us that Jacob "monitored the matter"? What exactly does this mean and where did it come into play? The story unfolds. Joseph's brothers tend their father's sheep, and Joseph is sent to them, initiating a chain of events that lead to Joseph's eventual bondage in Egypt. Jacob's "monitoring the matter" remains an enigma.

Let us look closely at these events as they ensued. Perhaps we can discern Jacob's wise and subtle hand trying to rectify the situation he was monitoring.

Jacob knew of his sons' jealousy and probably even hatred towards Joseph. He understood that two factors lay at the root of this jealousy: The brothers were afraid Joseph would supersede them, and there was also a lack of closeness between Joseph and his brothers. To rectify this, Jacob chose to increase the relative stature of his other sons and also to promote feelings of brotherhood among his sons.

What did Jacob do? He said to Joseph (37:14), "Go see to the welfare of your brothers and the welfare of the sheep."

Jacob had a threefold purpose in doing this: to enhance the stature of the brothers by demonstrating his concern for them; to minimize Joseph's status *vis-à-vis* his brothers by sending him on this errand on their behalf and also having him check on the sheep, enhancing the stature of the brothers by comparison; to engender feelings of comradeship among the brothers by having Joseph express concern about their well being.

This was not a casual mission by any means, a simple inquiry after the welfare of the brothers and the sheep. It was a foreboding mission simultaneously fraught with hope and danger, a mission consequential to the destiny of the Jewish people.

We find a sharp indication of the gravity of the mission in a single word of the narrative (37:13). "And Israel said to Joseph, 'Are your brothers not tending flock in Shechem? Go, I will send you to them.' And [Joseph] said, 'Behold, I am here.'" The phrase "I am here," *hineni*, is incongruous. It ordinarily occurs in the

Torah when a person is asked to go on a difficult mission and he expresses his full willingness to undertake it. The classic example is the *Akeidah*; Abraham's response to the divine calling to bring Isaac as a sacrifice to God at the *Akeidah* is, *"Hineni.* I am here."

Both Jacob and Joseph knew the mission would be treacherous and difficult; Joseph would be called upon to humble himself to his brothers. Nonetheless, Joseph declared, *"Hineni.* I am here. I am ready to do what must be done."

There is yet another indication that this was a hazardous mission in the use of the name Israel instead of Jacob. The name Israel, as noted, relates to his role as the patriarch of the Jewish people, whereas Jacob is a more personal name. It is Israel who sends Joseph to his brothers, not on personal business but on a mission of import to the future of the Jewish people.

It was in his role as Israel that Jacob felt he had the right to send Joseph on a dangerous mission to reestablish harmony amongst the future tribes. But the gears of a different destiny were already turning, for the brothers plotted as Joseph drew near. We find a hint to the divine hand guiding events in the appearance of the word ach, brother, or a cognate form of it, ten times in the story, equal to the number of brothers who had hated and plotted against Joseph — and with whom a true brotherhood would have to be established.

iv. *Hate From a Distance*

HATRED IS A DESTRUCTIVE EMOTION AND ALSO A MYSTERIous one. In the context of the story of Joseph and his brothers, the Torah offers us a profound insight (37:18), "And they saw [Joseph] from afar, and before he came close to them, they plotted to kill him."

The words "from afar, and before he came close" seem redundant, for if they saw him from afar, we know he had not yet come close. In fact, the entire phrase seems superfluous. It would have been enough to tell us that they plotted against him. What is added by informing us it was when Joseph was far away?

It would appear that the Torah is probing the sin of Joseph's brothers. Overcome with jealousy and hate, the brothers were only willing to see Joseph from a distance. They did not want to see him from up close. Had they allowed themselves to get closer, they might have identified more with him. They might have seen those sterling qualities that had inspired their father's special bond with him. But they kept their distance and only saw the object of their hatred.

What held them back?

It is the nature of a person to wish to preserve his sense of importance. It may have been threatening for the brothers to take a closer look at Joseph's nature, since it might have highlighted what they feared, namely their own relative insufficiencies next to Joseph. By avoiding a thoughtful examination of Joseph, his brothers preserved a negative image of him and convinced themselves that their father was misguided in his favoritism. This then is often the mechanism by which human beings condemn. They pass judgment from afar, not allowing the object of their hatred to come close.

The Torah gives us further indications of the extent of their hatred (37:24-25), "And they took him and tossed him into the pit … and they sat down to eat bread." It was callous to sit down to eat while Joseph was already in the pit, waiting to die of starvation. Similarly, when the Torah earlier states (37:4), "They hated him and could not speak with him peacefully," the Torah uses the word *leshalom*, which translated literally means "toward peace." The emphasis is on their unwillingness to reconcile with Joseph and to speak to him in a way that would lead toward peace and reconciliation.

In a totally different approach, the words "from afar" can actually be interpreted to the brothers' credit. The brothers knew of themselves that they were extremely compassionate people. At the same time, they felt objectively that Joseph posed a danger to the emerging nation. Wanting their decision to be completely rational and not colored by emotion, they judged him before he got close and aroused their natural compassion.

In the same vein, we can also explain their sitting down to eat bread right after they threw Joseph into the pit. According to the Talmud (*Sanhedrin* 56a), it is forbidden for judges to eat while they are considering a capital case. Once they judged Joseph, they sat down to eat to make the point that they had done so with clear conscience, iron will and in keeping with the law. Similarly, when the Torah earlier states that they could not speak with him "to peace," it also reflects on their strength and honesty. There was no hypocrisy. They could not feel one way and speak in another.

v. A Not So Empty Pit

EMPTY IS A RELATIVE WORD. THE TORAH TELLS US (37:24), "Then they took [Joseph] and cast him into the pit; the pit was empty, no water was in it." The Talmud analyzes the wording (*Shabbos* 22a), "Since it states that the pit was empty, doesn't it follow that there was no water? What does the expression 'there was no water in it' come to teach? There was, indeed, no water in it, but there were serpents and scorpions."

If we backtrack just a little bit, we will find a fierce argument taking place shortly before the brothers tossed Joseph into the pit. The brothers wanted to execute Joseph, but Reuben managed to dissuade them. Instead, he suggested that they throw him into the pit. Reuben's unexpressed intent was to return later to take him out of the pit (37:21-22). Now, if the pit was full of lethal creatures, what was the point of Reuben's suggestion? Joseph would quickly, if not immediately, be killed.

The Maharsha raises this question, and he answers that no one realized the snakes and scorpions were in the pit. This answer, however, raises another question in its turn. If no one knew about it, what is the Torah trying to convey by implying that the pit was far more dangerous than people realized?

Let us take a closer look at the phrase "they took him and cast him into the pit" (וַיִּקָחֻהוּ וַיַּשְׁלִכוּ אֹתוֹ הַבֹּרָה) Notice the subtle grammatical difference between the first and second verb. In Hebrew, the direct object of a verb can be attached to the verb as a suffix letter, or else it can stand as a word of its own when combined with the particle *es* (אֶת). The first verb of the verse, "they took him," appears as the single word *vayikachuhu* (וַיִּקָחֻהוּ). The second verb, "they cast him" is expressed as two words, *vayashlichu oso* (וַיַּשְׁלִכוּ אֹתוֹ), instead of the single word *vayaslichuhu* (וַיַּשְׁלִכוּהוּ). What is the grammatical difference between these two forms, and what is the significance for us here?

Rabbi Shamshon Raphael Hirsch explains that when the particle *es* (אֶת) appears as part of the direct object it is an indication that the verb is fully acting on its object; this may be connected to the relative positions of these letters in the Hebrew alphabet, the *aleph* being the first and the *tav* being the last. When the object appears simply as a suffix letter to the verb, it reflects a less intense effect of the verb on its object.

When the Torah tells us that the brothers grabbed hold of him, the one-word form, *vayikachuhu* (וַיִּקָחֻהוּ), is used. The physical taking possession of Joseph, even though it was for the purpose of harm, was done less emphatically by the brothers. Joseph was anathema to them, and they did not even want to get close to him.

But when the Torah tells us that they cast Joseph into the pit, the two-word form, *vayashlichu oso* (וַיַּשְׁלִכוּ אֹתוֹ), is used, with the particle *es* (אֶת) combining with the objective suffix to form its own separate word (אתו). They cast him away emphatically and without reservation.

This explanation may provide a clue to the Torah's oblique reference to the snakes and scorpions in the pit. It is human nature to hide from uncomfortable thoughts and feelings. The brothers had indeed resisted the overt act of willfully killing Joseph. Nonetheless, the emotions prompting their murderous intent still seethed within, but the brothers did not face up to them. When they threw him into the pit, however, they did it vehemently, not bothering to check if there were any lethal creatures in the pit. The suppressed desire to kill him surfaced in their failure to investigate.

There is also a second significance to Joseph's landing in a pit filled with deadly snakes and scorpions in that it conveyed a providential message to Joseph. Joseph saw clearly that his survival was miraculous, that God was protecting him in the pit from the lethal forces around him. In this way, God communicated to Joseph that He would watch over him throughout his twenty-two year ordeal, including thirteen miserable years of slavery and incarceration.

This message was reinforced shortly thereafter when the pack animals of the slave traders to whom he was sold were bearing unusually sweet-smelling spices (see *Rashi*, 37:25). This, too, presented a providential message to Joseph. For one thing, it showed divine consideration for his comfort while he was being led off into captivity. On a deeper level, the unusual fragrance hinted that Joseph's ordeal would be spiritually uplifting and end well.

vi. *Clever Plotters*

FTER SELLING JOSEPH INTO SLAVERY, THE BROTHERS dipped his coat in goat's blood to create the impression that he had been killed by a wild beast. But then they faced a serious dilemma. How could they break the terrible news to their father? The Torah tells us (37:32), "They sent the multicolored coat, and they brought it to their father."

There seems to be a redundancy here. Why does the Torah use two phrases, "they sent" and "they brought [the coat] to their father"? What additional information can be gleaned from the additional words?

There is a subtle indication here of the cleverness of the brothers' plot. First, they deliberately "sent" off the blood-soaked coat, planting the evidence in a place where it was certain to be found or they could contrive to have it found. Once the coat was brought to their father's camp, then "they brought it to him," with the explanation that someone else had found the coat and that an animal had presumably killed Joseph. All this to deflect suspicion from themselves.

Had they returned themselves with Joseph's blood-stained garment, their father, aware of their jealousy, might have suspected that Joseph had indeed reached his destination and that his brothers were covering up their own responsibility for his death.

There is also a hint of God's hidden providence in the language of the Torah. The word *vayishalchu* (וַיְשַׁלְּחוּ), "and they sent," resonates with the word *vayishlachehu* (וַיִּשְׁלָחֵהוּ), which appeared above, when Jacob "sent" Joseph to check on the welfare of his brothers. Jacob had sent Joseph to his brothers in an attempt to rectify the situation and effect reconciliation between him and his jealous brothers. But God had other plans. The brothers' sending would initiate a series of divinely directed events that would culminate in reconciliation twenty-two years later in Pharaoh's palace.

vii. *The Sale Is Final*

EFORE ENDING UP IN EGYPT, JOSEPH PASSED THROUGH several hands. First, his brothers sold him to a group of Ishmaelite peddlers. They in turn sold him to a group of Midianites. Finally, the Midianites sold him to Potiphar, the Egyptian minister of slaughterers.

The Torah's presentation of the sequence of events is puzzling. First, we are told (37:28), "And they sold Joseph to the Ishmaelites for 20 pieces of silver, and they brought Joseph to Egypt." But rather than telling us immediately the precise details of how Joseph ended up in Egypt, the Torah veers off onto a tangent (37:32-35), "And they sent off the multicolored coat, and they brought it to their father ... And Jacob tore his clothing and wrapped his loins I sackcloth ... And his father wept for him." Only afterward does the Torah supply the details of the final stage of Joseph's delivery into Egyptian hands (37:36), "And the Midianites sold him to Egypt, to Potiphar, Pharaoh's officer, the minister of slaughterers."

Why does the Torah not immediately supply all the details and then shift the scene to Jacob's discovery of the bloodstained coat? In fact, the entire mention of the sale to Potiphar seems superfluous, since it is mentioned again after the digression to Judah and Tamar.

According to the Torah, Jacob had observed his sons' antipathy toward Joseph, and presumably, they in turn were aware of their father's awareness. The brothers had to be careful to deflect suspicion from themselves. In order to accomplish this, they had to return first without him, professing not to have seen him. They also had to arrange for the bloodstained coat to be found only after they returned. In this way, they could further deflect suspicion from themselves by commiserating with their father and offering to search for the missing Joseph.

During this period, between the time they returned and the time the coat was "found," they must have observed their father's shock and grief as he fretted over his missing son's fate. At this point, they still had the opportunity to undo their dreadful deed. Seeing their father's anguish with their very own eyes, they should have intercepted the bloodstained coat before it reached him. Then they should have searched for Joseph and retrieved him from his captors. This is what they should have done. But they didn't.

This is why the Torah mentions the sale of Joseph without supplying the details of his coming to Potiphar prior to the discovery of the blood-soaked coat. Everything was still reversible until that point. The sale was not yet final. But when the brothers allowed the bloodstained coat to be delivered to their already grieving father, the last nail was driven into the coffin so to speak. Their horrible unbrotherly act could not be undone. Providence now directed that Joseph arrive in the hands of Potiphar, from where he would eventually emerge triumphant and be reunited with his family. Therefore, that sale is mentioned only after Jacob "learns" of Joseph's death.

viii. *The Seeds of Royalty*

JOSEPH IS CARRIED OFF TO SLAVERY IN EGYPT SETTING OFF A chain of events which would bring his entire family down after him and lead to centuries of Jewish bondage. At this moment of high drama, the scene shifts away to the story of Judah and Tamar (38:1ff). Judah falsely accuses Tamar of adultery, and when he realizes that he himself is the father of the unborn child, he acknowledges his paternity in a courageous confession. Then the story returns to Joseph in Egypt. It would appear that this interlude is somehow of crucial relevance to the divine plan of establishing the family of Jacob in Egypt. How is this so?

As we have seen from the beginning of Genesis, the underlying theme of the first Book of the Torah is the resolution of brotherly strife. The final third of the Book reveals the interaction of God's providence and the fledgling Jewish nation, which results in the personal growth of Jacob's children and the formation of a cohesive and loving family.

Rabbi Israel Chait, my teacher, has observed how each of the elements of the Jewish people had their unique challenges. Jacob's special attachment to Joseph and Benjamin, his sons from his beloved wife Rachel, interfered with the development of the nation. Joseph, blessed with talent and beauty, had to learn to direct his energies away from himself. And his brothers had to overcome their instinctive feelings of jealousy and accept their brother as he was — a superior person who was closer to their father and fit for leadership.

Against this background of spiritual growth, we encounter the subplot of Judah and Tamar. According to tradition, there will be two Messiahs, a preliminary one descended from Joseph, to be followed by a descendant of King David of the tribe of Judah. These two kingship strands begin at the point of Joseph's sale into slavery. Joseph descends to Egypt, and Judah turns away from his brothers because of their misgivings (see *Rashi,* 38:1). The strands come together when Joseph and Judah become the chief agents in the restoration and redemption of Jacob's family, as they will eventually come together in Messianic times. The interaction of Judah and Tamar holds the key to Judah's personal growth, making him worthy of kingship.

Judah's destiny for kingship probably began at he time of his birth when his mother Leah expressed gratitude to God. This trait is the cornerstone requirement of a Jewish earthly king. The honor and pomp associated with kingship cannot interfere with the obligation to recognize God's majesty.

Throughout the story of Joseph, we are keenly aware of Judah's leadership qualities. When Joseph's brothers decided to cast him into the pit it was Judah who initiated his sale to Egypt to avoid his being killed. All the brothers were righteous people devoid of conscious evil intent; they felt fully justified in imposing a death sentence on Joseph. It was Judah, however, who was able to step back from the precipice of murder and lead his brothers by his vision.

Later on, we see a repentant Judah vouch for the safety of Benjamin, Jacob's other favorite son, despite the preponderance of evidence that points to Benjamin's guilt. Judah was willing to sacrifice his own life to save his brother and rectify his sin. This is the heart of a king. The bond forged by this act of heroism lasted throughout history. The strip of the territory of Benjamin upon which the Temple stood was surrounded and protected by the territory of Judah. The tribe of Benjamin was also part of the Kingdom of Judah, unlike the tribes who were "lost." Most Jewish people today are descended from these two tribes.

In its broadest structure, the theme of the story of Judah and Tamar addresses Judah's erroneous first judgment of Tamar. In response to Judah's allegation, Tamar uses the same language the brothers used in reporting Joseph's death to their father (37:22). "*Haker na*," she says (38:25). "Please recognize [these things]." At that moment, when Tamar unwittingly confronted Judah with his own words, he realized his great sin against both Joseph and Tamar. Judah now understood that just as God had guided the events that led him to judge Tamar harshly and unjustly, so too might he have prematurely judged Joseph, leading to a tragic error.

Overcome by repentance, Judah said (38:26), "She is more righteous than I am." With his new insight, Judah gains the capacity to withhold judgment, which becomes manifest in his defense of Benjamin. The story of Judah and Tamar is, therefore, not a digression but an intrinsic part of the providential process that guided Judah, the progenitor of the Davidic dynasty, in his spiritual growth and prepared the way for his descendants to ascend to royalty.

ix. *She Grabbed Joseph's Garment*

OTIPHAR'S WIFE TRIED REPEATEDLY TO SEDUCE JOSEPH until, on one occasion, Joseph fled, leaving his garment in her clutched hand (39:7ff). Rejected, she used the garment as physical evidence to support her false accusation that Joseph had tried to seduce her. This is puzzling. After all, Joseph had rejected her advances a number of times, but he had never informed on her. What did she have to fear from him? Why did she slander Joseph after this incident? What was so unusual about it that the threshold of slander was crossed?

We find a clue in the *Midrash Rabbah* quoted by Rashi on the verse which introduces the event (39:11), "And it was like this day, and [Joseph] came to the house ... " Commenting on the words "this day," the Midrash explains that it was "a special day, a day of merriment, a religious day, that they all went to the house of idol worship."

On a simple level, the Midrash is describing the circumstances that allowed Potiphar's wife to be found alone with Joseph. On a deeper level, the Midrash is hinting at a profound spiritual longing Joseph was experiencing at the time, a longing that Potiphar's wife believed would make him vulnerable to her advances.

In the United States, it is customary for families to get together on Thanksgiving Day. Traditionally, they socialize, watch football and share a festive meal. Those who cannot make it to these family gatherings generally experience feelings of unusual loneliness, longing and melancholy. Although the celebration for most Americans is secular, the day touches people in a spiritual way by awakening memories of warmth, family and belonging to a greater whole. The inability to participate is frustrating.

Similarly, when the Egyptians celebrated their pagan holiday, the feeling of belonging to a greater whole aroused an element of spirituality, albeit corrupted, in the populace, as the Midrash would seem to indicate. At its source, this yearning stems from the soul's desire to cling to God in a service greater and more eternal than the body's temporal existence provides. This aspiration's importance is expressed in the Rosh Hashanah prayer in which we pray for mankind to form a single group in unified worship of God. Any national celebration taps into this spiritual yearning and diverts it into different channels.

Potiphar's wife sensed that the atmosphere of spirituality of the pagan holiday would touch Joseph and evoke within him feelings of longing for his own family. It was on that day that she again offered herself as a loving "surrogate family" with which to connect, a haven for Joseph's unrequited spiritual longing and loneliness. This approach is supported by Rashi, who states that Potiphar's wife sought to join with Joseph in this world and the next.

The Torah may also be alluding to another aspect of Potiphar's wife's plan (39:12), "And she grabbed him by his garment, saying, 'Lie with me.'" She may have been using the symbol of the garment to remind him of his own special garment that his brothers stripped from him and stained with blood before presenting it to their father. But on an even deeper level, it may be symbolic of a clever psychological ploy. The word for "garment," *beged*, is also the three-letter root word for betrayal. In this instance, the double entendre of the word *beged* reflects a profound insight into the nature of sin.

A person with a strong conscience, such as Joseph, cannot easily sin without rationalizing the guilty pleasure he is considering. One justification may take the form of rebellion, which can be liberating. The rebellious mind justifies sin by shifting blame to someone else. Potiphar's wife was playing on this by grabbing his "*beged*" and encouraging him to betray and rebel against his Jewish family and their values.

In effect, she was saying to Joseph, "Look, your family sold you away and has not even regretted it enough to search for you in all this time. Cling to me and not to them." Such an appeal would allow Joseph to have the pleasure that Potiphar's wife offered. In his rebellion, he could blame his actions on his treacherous brothers who had supposedly caused him to sin by putting him into this situation. Of course, we do not know how much Potiphar's wife had investigated Joseph's history. If she, in fact, did not know about his brothers, Joseph could have supplied the words for her in his own mind to rationalize his betrayal.

The Midrash (*Bereishis Rabbah* 86:7; *Tanchuma* 8:9) is sensitive to the seductive appeal of this rationalization. It states that the image of Jacob appeared to Joseph, and he refrained from sin. Joseph realized that this beckoning union was offering only an ersatz version of the spiritual life of his family that he missed. The image of his righteous father would not allow him to rationalize his sin.

Despite Potiphar's wife's attempt to grab Joseph in his "rebellion," Joseph nonetheless left the *beged* (garment, rebellion) in her hand, as the verse concludes.

When this happened, Potiphar's wife knew she had completely lost him. Furthermore, considering this her best opportunity for success, she had probably bared her soul to him as never before, and when he turned her down, the rejection must have been unbearable. Not surprisingly, the love she felt for him turned to hatred, and she turned on him with all her fury in an unbridled outburst of slander.

x. Four Versions of Flight

EARING THE ADVANCES OF POTIPHAR'S WIFE, JOSEPH LEFT his garment and fled. What exactly happened? Let us read on. First, the Torah tells us (39:12), "He fled and went outside." Potiphar's wife, however, notices something else (39:13), "And when she saw he had left his garment and he had fled outside." When she retells the events to her household staff, however, she reverts to the original version and says (39:15), "And he left his garment with me, and he fled and went outside." But when she tells her story to her husband, she reverts to the second version and says (39:18), "And he left his garment with me, and he fled outside." In these four descriptions of the same action, he sometimes "flees and goes outside (*vayivrach vayeitzei hachutzah*)" and sometimes just "flees outside (*vayivrach hachutzah*)." What is the significance of these discrepancies?

It would appear that the difference lies in the appearance of guilt. "He fled and went outside" describes the behavior of an innocent man who flees from sin because of his own conscience. He is not afraid of getting caught, because he has not done anything wrong. He only flees the scene of temptation; afterwards, he walks outside at a more leisurely pace. "He fled outside," however, would indicate a sense of guilt and fear of capture, which would require a hurried exit.

In the original description of the events, the Torah describes Joseph as fleeing simply to avoid her embrace. Not burdened by guilt or a sense of danger, he could flee the room and then casually go outside. "He fled and went outside."

Joseph, though, did not realize that this time was different; danger loomed in proportion to his ardent pursuer's feelings of rejection. The Torah confirms this view in the next verse when describing her reaction from her perspective. She sees Joseph fleeing from her completely to the outside, a total rejection. "He fled outside."

In her first retelling of the story to her household, Potiphar's wife recounts the event accurately, perhaps because it was humiliating for her to recall the greater rejection suggested by the words "he fled outside." She only says, "He fled and went outside."

By evening, however, her embarrassment subsides, while her rage reaches volcanic levels. She wants revenge! Therefore, she is careful to frame Joseph in a believable fashion. She claims that "he fled outside," like a man guilty of attempted seduction fleeing for his life.

xi. *Joseph's Power of Deduction*

REAMS UNCOVER MANY BITS OF IMPORTANT INFORMATION, but they are still notoriously difficult to interpret. Nonetheless, when Joseph found himself in prison with two royal ministers, he offered to interpret their dreams, and then he predicted their fates with uncanny accuracy. How did he know that his interpretations were correct? Was it divine inspiration without any rational basis?

Let us look closely at the verses. The Torah tells us (40:16), "When the minister of the bakers saw that [Joseph] had interpreted [the dream of the wine steward favorably], he said to Joseph, 'I also had a dream…'" The wine steward had asked for an interpretation without knowing what the result would be, but the baker only asked to have his dream interpreted after he heard the favorable interpretation of the first dream. Joseph immediately saw that the baker was motivated solely by self-interest. This was not the case with the wine steward, who was interested in the truth.

Joseph's perception of the baker was confirmed when he recounted his dream. Pharaoh's cakes were negligently exposed while the other cakes, presumably his own, were better protected. The baker, in contrast to the wine steward, lacked the devotion and loyalty necessary for the service of the king. The original crimes also confirmed this evaluation. The Midrash tells us (*Bereishis Rabbah* 88:2) that the baker allowed a pebble into Pharaoh's bread and the wine steward failed to prevent a fly from entering into his wine. A pebble can be avoided with sufficient care, while it is much more difficult to protect against an animate fly. The baker was the more negligent of the two. The Torah hints at this distinction (40:1), "After these things, the wine steward to the king of Egypt and the baker sinned." The wine steward is identified by his service to the king, while the more self-centered baker is not.

Joseph also understood that the cases of the two ministers were likely to be reviewed on Pharaoh's birthday, which was coming up in three days' time. The appearance of the number three in both of their dreams — three layers of cakes in the baker's dream and three clusters of grapes in the wine steward's, — hinted strongly at their anticipatory anxiety.

Then Joseph combined this information with another insight. The Torah tells us that the birthdays of the Egyptian pharaohs were celebrated as national holidays (40:20). Since the pharaoh was worshiped as a deity, his birthday also had religious significance. Appeals for clemency presented publicly on that day gave him the opportunity to showcase his godlike control over life and death. Joseph reasoned that Pharaoh would demonstrate his full control by simultaneously granting life to one supplicant and decreeing death for another.

Joseph then made a summary of what he had learned and deduced. He knew that both the baker and the wine steward were coming up for review within three days. He presumed that Pharaoh would pardon one and condemn the other. And he knew that the baker was more negligent, less loyal and, therefore, the more likely candidate for execution.

פרשת מקץ
Parashas Mikeitz

i. A Shot in the Dark

WHEN PHARAOH NEEDED AN INTERPRETER FOR HIS DREAM, the wine steward recommended Joseph (41:9-13). "Then the wine steward spoke before Pharaoh ... '[The chief baker and I] had a dream on the same night ... And it came to pass just as [Joseph] interpreted for us, [Pharaoh] restored me to my post, and [the baker] was hanged.' "

The wine steward offered Joseph's accurate interpretation of his own dream as well as that of the baker's dream in support of his recommendation. Why was this necessary? Wouldn't the one dream alone have been sufficient proof of Joseph's powers?

Apparently, one serendipitous prediction would not have demonstrated Joseph's great wisdom neither to the wine steward nor to Pharaoh later. His success could easily have been construed as grasping at straws, a shot in the dark. It would have been a low-risk guess to give the wine steward a favorable interpretation. If Joseph was right, he would look great, and he might expect some considerations in the future. And if he was wrong, no harm done. The wine steward would be hanging from a tree, in no position to complain or retaliate.

But when Joseph interpreted the baker's dream unfavorably, he was really going out on a limb. For if it turned out he was wrong and the chief baker was reinstated, he would have been in deep trouble. The baker could have easily exacted revenge on the hapless slave who had caused him unnecessary heartache. Joseph's interpretation stemmed from his great confidence in the wisdom God had granted him. It established his abilities as genuine.

ii. *Think Quick and Act Fast*

AVING HEARD ABOUT JOSEPH'S ABILITY TO INTERPRET dreams, Pharaoh orders that he be brought before him (41:14). "And Pharaoh sent and summoned Joseph, and they rushed him from the pit, and he shaved, and he changed his clothing, and he came before Pharaoh."

Why this preponderance of predicates: rushed ... shaved ... changed ... came? Why could the Torah not simply tell us "they brought Joseph to Pharaoh"?

Our Sages tell us that Joseph stayed in prison for an additional two years because he had asked the wine steward to intercede for him with Pharaoh (*Targum Yonasan* 40:14; *Rashi* 40:23; *Bereishis Rabbah* 89:3). The wine steward, however, forgot all about him. The Midrash states that Joseph was punished because he failed to trust in God. But what was wrong with Joseph's striving to free himself? It is a basic Jewish tenet not to rely on miracles when normal efforts may succeed.

Perhaps we can say that Joseph's error, in part, was in the way he tried to free himself. After having his prophetic dreams, and after surviving the snakes and scorpions in the pit where his brothers had thrown him, he knew God was watching over him and guiding him toward an important destiny. He also knew from his dreams that he was slated to serve as an agent of the divine plan and a leader of his people. If so, petitioning Pharaoh through the wine steward with a prisoner's tale of woe was not the route to respect and elevation. Apparently, Joseph's main focus when he asked for pity was to save himself. He gave insufficient thought to how the form of his request would affect his greater mission. In this instance, he should have relied on God's guidance, and so, he was punished.

Two years later, when the palace guards came to bring him from the prison (pit) to the palace, he did not make the same mistake. Even as he was "rushed" up from his cell in the dungeon, he assessed the situation with great presence of mind and seized control of it. He reacted brilliantly.

He knew his destiny was to become a powerful person in order to benefit his family. Joseph understood that if he was about to meet Pharaoh, it was because Pharaoh wanted something from him. Further, he knew that if he were ever to obtain continued access to power, he would somehow have to gain Pharaoh's respect and admiration. In Joseph's current state, as a dirty and disheveled prisoner, it would be difficult for Pharaoh to see him as a potential high official and advisor. He had to think quickly and act fast.

The palace guards probably had no affection for the imprisoned Hebrew slave, and they were prepared to rush him to the palace as he was. Joseph may have warned them that it would be disrespectful to the king to bring him an ill-groomed slave. He may have hinted at his future powers and made some veiled threats. In any case, he persuaded them to allow him to shave. With further guile, he then persuaded them to bring him fresh clothing. Finally, the Torah records, Joseph came before Pharaoh, not rushed like a slave taken straight from jail but walking like a free man, well-groomed and well-dressed. In a brief moment,

Joseph brilliantly assessed and took control of the situation. Comparably, in a few brief words, the Torah reveals his genius.

There is another illustration of intuitive psychological brilliance in the Talmud (*Berachos* 48a), tangential to a discussion concerning blessings. The Talmud tells about King Yannai, of the Hasmonean dynasty, who murdered hundreds of rabbis. The queen's brother, Rabbi Shimon ben Shatach, a leading sage of that generation, managed to escape. A short while later, Yannai wanted a rabbi to lead the *Birchas HaMazon* blessing after the meal, and he asked the queen to invite her brother. The queen, however, refused to reveal her brother's whereabouts until the king swore he would do him no harm.

Seated at the table with his wife and brother-in-law, the king boasted about the honor he was bestowing on his brother-in-law by giving him the privilege of leading the blessings. Rabbi Shimon responded that the Torah was actually the cause of his honor, and he proceeded to quote a verse. Despite being angered by Rabbi Shimon's seemingly ungrateful response, Yannai gave him the ceremonial cup to recite the blessing.

"Shall I bless God from whose bounty Yannai and his friends have eaten?" Rabbi Shimon asked sarcastically. In other words, how could he recite the blessing if he had not partaken of the meal? This sharp comment further angered Yannai. Notwithstanding, he gave him some wine so that he could also be considered a participant in the meal.

The Talmud proceeds to analyze this incident to derive a ruling as to which foods someone must eat in order to qualify as a participant in the meal and participate in the blessing afterward.

But let us consider another aspect of this story. How did Rabbi Shimon ben Shatach have the audacity to insult Yannai twice? Wasn't he afraid for his life? True, Yannai had promised that he would do Rabbi Shimon no harm, but was his oath enough of a safeguard? After all, Yannai had slaughtered so many rabbis. Wasn't Rabbi Shimon worried that Yannai might break his oath if provoked? If he could kill innocent rabbis in his anger, he could certainly not be trusted to keep his word. Would it not have been more prudent for Rabbi Shimon to maintain a low profile and avoid angering Yannai? What could he gain by being provocative?

The answer is that he could gain a lot. Everything, in fact. What he did reflected his intuitive psychological brilliance. He had penetrated to the essential nature of Yannai's personality.

Successful and powerful wicked people, such as crime lords, have a strong sense of self-importance. Thus, if they give their word on something, it is meaningful. They consider their word to be part of themselves. If they took a cavalier attitude towards their word, they would be belittling themselves. In their thinking, they are extremely important, and their word as an extension of themselves is likewise. As time passes, however, the power of the given word begins to wane. Other desires crowd into the wicked man's heart, and a promise given much earlier may be rationalized away or pretended to be forgotten; the wicked have no particular problems with being hypocritical.

Understanding this psychology, Rabbi Shimon challenged Yannai's promise immediately, while it was still fresh. In doing so, he indicated that he took the promise seriously and believed Yannai would not hurt him regardless of his provocative behavior. Since it was still too early for Yannai to rationalize away or pretend to forget his promise, he was forced to act in accordance with his word. The promise was thus confirmed in such a way that, even later, Rabbi Shimon was indeed safeguarded by Yannai's then-perhaps-regretted oath of protection.

Had Rabbi Shimon initially behaved cautiously, he would have accomplished the exact opposite result. By showing himself to be fearful that Yannai might not keep his word, he would unwittingly be giving him subtle permission to break it. Yannai would have thought, *If Shimon doesn't take my promise seriously, it is because he understands that I never meant to give my word.* This would free Yannai to do as he pleased.

Clearly, Rabbi Shimon ben Shatach, like Joseph before him, had a quick and deep grasp of human nature.

iii. *The Growth Catalyst*

COINCIDENCES DO NOT OCCUR IN THE TORAH, CERTAINLY NOT if the associations are numerous and frequent. Therefore, there must be some profound significance to the association that we consistently find between Joseph and the number two.

Let us mention some. Joseph has two dreams. He is separated from his father for twenty-two years. While in prison, he interprets the dreams of two royal ministers. Then he remains there for an additional two years. Finally, he is released and interprets Pharaoh's two dreams. He is one of his mother's two sons, and he eventually has two sons of his own. The expected seven lean years are reduced to two when his father arrives. His father treats him like the firstborn by giving him a twofold share in that his two sons become two tribes. His very name Joseph means to add another. He is referred to by double names, such as Tzafnas Pane'ach and Ben Poras. Joseph's is the only death recorded twice, both in Genesis and in Exodus.

Furthermore, Pharaoh calls him a prodigy, *avrech* (אַבְרֵךְ), and gives him a chariot, *rechev* (רֶכֶב). The numerical values of the letters of *rechev* (רֶכֶב) are 200, 20 and 2, while *avrech* (אַבְרֵךְ) has the same letters but preceded by an *aleph* (א), whose value is 1. Again, we see Joseph surrounded by a multiplicity of twos.

The Midrash states that the Torah could not begin with the letter *aleph* since it is the first letter in the word *arur* (אָרוּר), cursed. Instead, the Torah begins with a *beis* (ב), which is the first letter in the word *berachah* (בְּרָכָה), blessing.

The Maharal in *Tiferes Yisrael* explains that creation is the ultimate expression of unity transformed into plurality, whereby God effects, so to speak, a transition from His singular existence to a universe of multiplicity, or *ribui*. This is the idea of the root word for blessing (ברך), whose letters have the numerical values of 2, 200 and 20. It is a petition to God to expand the manifestation of His presence in His creation. The Maharal goes on to explain that while it is our eventual goal to reunite the disparate elements of creation into one composite (אֲגֻדָּה אַחַת) united in the service of God, that synthesis has yet to occur. In the world of created things, one is associated with curse, for there is no other "one" outside of God (אֵין עוֹד מִלְבַדּוֹ). Therefore, concludes the Maharal, the Torah begins with a *beis* instead of an *aleph*.

In going down to Egypt, the Jewish people were about to undergo a historic metamorphosis. They were to be transformed from a family into a nation predicated on their singular values and beliefs. Joseph was to be the catalyst and facilitator for this expansion (*ribui*) or blessing. Indeed, Joseph's being called an *avrech* (אַבְרֵךְ) indicates that he is the single agent (*aleph*) who generates growth in the world of twos. He is the primary fount of blessing; indeed, both in Jacob's blessings issued to his twelve sons and in Moses' later blessings to the twelve tribes, the blessing given to Joseph is longer than any of the others.

Moreover, Jacob calls Joseph by the name Ben Poras, which also implies fruitfulness and multiplication. Joseph also names his second son Ephraim (41:52), because "now we will multiply in the land." Again, we encounter the theme of fruitfulness and multiplication.

Joseph's role as the catalyst of growth for the Jewish people was critical. The transformation of a family into a nation is fraught with perils, and for the Jewish people, these actually materialized; the Midrash relates that the Jewish nation came to the brink of dissolution as they degenerated to the forty-ninth level of impurity in Egypt. The critical point for their ultimate survival was at the very beginning, when the seed of the nation was planted in Egypt.

It is well known that in human embryology the most severe genetic defects occur earliest in fetal development. It is not much different for a nation. If the inception is flawed, severe defects will show up later, perhaps causing the nation to disintegrate into irreconcilable splinters and factions. It required leadership of the highest order to guide that transition to nationhood.

By its very nature, leadership provokes resentment. People see the trappings of power and prestige, and they feel resentful. Some may feel that they are worthier of the position. Others may simply disparage the qualities of the leader. A psychological source of this resentment often exists in the nuclear family when, during childhood, siblings compete for the love and recognition of their parents. To his great credit, Joseph was eventually accepted by all his brothers. He united them and shepherded their further development from a family toward a multitudinous nation.

Rabbi Yitzchak Hutner, in *Pachad Yitzchak*, notes that Joseph's death is mentioned both at the end of Genesis and the beginning of Exodus. This, he explains, reflects Joseph's status as both an *av*, national patriarch, and a *shevet*, tribal patriarch. Pursuant to this concept, it is noteworthy that Joseph is the only one among the brothers of whom the Torah states specifically (50:23) that he saw his grandchildren. Joseph was the transforming agent who guided the Jewish people's transition from family to nationhood.

Other aspects of Joseph's personality also singled him out for leadership. Both as Potiphar's slave and in prison, the Torah relates (39:4; 39:21) that Joseph found *chen* (חֵן), grace, in the eyes of those around him. This quality of "grace" emanated from Joseph's disposition toward other people with no condescension. He had learned well from his mistakes with his brothers and had nurtured within himself character traits which defused the animosity and envy of others.

When Jacob sent Joseph off to check on his brothers, he responded (37:13), "*Hineni*. Behold, I am here." In courageously accepting the perilous task of repairing the family schism, he also demonstrated real leadership qualities.

Finally, perhaps the greatest expression of Joseph's shepherding leadership came after Jacob's death, when the brothers begged Joseph not to take revenge on them (50:18). Joseph responded that, despite their evil intent, he considered everything that transpired to be the unfolding of the divine plan. Joseph's response reflects his acceptance of the hardships he had borne. And despite being in a position of power where he might have come to feel himself superior, Joseph displayed the self-abnegation of a great leader.

We find an indication that Joseph fully accepted the yoke that had descended upon his shoulders, despite the tremendous hardship, in the curious expression Joseph used in naming his first-born son. He named him Menasheh (41:51), because "God has made me forget all my struggle and the house of my father."

Paradoxically, Joseph seems to be expressing relief or even pleasure in his ability to forget "the house of my father." Is this the same Joseph who later demonstrated such great concern for his father when his brothers arrived in Egypt? Is this the righteous Joseph, the favorite of his father, the loving and dutiful son?

There is also another mystery in the story of Joseph that needs to be explored. Not long after arriving in Egypt, Joseph became the overseer of the estate of Potiphar, an important Egyptian minister. In this position, he undoubtedly had ample opportunity to contact his father, yet he did not. Why didn't he do so?

Apparently, the prophetic nature of his earlier dreams convinced him that his divinely ordained role in the development of the Jewish people had led him to Egypt and that he was destined to achieve a position of power. Contacting his family and returning home would have interrupted that destiny. Joseph chose to be silent and bear suffering and loneliness for the sake of the budding Jewish nation. His hopes were dashed once when he was thrown into prison, and then again when the wine steward forgot him for two years. At those times, it would have been easy for Joseph to succumb to despair and self-recrimination, but he did not lose faith.

Then opportunity suddenly came his way, and he seized the moment to attain a position of great power. He understood from Pharaoh's dreams that a famine was coming and that his family would eventually be forced to purchase grain in Egypt, and he knew that he would be in a position to heal the rupture in the family. The wait and the silence had finally paid off.

In his naming of Menasheh, Joseph declares that he sees God's plan in all his suffering of separation from his family. He recognizes that by revealing the divine purpose God has allowed him to "forget," or perhaps better translated "remove," his suffering, for all the suffering he endured would be resolved in time with God's will. Under these circumstances, the hardships were more than bearable. They were of eternal value.

iv. To Face the Truth

ROM THE MOMENT JOSEPH SAW HIS BROTHERS ARRIVE IN Egypt, he initiated a campaign to stimulate their introspection and repentance. He summoned them into his presence and accused them of being *meraglim*, spies. Then he repeated the charge when they tried to defend themselves (42:9-14). Why did he level this charge at them?

For one thing, it gave him a pretext to take Shimon hostage and thereby force his brothers to bring Benjamin to Egypt. It is also likely that Joseph believed these particular words would cause his brothers to address their shortcomings that led to their selling their own brother into bondage.

The essence of a spy is to dissemble. He passes himself off with one intent and one loyalty, while in fact others lie beneath the surface. Joseph's brothers were also dissemblers, passing themselves off to their father as what they were not. Indeed, their hatred for Joseph stemmed from Joseph's attempts to unmask them.

The Torah relates (37:2), "And Joseph would report their evil doings to their father." Apparently, Jacob would otherwise not have known about their questionable activities. The Midrash assures us (*Tanchuma* 7; *Bereishis Rabbah* 84:7) that there was some justification for all the brothers' seeming indiscretions. Nonetheless, they concealed their acts from their father, suggesting a tincture of misdeed and guilt. Joseph wanted his father, whose abiding virtue was truth (*emes*), to know exactly what was going on. True, Joseph would have been better advised to find a more sensitive and diplomatic means of accomplishing his end. But at its root, the issue of truth sparked the conflict between Joseph and his brothers. Joseph wanted to reveal it, while his brothers wanted it concealed.

This was the more profound intent of Joseph's initial words to his brothers, "You are spies!" On some level, he wanted to reach them and cause them to think about what they had done. He wanted them to acknowledge, at least to themselves, that they had lived in their father's house as spies, concealing their own indiscretions and flaws. He wanted them to realize that their role as dissemblers had led to the heinous crime they had committed against their own brother. He wanted them to face the awful truth that in order to cover up their crime they had lived a lie for twenty-two years, witnessing their father's unnecessary grief and pretending to share it.

This endemic deceptiveness returned to haunt the Jewish people hundreds of years later when they were in the desert. Joseph's brothers had accused him of *dibah*, slander, in reporting their "evil doings," and he in turn had accused his ten brothers of being duplicitous *meraglim*, spies. So, too, ten of the twelve *meraglim* sent to scout the land of Israel before its conquest returned with *dibah* against the land (*Numbers* 13:32). Moses calls them an *eidah raah*, an evil congregation.

By using the words *meraglim* (spies), *raah* (evil) and *dibah* (slander), language resonant with the sin of Joseph's brothers, the Torah encourages us to make a connection between these events. The ten scouts who slandered the land were spies in a more profound sense. They were already seeking a pretext to avoid the challenges and responsibilities that living in Israel would entail, but they concealed their predisposition against the land from the rest of the people. According to our Sages, we are still suffering the consequences of these two sins — the sale of Joseph and the ten spies. A common theme runs through both of them.

This connection is also manifest in another aspect of these two seminal episodes. Arguably, the central characters in the process of reconciliation between the brothers and the expiation of the sin of the sale are Judah and Joseph. They struggle most over the deed, and they gain the most from their struggle. It is appropriate, therefore, that it is the two descendants of Judah and Joseph who resist the conspiracy of the spies in the desert — Joshua from the tribe of Ephraim and Caleb from the tribe of Judah.

v. *The End of the Buts*

INALLY, AFTER TWENTY-TWO YEARS, THE BROTHERS acknowledged their grievous sin (42:21). "Then they said to each other, 'We are indeed guilty concerning our brother.' " The word used here for "indeed" is *aval* (אֲבָל). With this single word, the brother expressed their guilt and contrition over the sale of their brother Joseph.

The word *aval* (אֲבָל) is a fascinating one by virtue of its multiple, even contradictory meanings. It may mean "indeed," "but" or "mourner." The first two meanings express opposite ideas. "But" is used to contradict a previous thought, whereas "indeed" confirms it. While it is not unusual for single root words in Hebrew to have opposite meanings, a common source can be discerned when one explores deeply. For instance, *kadosh*, holy, and *kadeish*, promiscuous, share the same three-letter root (אדש). Both refer to something unusual or separated, albeit on opposite ends of a spectrum. What then is the commonality between "indeed" and "but"? And what is the connection to "mourner," the third partner to this root word?

Modern psychology has investigated and dissected the human response to loss. Different paradigms are offered to catalogue the various natural stages of mourning. Common to them all is the initial natural tendency to deny the loss. If the mourning proceeds normally and healthfully this denial evolves into an acceptance. Mourning, therefore, begins with a "but," a word that expresses denial of the death of the loved one, and it terminates with an "indeed," a confirmation and acceptance of the loss.

This gives us a further insight into the connection between "but" and "indeed" in the Hebrew language. Because they share the same root, when *aval* is used as indeed, it carries a vital connotation not present in English. It means confirmation despite the presence of any argument, rationalization or "but" to the contrary. It is a confirmation that brooks no excuses. This was the brother's admission in its most profound sense. Regardless of any arguments there may have been to justify their behavior with their brother Joseph, the core corruption of their personalities was inexcusable. This was the painfully honest confession they made with the word *aval*.

This concept allows us a deeper understanding of one aspect of our Yom Kippur liturgy. The section of confession (*vidui*) which occurs in each *Amidah* (main standing prayer) begins with the words "indeed (*aval*) we have sinned." With a single word of introduction, *aval*, we acknowledge that, despite all buts or excuses, at our core we are guilty and have sinned.

vi. We Paid No Heed

GUILT SOMETIMES DOESN'T SURFACE UNTIL MANY YEARS later. In the case of Joseph's brothers, it took twenty-two years. The Torah tells us (42:21), "We are indeed guilty concerning our brother; inasmuch as we saw his anguish when he pleaded with us yet paid no heed; that is why this suffering has come upon us."

Joseph's brothers acknowledge their failure to respond to his anguished pleas from the pit. We cannot help but wonder, however, at what they failed to mention. They speak only about turning deaf ears to his pleas from the pit, but they do not mention the very act of selling their own brother into slavery. Nor do they acknowledge any guilt for inflicting so much grief on their father Jacob, who was inconsolable for twenty-two years. Were these not more serious crimes than ignoring Joseph's pleas for leniency?

Furthermore, if we examine their words from another perspective, we are presented with difficult questions of an altogether different kind. The brothers did not sell Joseph into slavery in an act of impulsive rage. They sat in sober judgment and discussed the question in great detail. They then determined that the inclusion of Joseph in the nascent Jewish nation would introduce a destructive element that would ultimately lead to disaster. They condemned him and removed him from their midst.

The judgment, on the face of it, may seem harsh to us in retrospect, but at the time, Joseph's brothers considered it painful but just. What if a murderer sentenced to death pleads with the judges of the court for mercy? Clearly, they have to be strong in their resolve. Otherwise, if the consequences of crime can be avoided through pleading, the rule of law would break down. If so, why do the brothers confess that "we are guilty concerning our brother, inasmuch as we saw his anguish"? At the time, they had established that their actions were justified in that they sought to protect the future of the Jewish nation, Joseph's pleas notwithstanding.

Our Sages state that truth is recognizable (*nikarim divrei emes*); truthful words have "the ring of truth." Nonetheless, the brothers' earnest and truthful protestations of innocence seemed to have no impact on the Egyptian viceroy, who unbeknownst to them was Joseph. The brothers had pleaded with the viceroy and passionately protested their innocence, but all to no avail. The brothers were, therefore, dumfounded. How could such a thing be? How could a fair judge turn a deaf ear to the truth? How could their manifestly truthful protestation not have caused him to reexamine his ruling?

The brothers then recalled something of their own past as they wondered why providence was causing them to be subjected to such an unfair reception. They turned the spotlight of their scrutiny inward and remembered that this was exactly what Joseph had intended to accomplish with his heartrending pleas from the pit. They were now on the road to repentance.

In their new state of awareness, the brothers reviewed the trial and condemnation of their long-lost brother Joseph. Why had they turned a deaf ear to him? Why hadn't they been moved by his pleas to rethink their ruling, to reaffirm for their own peace of mind that there had been no miscarriage of justice? They concluded that their behavior had not been guided exclusively by pure rationality. Jealousy, emotion and bias had been present, and if so, what validity did their judgment have?

If they had turned a deaf ear to Joseph's cries of innocence, unwilling even to reconsider, their verdict could not be considered fair and just. This was where logic led them once they conceded the first point of insensitivity. And indeed, this is what Reuven immediately told them (42:22), "Did I not speak to you, saying, 'Do not sin against the boy'? but you would not listen!"

vii. *A Cleverly Crafted Plan*

HE VICEROY OF EGYPT IS REALLY THEIR LONG-LOST BROTH-er Joseph, but Jacob's ten sons do not recognize him. He accuses them of espionage, and they profess their innocence. He detains Shimon as a hostage and sends off the others to bring Benjamin to Egypt as confirmation of their story (44:3). "The morning grew light, and the men were sent off."

The Talmud (*Pesachim* 2a) understands from this verse that "a person should be careful to leave and arrive at his destination, when it is light." Where exactly does the Talmud find a hint in this verse that a concern for safety prompted the brothers to leave at daybreak? Furthermore, what is the purpose of telling us exactly when they left in the context of the story? What useful information does it convey?

It is clear from the broader framework of the events that Joseph was not trying to torture his brothers before he revealed his identity to them. He had devised a very clever plan to facilitate his brothers' repentance. Originally, they had sinned by acting on their jealousy in their perception of Joseph as Jacob's favorite. Joseph's plan was to design a similar situation that would provoke jealousy and give the brothers the opportunity to overcome their jealous instincts. This would be a proper expiation of their guilt.

Specifically, Joseph decided to convince his brothers that Benjamin was favored, as Joseph had been, and that he was truly guilty of stealing the goblet he would later plant on him, just as they had deemed Joseph guilty of slander. And he took several steps to achieve this.

First, Joseph established himself in their minds as a fair ruler. He imprisoned them on suspicion of espionage, but he listened sympathetically to their protestations of innocence. He then generously released all except one, whom he kept as a hostage until they brought verification of their story in the person of their younger brother

Benjamin. Why was he being so generous? Because, he explained, he "feared the Lord." Clearly, he was an eminently fair man.

When the brothers returned to Canaan, they were aghast to discover the original purchase money still in their saddlebags, where Joseph had ordered it planted. Eventually, they returned with Benjamin to try to gain the release of their detained brother. When they tried to return the money they had found in their saddlebags, Joseph magnanimously waved it aside and told them to keep it. It was a mistake, he says, just their good fortune. As a result, Joseph gained further credibility with the brothers. The money in the saddlebags was obviously not meant to entrap them. It was clear the generous viceroy did not harbor any animosity toward them.

Upon Benjamin's arrival, Joseph hosted an elaborate banquet for all the brothers. He deliberately seated them in their birth order and conspicuously gave Benjamin privileged treatment. He thus replicated the family situation in which their jealousy had been aroused against himself. Benjamin was now the object of their potential jealousy.

Joseph then sent all the brothers back to their father in Canaan. As soon as they were under way, he sent his officers to stop and search them, and his own goblet was discovered in Benjamin's saddlebags, where he had planted it to frame him.

What went through the brothers' minds? Would Joseph be framing them? Surely not. He had always shown himself to be fair and equitable. Furthermore, as the messenger Joseph sent to overtake the brothers points out, the stolen goblet was used by the viceroy for divination. It was undoubtedly well known in Egypt that Joseph had attained his power because of his seemingly mystic clairvoyance. Presumably, the goblet would be very important to him, and he would not risk planting it on Benjamin when he could just as easily plant money. For his part, Benjamin had the opportunity to steal the goblet because he had sat next to Joseph during the dinner.

The only solution seemed to be that Benjamin was indeed guilty. But could it be true? If they had allowed their jealousy to be sparked against Benjamin, they would have accepted the libel as the truth. But they did not. Led by Judah, they passed the test and resisted jealousy and distortions that jealousy may have aroused. They remained certain of Benjamin's innocence and were prepared to come to his defense.

This understanding allows us to decipher the perplexing verse quoted above. Just before the brothers left for home with the goblet in Benjamin's saddlebags, Joseph did one more thing to gain credibility with them and allay their suspicions. The verse states, "The morning grew light, and the men were sent off." The use of the passive verb form implies that their leaving was not under their control; they were being sent. In what way was their leaving out of their control? Weren't they free to go? They should have been, but Joseph held up the time of their departure until "the morning grew light." Presumably, once Shimon was free and they had purchased another load of grain, the brothers were eager to return immediately to their suffering father. Nonetheless, Joseph detained them until daybreak. Why? Because he wanted to demonstrate his concern for their safety and further gain their trust and confidence.

We can now understand how the Talmud derived from this verse the importance of leaving on a journey after daybreak. At first glance, this verse seems to have no significance in the context of the story. This leads us to extrapolate that it is meant to show, as explained, that Joseph showed his concern for them to gain their trust, since leaving before daybreak would be considered unsafe.

This explanation also clarifies the seemingly superfluous concluding words of the verse, "… they and their donkeys." Why mention their donkeys? We already know that they had donkeys. This is a subtle hint that their daylight departure was connected to their donkeys. Their departure was delayed until after daybreak to reinforce their confidence in the Egyptian viceroy, so that he could successfully frame them by placing his goblet in the donkeys' saddlebags.

viii. A Strategic Move

JOSEPH'S PLAN IS INTRICATE AND ELABORATE. AFTER HIS first encounter with his brothers in the royal palace, Joseph retains Shimon as a hostage and sends the others back to their father in Canaan. Before they go, he clandestinely plants their original purchase money in their sacks, and they do not find it until they stop for the night. The Torah tells us (42:27), "And the one of them opened his sack to give fodder to his donkey at the inn, and he saw his money, and behold, it was at the opening of his sack."

It is odd, though, that only one brother finds the money on that first night out of Egypt. The other brothers do not discover their money until they return to their father Jacob in Canaan and empty their sacks (42:35). Why didn't they all discover the money at the same time their brother did? Didn't they also need to feed their donkeys? Moreover, wouldn't curiosity have led them to inspect their own bags after the first brother found his money in the sack?

A careful reading of the verses reveals that the other brothers may very well have checked their own sacks but to no avail. The one who found his money had discovered it at the opening of his sack, right on top, just asking to be found. The others, however, did not find it until they "emptied their sacks" back in Canaan. Apparently, Joseph had placed their money at the bottom of their sacks, where it would be difficult to find. When the one brother found his money at the opening of his sack, the other brothers probably checked their sacks as well. They may even have dug a little deeper into the fodder just to make sure, but they did not empty the sacks completely, and therefore, they did not find their money until they were back in Canaan.

But why would Joseph do such thing? Why have one brother discover his money immediately and the others only at the very end of their journey?

Let us consider the identity of "the one of them" who found the money right away. Rashi, quoting the *Targum Yonasan*, notes that the odd expression "the one" reveals his identity. He was Levi, the brother who suddenly found himself alone, separated from his partner. Shimon and Levi were always in tandem, but with Shimon hostage in Egypt, Levi was now "the one."

In fact, it was precisely because Shimon and Levi were such a pair that Joseph chose Shimon to be his hostage. Rashi, quoting from the Midrash (*Bereishis Rabbah* 91), explains that Joseph separated Shimon and Levi in order to avoid trouble. Shimon and Levi had colluded to destroy the city of Shechem after the violation and capture of their sister Dinah. Among the brothers, they were most inclined to react to provocation with action rather than introspection. They might very well have responded with violence to Joseph's manipulations. By taking Shimon hostage, Joseph defused a potentially explosive situation.

But Levi was still at liberty, and he was a dangerous man. Even by himself, Levi posed a threat to Joseph's carefully laid plans to lead his brothers to repentance. Therefore, Joseph drove a slight psychological wedge between Levi and his brothers. He returned the purchase money to all the brothers in order to show that he had no malicious intent toward them, as previously noted. But now he did it in a way that would isolate Levi. He planted Levi's money in the opening of his sack, right where it could be easily found. When the others investigated and found no money in their sacks, it would naturally raise subtle but significant suspicions about Levi. Any violent plans he might thereafter propose would be met with reserve, thereby rendering him ineffective.

Joseph knew that they would discover their own money at the bottom of their sacks. With his sharp insight into human nature, he also knew that once a person comes under suspicion, even if he is later cleared, a residue of the suspicion lingers on. Consequently, even when they returned to Egypt, the impact of Levi's possible exhortations to violent solutions would be neutralized.

ix. *The Unexpected Goblet*

O SOONER HAD THE BROTHERS LEFT THE EGYPTIAN CAPITAL than Joseph in his guise as viceroy called them back. One of them, Joseph's messenger insisted, had stolen the viceroy's precious goblet. The brothers protested their innocence indignantly (44:8-9), "How could we have stolen any silver or gold from your master's house? If it is found with whomever of your servants he shall die, and we too shall become slaves to my lord."

At first glance, this seems quite a rash statement. After all, on their first visit to Egypt, unknown parties had planted money in their saddlebags. Wasn't it possible that these same phantoms were scheming once again and had planted the viceroy's goblet in one of their saddlebags? Why were the brothers so sure that none of them had taken the goblet?

It seems reasonable to assume, in the light of their prior experience, that the brothers checked their saddlebags carefully before they left on their return journey and found nothing. The only other person who would have had access to their saddlebags up to the very last minute was the all-powerful viceroy. If the goblet was in one of the saddlebags, it could only have been put there by the viceroy himself or by one of the brothers. Both were out of the question.

The viceroy had already had an opportunity to incriminate them when the money was found in their saddlebags, and he had declined to do so. Furthermore, we are told (44:5) that the missing goblet was "the one from which my master drinks, and with which he divines." The brothers knew this; it was highly unlikely that he would plant his favorite goblet, the supposed repository of his occult powers, in a visitor's saddlebags and risk losing it for no conceivable reason. The brothers also knew that they were not thieves. It is then no wonder that the brothers were so confident that there was no goblet in their saddlebags and they were taking no risk with their seemingly rash statement.

x. An Eerie Echo

PURSUIT OF A DEPARTING CARAVAN. HARSH ACCUSATIONS. Stolen religious articles concealed in saddlebags. As we read about the pursuit of the departing brothers and the discovery of the viceroy's goblet of divination (*nichush*) in Benjamin's saddlebags, we cannot help but experience a feeling of déjà vu. Doesn't all of this sound like an eerie echo? Haven't we been through something like this once before? Indeed, we have.

One generation earlier, when Jacob and his family took flight from his father-in-law Laban's house, a similar event occurred. Laban pursued Jacob and accused him of stealing the idols he used for divination (30:27; 31:30ff, *Ibn Ezra* and *Ramban*). Jacob knew nothing about the missing idols, but in fact, his wife Rachel had taken them. The Midrash tells us (*Bereishis Rabbah* 75:5) that her intention was to prevent her father from practicing idolatry. With all the righteous indignation of an innocent man, Jacob responds to Laban's accusation by declaring that whoever possesses the idols should die. Our Sages (*Bereishis Rabbah* 75:9) attribute Rachel's death about a year and a half later, while giving birth to Benjamin, to Jacob's unwitting curse.

Now, a generation later, this same Benjamin finds himself in a situation with numerous striking parallels to the one that led to his mother's death. His brothers unwittingly curse with death whoever possesses the viceroy's divination goblet. How do we account for this? What is it meant to tell us?

Normally, we can attribute parallels between different generations to the concept of "*Maaseh avos siman levanim*, The deeds of the fathers become the paradigm for their children." In this case, however, this will not suffice. Despite all the parallels, there are also important differences. Rachel willingly took her father's object of divination, whereas Benjamin was completely unaware of its presence in his saddlebags. Rachel's purpose was to prevent her father's idolatry, whereas Joseph's intent was psychological manipulation to steer his brothers toward repentance.

Perhaps, though, there is a thread of similarity in the efficacy of the curses. Our Sages tells us (*Makkos* 11a) that when a righteous person utters a curse, even in error or on condition, it is fulfilled. In a general sense, this may be understood to reflect the partnership between God and righteous people in determining the specific path of God's providence toward His ultimate plan.

According to the Midrash, Jacob's unwitting curse caused Rachel's untimely death. Do we have any indication that the unwitting curse of the brothers had a negative effect on Benjamin? Of course, it could not have been fulfilled exactly as they said, because according to oral tradition, God has decreed that no tribe (*shevet*) shall ever be completely destroyed (*Bava Basra* 115a). But do we find any partial destruction in connection with Benjamin that might be attributable in part to the brothers' curse?

Actually, we find two.

One instance occurs when the Jewish people leave Egypt two hundred and ten years after the brothers' curse. In the enumeration of the tribe of Benjamin at that time, five of the original ten sons of Benjamin are omitted. Apparently, they were lost in Egypt.

The other possible incident of near annihilation occurs in the Book of Judges as a consequence of the events of the concubine of the tribe of Benjamin (*pilegesh b'Givah*). The Torah describes an internecine war between Benjamin and all the other tribes. The war nearly eradicated the tribe of Benjamin. Only six hundred males survived. God had promised that no tribe would be eradicated, and six hundred male survivors constituted a viable nucleus of a tribe. The Maharal ascribes special significance to the number six hundred, since six symbolizes completeness, as seen in the six days of creation or 600,000 men who left Egypt. Moreover, the letter *samech,* which has the numerical value of sixty, is completely round, with no beginning or end. Thus, the survival of six hundred men of Benjamin constitutes the survival of the tribe, while the death of the rest may have been connected to the brothers' curse.

פרשת ויגש
Parashas Vayigash

i. The Gift of Grace

OU WOULD HAVE THOUGHT JOSEPH HAD LEARNED HIS lesson from his own experiences. His father gave him a special coat, thereby arousing his brothers' jealousy and setting off a chain of events that delivered him into slavery. And yet, Joseph himself made the same sort of provocative gesture after the reconciliation with his brothers (45:22). "[Joseph] gave each man an additional garment, but he gave Benjamin 300 silver coins and five changes of clothing."

How very odd that the wise and righteous Joseph should make a public expression of favoritism. The Talmud raises this issue (*Megillah* 16b) and explains that the five changes of clothing are an allusion to the five royal garments King Ahasuerus awarded to Benjamin's descendant Mordechai after his triumph over Haman.

This answer, however, does not seem to respond specifically to the question. How does an allusion to garments given to

Mordechai about a thousand years later justify the anguish Joseph may have caused his brothers by favoring Benjamin?

Perhaps Joseph's actions can be explained by a twofold motivation. First and foremost in his mind was to facilitate his brothers' expiation of their sin. In order for their repentance to be truly meaningful, he needed to replicate as closely as possible the situation that had given rise to their jealousy in the first place. Therefore, from the very beginning, he was consistently more felicitous toward Benjamin, seating him at the head of the banquet table and speaking to him with especial kindness. He also engineered a false criminal accusation against Benjamin under circumstances that pointed strongly to his guilt. He gave his brothers every opportunity to respond to Benjamin with jealousy and turn on him, but they resisted. Led by Judah, they overcame any nascent jealous feelings and stood loyally by Benjamin's side. Their repentance was nearly complete.

Joseph now gave them one final test through a display of favoritism to ensure that their repentance and the expiation of their sin were indeed complete. He gave them an opportunity to become aware of and eradicate any latent tendencies towards jealousy by exposing them again to blatant favoritism. The brothers passed the test.

As Joseph saw his brothers conquer their jealousy, he perceived something more than repentance in the interplay between Benjamin and his brothers. Joseph saw in Benjamin the rare ability to find so much favor in his brothers' eyes that any privilege he enjoyed did not evoke feelings of jealousy in them. This trait is called *chen* (חֵן), grace. Benjamin enjoyed the blessings of grace.

When Joseph first saw Benjamin in Egypt, he immediately said to him (43:29), "May the Lord give you grace, my son." Joseph knew that the virtue of grace would be Benjamin's best protection from the fraternal jealousy he was planning to instigate. Joseph himself had been deficient in grace, and he had borne the full brunt of his brothers' jealousy.

As soon as he was tossed into the pit, Joseph realized wherein lay his deficiency, and he attempted to correct it. The Torah relates (42:21) that Joseph's brothers, after they began to experience difficulties in Egypt, reflected on their error in ignoring their brother's pleas *"behis'chaneno eileinu* (בְּהִתְחַנְנוֹ אֵלֵינוּ), when he pleaded with us." The root word of *lehis'chanen,* to plead, is *chen,* grace. To plead is to seek grace. Immediately upon being cast into the pit, Joseph realized his error. He tried to reach his brothers through grace, but he was unsuccessful.

Subsequently, he studiously cultivated this character trait in himself. The Torah notes that both in Potiphar's home and in jail he found "grace" in the eyes of those around him. During the years of famine, we find another echo of the trait of grace when the hungry Egyptians pleaded with Joseph (47:25) that "they find grace in his eyes." Joseph, at the apogee of his political life, had become the source of grace for the entire nation.[1]

This then was Joseph's second intent in giving the extraordinary gift to Benjamin. He wanted to secure the gift of grace for Benjamin for the future so that his descendants would be the conduits of blessing for all the Jewish people. As our Sages have said, "*Masseh avos siman levanim,* The deeds of the fathers become the paradigm for their children." Joseph gave Benjamin five suits of fine clothing over and above what he gave the others, and they did not react negatively.

One thousand years later, Mordechai would be in a position of leadership as viceroy to the king, just as Joseph had been. High office, with its power and prestige, arouses envy in others. It was this natural trait of Benjamin's, which Joseph had encouraged, that enabled Mordechai, Benjamin's descendant, to wear the five robes of royalty without provoking the jealousy of his brethren; as we read at the end of the Megillah, "And Mordechai was appreciated by the multitudes of the people." By his actions, Joseph

---

1. Interestingly, a generation later, the ungrateful Egyptians forgot Joseph's grace and enslaved his descendants. Therefore, God responded to their ingratitude during the Exodus (11:3). "And God granted the [Jewish] people favor (*chen*) in the eyes of Egypt," and they gave many precious gifts to the Jews on the eve of their departure.

nurtured grace in Benjamin so that his descendants would carry their good fortune with grace such that the rest of the Jewish people would accept it without jealousy.

What quality lies at the root of this grace? What exactly is it that deflects the envy of others? We find a clue in the blessing Jacob gave Benjamin before his death (49:27), "Benjamin is a voracious wolf; in the morning he eats his prey, and in the evening he divides the spoils." In none of the blessings to his other children does Jacob describe the beneficiary as sharing his blessings with others. This is the key to Benjamin's grace. Benjamin saw his blessings as a means of helping others rather than a private route to self-esteem and importance.

Some people are reluctant to share, because they feel they are giving away part of themselves. In essence they are attaching their blessings tightly to themselves and their self-esteem. They feel their possessions make them better than others, and presently, others accept this notion and become jealous. People who share gladly, however, enjoy their blessings thoroughly but are not so exclusively connected to them. They do not arouse jealousy in others.

Targum Onkelos sees in Jacob's blessing to Benjamin a metaphor of the Temple, which was in Benjamin's territory. From a religious perspective, the ultimate material possession in this world is the Temple. It was Benjamin's trait of selfless sharing that made him the appropriate receptacle for this blessing. With the Temple in his portion, it would be best shared with the rest of the Jewish people.

Benjamin's willingness to share was also manifest in the names he gave his ten children, all of which, as Rashi tells us (43:30), recalled Joseph's tragic disappearance. As in a Levirate marriage (*yibum*), Benjamin sought to preserve the memory of his lost brother; he was willing to share his children with Joseph in the sense that he used their names to eternalize Joseph's memory.

ii. The Good Fight

AFTER JOSEPH REVEALS HIMSELF TO HIS BROTHERS, HE sends them to retrieve their father with a mysterious warning (45:24), "Do not become agitated along the way." The Talmud (*Taanis* 10b) explains that Joseph admonished his brothers to refrain from halachic discussions that might cause them to become agitated. The Tosaphists quote another Midrash that states the exact opposite. Joseph was telling his brothers not to refrain from halachic discussions.

These two views seem diametrically opposed. How could our Sages express such completely contradictory views as to whether Torah discourse would foster acrimony among Joseph's brothers?

Very often, when people converse or discuss a certain topic, there may be an entire dynamic at work that is not readily visible on the surface. When people suppress their hostility and resentment, these feelings will frequently find ways of escaping and finding expression.

Thus, if two people harboring a suppressed feud engage in an academic debate in an area unrelated to their quarrel, the passion of the undeclared resentment will seep into the argument. Disagreements burst forth with unjustified vehemence and rancor. This leads to further acrimony and hurt feelings, which are harder to heal since the real emotional issues that cause them remain hidden.

On the other hand, if two people have been open with each other about their grievances or resentments, a discussion in an unrelated area, especially if it is a Torah discussion, may provide a healing distraction from their resentments. It can help them forge and solidify a bond as they participate together in their holy activity.

These then may be the two sides of a single coin the Midrashim are articulating. Joseph counseled his brothers not to engage in Torah learning if they had not yet aired their mutual recriminations over the sale of their brother and dealt with them honestly. If simmering issues remain not fully addressed, there was a danger that animosity might seep into their halachic discussions, which are already contentious by their very nature. In the already dangerous situation of travel, this might lead to disastrous consequences. Joseph warned against it.

If, however, they had already aired their thoughts and feelings and addressed their differences, they should by all means engage in halachic discussions. Not only would doing so be Torah study, it would also be a healing process.

iii. *Who Sent the Wagons?*

HO SENT THE WAGONS TO BRING JACOB DOWN TO EGYPT after the brothers were reconciled? There seems to be a discrepancy here. First the Torah quotes Pharaoh as saying (45:19), "And you [Joseph] are so instructed, this is what you shall do: take wagons for your children and your wives, and you shall transport your father and come." Apparently, Pharaoh sent them. Yet, when the wagons arrive in Canaan (45:27), "[Jacob] saw the wagons Joseph had sent to transport him, and the spirit of their father Jacob was revived." In this instance, the Torah seems to be giving the credit to Joseph. Who really deserved the credit?

Rashi appears to address this discrepancy. According to the Midrash (*Bereishis Rabbah* 94:3), the Torah subject Jacob and Joseph had discussed before being forcibly separated for twenty-two years concerned the laws of the *eglah arufah* (literally, broken-necked calf). The Hebrew word for wagon, *agalah* (עֲגָלָה) uses the same root letters as the word for calf, *eglah* (עֶגְלָה). By sending the wagon, Joseph was signaling his father that he was really alive, since only he knew that they had discussed *eglah arufah* on that day. Moreover, seeing that Joseph was still involved with Torah and had not assimilated, Jacob's spirit revived.

A close examination of the verses suggests how Jacob understood that this was Joseph's intent. Pharaoh had only instructed that the wagons be sent to help with the women and children, and that Jacob should be brought. When Jacob was told that Joseph had specified that the wagons were for him as well, Jacob deciphered the additional message that Joseph wished to convey.

There is also a deeper meaning in the message of the *eglah arufah*. These laws come into effect when a Jew is found murdered in the countryside between two towns and the perpetrator of the crime is unknown. The Torah requires that the sages of the town nearest to the corpse break the neck of a calf that has never worked. Afterwards, they wash their hands and declare (*Deuteronomy* 21:7), "Our hands have not spilled this blood, nor have our eyes seen anything." They then proceed to ask God for atonement on behalf of the Jewish people.

Jacob had initiated the discussion of *eglah arufah* when he observed the growing enmity of Joseph's brothers toward him. The laws of *eglah arufah* emphasize the responsibility of the leaders of the generation for the moral and physical welfare of the nation. Standing next to the dead calf, they declare that they have not been negligent in attending to the people's needs (*Sotah* 48b). According to the Midrash, Jacob wished to impress upon Joseph, whom he was grooming for leadership, the importance of heading off the hatred and violence he saw looming on the horizon.

This then was the essence of Joseph's message. Just as the *eglah arufah* was the sign of the exoneration of the people of any guilt in allowing a murder to take place, so too were the brothers exonerated of guilt and forgiven for their crime against him. The wagons, with their allusion to the *eglah arufah*, were a confirmation that closure had been achieved.

iv. Pharaoh's Rude Question

ACOB ARRIVES IN EGYPT, AND JOSEPH PRESENTS HIM TO Pharaoh. Jacob greets Pharaoh and blesses him. But Pharaoh's response is on the strange side. Loosely translated, Pharaoh asks Jacob (47:8), "How old are you?" Why does Pharaoh ask such a peculiar, even intrusive question? Why is he even interested? Moreover, following Jacob's generous greeting, Pharaoh's first words seem positively rude.

According to the Talmud (*Bava Metzia* 87a), prior to the time of Jacob, people did not become infirm as they grew older. Jacob, however, prayed for this change in human physiology so that people would be reminded of their mortality and be more inclined to repent. Additionally, old-looking people may have been unknown in Egypt, as this tendency in human physiology had only recently begun. Indeed, the Ramban understands that it was Jacob's uniquely wizened appearance that prompted Pharaoh's question. Looking at Jacob, Pharaoh saw the specter of death, and he was disconcerted.

The Egyptians viewed the Pharaohs as gods. The great pyramids were transient homes for their deceased kings on their journey to their next physical existence. When Pharaoh saw Jacob, he realized that the body, left to its own devices, wears away and that embalming fluids could only artificially retard the decay of living flesh. This was a threat to Pharaoh's entire worldview, and he immediately questioned Jacob about his age.

Jacob replied (47:9), "I am 130 years old, my life had been brief and hard in comparison to my forefathers." The Jews were in a precarious position as foreigners in the land, and Jacob wished to allay Pharaoh's anxieties. He stressed to him that his life had been particularly difficult, that he was the exception and not the rule.

פרשת ויחי
Parashas Vayechi

i. The End of Life

RDINARILY, THE TORAH TELLS US A PERSON'S AGE AFTER he or she has passed away. Contrary to this practice, the Torah lets us know that Jacob lived 147 years well before the momentous events that marked the end of his life. He has not yet instructed Joseph to bury him in Hebron, nor has he elevated Ephraim and Menasheh to the status of tribes, nor has he conferred individual blessings on all his sons, and already, the Torah is telling us his age.

At the beginning of this *parashah*, we learn that Jacob lived in Egypt for the last seventeen years of his life. Why do we need to know this information? And if we do, we can easily figure it out with a simple calculation. When he first arrived in Egypt, Pharaoh asked him how old he was, and he replied that he was 130 years old. Then the Torah tells us that he was 147 years old when he passed away. That means he lived in Egypt for seventeen years. Why do the arithmetic for us?

After giving us these statistics, the Torah continues (47:29),

"And the days for Israel to die came close, and he called to his son Joseph and he said to him, ... please do not bury me in Egypt.' " The verse implies that Jacob's imminent death prompted him to instruct Joseph to bury him in the Cave of the Machpelah. How did Jacob know that he was going to die? It is only an unspecified time after this exchange that we are told of Jacob's falling ill. And even then it was apparently not serious enough for him to summon Joseph's children to install them as full-fledged tribes. Joseph did so on his own when he learned of his father's illness (48:1).

Let us take a closer look at some of Jacob's remarks in the context of conferring full tribal status on Ephraim and Menasheh. Jacob pronounces (48:5), "And now, your two sons, born to you in the land of Egypt before I came to Egypt for you, they shall be mine; Ephraim and Menasheh shall be like Reuben and Shimon to me." Why does Jacob add the words "before I came to Egypt for you"? How are they relevant to his decision to elevate them to full tribal status?

If we look back in Genesis, we find that the only previous mention of the passage of seventeen years occurs only once. Prior to the events leading up to the sale of Joseph, the Torah relates (37:2) that he was 17 years old. Perhaps this is why the Torah makes a point of telling us that Jacob lived in Egypt for seventeen years. The first seventeen years of Joseph's life had brought Jacob's family fraternal strife and tragedy. In counterpoint, however, the final seventeen years, during which his father was with him in Egypt, brought healing and the reparation of that earlier schism.

After these seventeen years, the formation of the embryonic Jewish nation out of the seventy souls who descended to Egypt was accomplished, and Jacob's life work was complete. He had succeeded in his life work; it is with good reason our Sages declare (*Taanis* 5b) that "Jacob did not die." Death normally effects a benefit on the soul by stripping away the distracting and potentially deluding aspects of physical existence. Jacob, however, was beyond death, because he had reached his full potential and accomplished his purpose in life. In fact, as *Targum Yonasan* indicates (28:12), Jacob reached such a high level of perfection that his image is imprinted on God's Heavenly Throne. That is why we are told the full number of his years, even before he passed away. His life was complete even as he walked among the living. He knew it was time to pass on to a higher form of existence, and therefore, he left instructions for his burial even before his final illness.

Jacob had guided the upbringing of all of the seventy souls that formed the nucleus of the Jewish nation, except for Ephraim and Menasheh, who had grown up in Egypt without the benefit of his guidance. However, by conferring the status of tribes on Ephraim and Menasheh, Jacob linked them directly to himself and thereby completed his life's work.

ii. *Of Swords and Bows*

BEFORE JACOB'S DEATH, HE BEQUEATHED TO JOSEPH, AS A special inheritance, the city of Shechem. Shimon and Levi devastated Shechem in retaliation for the abduction of Dinah, and it seems to have remained in Jacob's possession. In giving away this property, Jacob identifies the land by the mode of its conquest (48:22). It is the land "that I took from the Amorites with my sword and bow" (אֲשֶׁר לָקַחְתִּי מִיַּד הָאֱמֹרִי בְּחַרְבִּי וּבְקַשְׁתִּי).

Targum Onkelos translates this verse as the land "that I took from the Amorites with my prayers and supplications." The word בְקַשְׁתִּי, *bekashti*, with different vowels, can be read as *bakashasai*, "my supplications." This homiletic reading is somewhat surprising. Onkelos almost always translates into Aramaic according to the literal meaning of the words for those who did not know

Hebrew. The chief exception is when a literal translation might be misleading. For instance, when the Torah tells us (18:1) that "God appeared to Abraham," an unschooled reader might think Abraham actually saw God. In order to remove the anthropomorphism, Onkelos translates the verse as "God was revealed through his communication to Abraham."

In our case, however, why couldn't Onkelos translate the verse literally as "with my sword and with my bow"? Wasn't it true that Jacob's family had forcibly captured Shechem?

Apparently, Onkelos felt that a translation that seemed to imply that the land was gained by force would also be misleading to the unschooled reader. Jacob knew that, unlike other lands that can be acquired by natural means, Eretz Yisrael, the Promised Land, could be acquired and retained by the Jewish people only through specific divine providence. The only weapons that would be efficacious for them were prayers and supplications to bring them closer to God. They would never acquire or maintain it in their possession by force of arms without a continual correct relationship with God. The true cause of Jacob's ownership of the land was his relationship with God, and Onkelos avoided any language that might be construed otherwise.

iii. Egyptian Mourning

ACOB'S FUNERAL PROCESSION, LED BY JOSEPH, VICEROY OF Egypt, was accompanied by a vast royal entourage all the way to the threshold of Canaan (50:10-11). "And they came to Goren HaAtad that was across the Jordan, and they delivered great and weighty eulogies, and [Joseph] sat in mourning for his father for seven days. And the Canaanite inhabitants of the land saw the mourning at Goren HaAtad, and they said, 'This is a heavy mourning for Egypt,' therefore, they named the place Egyptian Mourning Across The Jordan."

Why does the Torah inform us of the reaction of the indigenous population of Canaan? And why is it relevant for us to know what they named the place and that they mentioned Egypt in it? Finally, why is it important that the mourning occurred specifically "on the other side" of the Jordan River?

Since the time of Abraham, he and his successors had taught the ideas of monotheism to the inhabitants of the region. It is likely that they also spoke to the people of God's plan to establish a nation on the soil of Canaan with the mission to spread these ideas to mankind.

When Joseph and his brothers returned to Canaan to bury their father, the local inhabitants saw that the descendants of Abraham had already grown into a large clan, the first stage in the birth of a new nation. They knew that this embryonic nation had already been living in Egypt for seventeen years and that they were returning to Egypt after the funeral. And they were happy about it. Perhaps these people would do their missionizing work in Egypt and leave Canaan alone. They did not know, of course, that the fledgling nation would return en masse two centuries later and conquer the land.[1]

The local inhabitants expressed their wishful thinking that the great outpouring of grief they were witnessing at Goren HaAtad had relevance only to Egypt. They even named the place Egyptian Mourning Across The Jordan to emphasize and memorialize their sense that this was exclusively an Egyptian phenomenon on the other side of the Jordan River. The local Canaanites felt threatened by Abraham's family's claim of "manifest destiny" to the land. They wanted no part of the divine mission Abraham had bequeathed to his family.

---

1. Two hundred and ten years in Egypt, plus forty years in the desert, minus the seventeen years they were already there. Thus, it would be two hundred and thirty-three years before they returned to the land of Israel.

שמות
EXODUS

פרשת שמות
Parashas Shemos

i. *Pharaoh's Hidden Fear*

PHARAOH LOOKED UPON THE BURGEONING JEWISH POPU-
lation in Egypt with dread, but he had a plan (1:9-10),
"And he said to his nation, 'Here is a nation, the people of Israel, they are more numerous and stronger than we are.
Come, let us outsmart them lest they multiply, then should there
be war, they may also join our enemies and wage war against us,
and go out from the land.' "

Pharaoh attempted to solve the problem of Jewish overpopu-
lation (1:16). "And [Pharaoh] said [to the Hebrew midwives], 'If it
is a son, you are to kill him, but if it is a daughter, she shall live.' "

Did Pharaoh really think killing the male children and leaving
the females alive would control the Jewish population? Haman,
who tried to destroy the Jewish people during the time of the
Persian Empire a thousand years later, thought that Pharaoh's plan
was laughable (*Vayikra Rabbah* 27:11). "Haman said, 'Pharaoh
must have been mad to order that every boy be cast into the Nile

but every girl be allowed to live. Didn't he understand that the women would somehow find a male partner and reproduce?' "

Pharaoh's plan is indeed strange. If his concern was an immediate military threat, the adult males should have been the targets of his decrees. If population control was his object, then the killing of the newborn girls, or women in general, would have been more effective.

The Jewish people in Egypt did something no other people ever did before or since. They did not assimilate. Historians and anthropologists have observed that conquered or second-class citizens always strive to adopt the mores and customs of the dominant culture of their host societies. By blending in, they seek to share the perks and privileges.

The Jewish people in Egypt resisted these assimilationist tendencies. They preserved their language, their modes of attire and their distinctive Jewish names. At the root of this resilience was a core belief and value system to which they steadfastly clung and for which they were willing to sacrifice the rewards of assimilation.

Pharaoh and the Egyptians found this resistance highly offensive; they considered theirs the most sophisticated and advanced culture on the face of the earth. Pharaoh may have expressed fears of a potential fifth column in their midst, but these were not the grounds for his anxiety. His hidden fear was the moral threat the Jewish people posed to his empty and even evil belief system. Pharaoh therefore planned to eradicate the Jewish ideology. To achieve this, he would kill the males, who are generally perceived as the proponents and communicators of ideologies.

But Pharaoh was mistaken, as Haman saw with clear hindsight a thousand years later. Pharaoh failed to recognize that Judaism is also an integrative experience, involving beliefs and practices that blend with and color the personality. God gave primarily to the mother the responsibility of knitting Judaism into the fabric of young Jewish personalities. Just as the woman brings the male seed from its potential to physical fruition in the womb of her body, so is she also charged with bringing the child's Jewish personality to fruition within the sanctum of the Jewish home.

This is the hidden element of Jewish life, accomplished with characteristic modesty, that Pharaoh failed to recognize. Attacking a generation of men would not eradicate Judaism. Haman, the embodiment of Amalek, sworn enemy of an ideology that places God rather than man at the center of the universe, knew that Pharaoh had erred in not seeking to eliminate the women. But he had the benefit of seeing that for a thousand years the continued Jewishness of the Jewish people had been to the credit of both the men and the women.

ii. Crushing Labor

OST OF US HAVE SEEN CONSTRUCTION WORKERS DOING manual labor so arduous that we might collapse after a minute or two should we attempt it. And yet, these workers are not crushed by their strenuous tasks.

Manual laborers thrive on heavy labor; often, they actually enjoy it. So how are they different from the rest of us? The answer is simple. They are not. Such is the nature of human physiognomy — the more exercise we do the stronger we become.

With regard to the enslaved Jewish people, however, the Torah tells us (1:13): "And the Egyptians enslaved the people of Israel with *perach*." What does *perach* mean? The Talmud explains (*Sotah* 11b) in the name of Rabbi Shmuel bar Nachmani that it means crushing labor. Rashi expresses it as "labor that breaks apart the body." What kind of labor crushes the body? Labor doesn't crush the body; it strengthens it.

Let us now consider another statement we find in the Talmud

(ibid.). Once again, it is Rabbi Shmuel bar Nachmani speaking. *Perach*, he explains, refers to assigning women's work to men and vice versa. At first glance, this would seem puzzling. Is it indeed so utterly difficult for men to do women's work? Would that be considered crushing labor?

Here lies the answer. Physical labor is ordinarily not crushing. There is, however, one instance when it does crush. When the labor takes away one's sense of self, one's very identity, it can be devastating. And the damage is not limited to the psyche alone. It is well-documented that under such demoralizing conditions the immune system breaks down and very real physical illness results.

When a man is forced to perform women's work, when he is made to feel he is not a man, he is humiliated and crushed. Likewise, a woman feels her selfhood eviscerated when forced to do men's work. In such circumstances, every single act goes against the self and is filled with self-loathing. This is what the Egyptians set out to do to the Jewish people, to crush them emotionally, mentally and physically.

In this light, we gain new insight into the statement of the Torah (*Leviticus* 25:46), "As for your brothers, the people of Israel, you shall not encumber him with *perach*." Again we come across this unusual word, *perach*. What does it mean here?

According to Rashi, based on *Sifra*, this prohibition forbids the master of a Jewish slave to give him unnecessary work, to make him work for the sake of work with no other purpose in mind. Since the master's sole intent in assigning these superfluous labors is to demonstrate his power over his fellow Jew who had the misfortune to have become his slave, this is considered *perach*, crushing labor.

A master who seeks to impress a sense of inferiority upon his slave is crushing him, just as the Egyptians were crushing the Jews by denying them their sense of self.

iii. *Alias Shifrah and Puah*

OCHEVED AND MIRIAM WERE THE FIRST HEROINES OF THE Exodus story. The Torah describes their courage (1:15-17), "The king of Egypt said to the Hebrew midwives, of whom the first was named Shifrah and the second was named Puah, and he said, 'When you deliver the Hebrew women, and you see them on the birthing stool, if it is a son, kill him, but if it is a daughter, let her live.' But the midwives feared the Lord, and they did not do as the king of Egypt told them, and they caused the boys to live."

Although the Torah refers to them as Shifrah and Puah, our Sages identify them as Yocheved and Miriam. Yocheved was called Shifrah because she would beautify the newborn children (*meshaperes*). Miriam was called Puah because she would soothe the infants by cooing to them (*po'ah*). In other words, Yocheved saw to their physical needs, while Miriam attended to their emotional needs. Later on, Yocheved provided the physical needs of the people by giving birth to Moses, their redeemer, while Miriam tended to their emotional needs, as reflected in her leading the women in a song of exultation after the Splitting of the Sea.

We can safely assume that the names Shifrah and Puah are mentioned here in order to inform us of the heroism and kindness of these two women. What additionally does the Torah convey by revealing their virtues in this circuitous manner?

There are many circumstances in life that lead people to perform acts of kindness. Some people tend to an infirm relative. Others offer homeless people a place to stay. During the Holocaust, some gentiles gave shelter to Jews at great personal risk. In all these instances, as time goes on the enthusiasm of the benefactor tends to wane. He may continue to be gracious externally, but underneath his benevolence, his patience may begin to wear thin. Small signs of his resentment may leak out. His greeting may become less friendly, he may avoid eye contact, or he may even become short tempered. He is caught between his desire to do good and the cumulative burden of his benevolence. This is a common occurrence.

This was not the case with Yocheved and Miriam. Although their role as midwives continually put their lives at risk, their devotion to the Jewish mothers and their newborn children never waned. Even after the children were born, Yocheved and Miriam continued to place their lives in jeopardy, tending to them without hesitation and doting on them. This may be what the Torah teaches us by expressing their virtues in the names Shifrah and Puah. The devotion of these midwives to the physical and emotional needs of the Jewish infants was part of their very essence, not an undertaking born of duty and fraught with conflict, as ambivalence toward their newborn charges might have indicated. No, even after delivery, they coddled and cooed at the infants.

iv. *The Names Are Missing*

HERE IS A SINGULAR LACK OF NAMES IN THE STORY OF THE birth of Moses (2:1-2). "And a man from the house of Levi went and took Levi's daughter [in marriage]. She conceived and gave birth to a son, and she saw he was good." We know, of course, that the parents were Amram and Yocheved and that the child was Moses. For some reason, however, their names do not appear in the story.

Earlier, we encountered another case of missing names. We meet Shifrah and Puah, the heroic midwives who saved the Jewish children during the time of Pharaoh's infanticide decree (1:15-17). Who were these women? By tradition, we know them as Yocheved and Miriam, Moses' mother and sister. Here too their real names are absent.

Our Sages point out (*Rashi; Sotah* 12a) that Moses' parents had already married once, and Yocheved had given birth to Aaron and Miriam. They separated, however, after Pharaoh decreed that all newborn sons should be slaughtered. At Miriam's urging, Amram and Yocheved courageously remarried; the marriage recorded by the Torah is actually a remarriage. Once again, we wonder why the Torah hides their noble act in anonymity.

Why do people want to have children? Among the driving forces are a vicarious sense of accomplishment and a feeling of immortality through having their lineage extend into the future. The names people give their children may reflect these wishes. Names are a reflection of our sense of self-importance; people will say, "He wants to make a name for himself." When people pass their names on to their descendants, either as personal names, surnames or patronymics, they often feel they have perpetuated themselves.

Amram and Yocheved made a decision to remarry and have children for purely altruistic reasons. Their decision had nothing to do with the perpetuation of their own names. The Torah subtly reveals this to us by hiding their names.

Yocheved and Miriam, who risked their lives as midwives to Jewish mothers, also demonstrate this same selflessness and humility. They did not do it for honor, glory or any form of personal gain; the Torah again reveals this to us by concealing their real names.

The profound humility of Amram and Yocheved resulted in the birth of Moses, the "humblest man who ever lived." Here, too, the Torah does not divulge the birth name his parents gave him; the Midrash identifies it as Tuviah. By omitting the names of these exalted parents and son, the Torah declares their transcendent humility. Moses did not achieve the epitome of humility in a vacuum. The wellsprings were already present in his family.

There is yet another instance of a name hidden in this *parashah*. The Torah relates (*Genesis* 46:27) that "seventy souls went down to Egypt," yet the recorded names add up to only sixty-nine. Our Sages explain that the missing name is that of Yocheved, who was born as Jacob and his family passed through the gateways of Egypt. Yocheved's anonymity foreshadows her future humility.

Moreover, we may add, just as the birth and name of the mother of the redeemer of the Jewish people was obscured by the walls of Egypt as that exile began, so are the seeds of our own redemption already present, but obscured by our protracted exile.

v. *Mother's Milk*

IRIAM, MOSES' SISTER, SUGGESTED TO PHARAOH'S DAUGHter that she give Moses to his mother Yocheved to be nursed (2:7). Ordinarily, Pharaoh's daughter would not have allowed the child she hoped to raise as her own to be nursed by a Jewish woman. However, as Rashi quotes from the Midrash, Moses refused to nurse from any non-Jewish nursemaid. Pharaoh's daughter had no choice but to accept Miriam's suggestion. As a result, Moses' own mother raised him in his formative years.

Clearly, this was a supernatural occurrence. Presumably, without specific providence, a hungry Jewish baby would nurse from a non-Jewish woman. What was the reason for this divine intervention? The Midrash states (*Shemos Rabbah* 1:21) that since Moses was destined to speak daily with the *Shechinah*, the Divine Presence, he could not take into his mouth anything impure, such as the milk of an idolatrous woman.

What exactly is the connection between the milk Moses drank as a child and the prophecies he would experience eighty years later?

In psychological terms, it is impossible for a person not to find some level of identification with or connection to a person with whom he has formed his first attachment. This is normally the mother. The newborn infant only knows its own needs and strives to satisfy them. This is called primary narcissism. As he becomes aware of his surroundings, he forms attachments or cathexes to objects onto which the primary self-love is now projected, foremost of which is the mother-nurturer. This concept is implicit in the command to love one's neighbor as oneself. The love for others is a derivative of a proper primary self-love.

Moses was to be the redeemer of Israel. He was to reach a level of prophecy no human before or since would ever attain. Suckling from an Egyptian steeped in idolatry might have created a level of identification, albeit unconscious, and it would have become part of Moses' personality. Such identification, even at a slight level, would have inhibited Moses from achieving the spiritual growth necessary to speak "mouth-to-mouth" with God.

vi. *Expect No Appreciation*

ONCERNING THE PIVOTAL MOMENT IN MOSES' LIFE WHEN he killed an Egyptian to save a Jew, the Torah records (2:12), "And [Moses] turned this way and that and saw that no man was present, and he struck down the Egyptian." The Midrash offers various explanations for his turning hither and thither, but according to the plain meaning of the verse, Moses was simply checking to see if it was safe to strike down the sadistic Egyptian overseer.

Why does the Torah need to tell us that Moses tried to avoid detection? All we really need to know is that Moses was found out and subsequently had to flee. Is there a lesson for us to learn from Moses being discovered despite being careful?

Furthermore, as my teacher Rabbi Israel Chait asked, if Moses looked, how indeed did it come to pass that he was found out? Only one person could have told, he explained, the one Moses never would have suspected of betraying him. Who was that? The Jew whose life Moses saved!

Perhaps then, this was a lesson that God wanted Moses to learn early on, as he took his first steps toward his role as leader of the Jewish people: The man whose life he had just saved places him in mortal danger the very next day. A leader who seeks *hakaras hatov*, gratitude, is asking to be disappointed. Such a leader will likely be ineffective. If you want to be a great leader, expect no appreciation!

vii. *Buried in the Sand*

AFTER KILLING THE EGYPTIAN OVERSEER, MOSES DISPOSED of the body carefully (2:12). "And [Moses] turned this way and that and saw that no man was present, and he struck down the Egyptian and hid him in the sand."

It is odd that Moses would choose to hide the dead Egyptian in the sand. If the reference here were to ordinary soil, the Torah would have used the word *adamah* or *eretz*. The word *chol* refers specifically to sand. But why choose material that is likely to shift and reveal its secrets? And even if there was nothing at hand but sand, why does the Torah refrain from the more generic terms for land? Why add words to identify the material in which he was hidden? Suffice it to say that he was hidden.

Before killing the Egyptian, Moses "turned this way and that." What does this mean? Rashi explains that Moses looked to see if any of the Egyptian's future descendants would convert. When he found that "no man was present," he proceeded to kill the Egyptian. Why was this a consideration? A woman condemned to death by the courts is executed even if she is pregnant. If the Egyptian deserved to die, surely potential converts among his descendants should not exonerate him.

The Maharal finds a profound significance in the derivation of Moses' name. Pharaoh's daughter found him in the river and drew him out, and she named him Moses (2:10) *"ki min hamayim meshisihu,* because I drew him from the waters." Moses' name, according to the Maharal, does not merely reflect the circumstances of his rescue. It reflects his very essence.

Water lacks form, color, taste and smell; it represents the undifferentiated potential of the material world. Moses is the antithesis of this, the maximized realization of potential. In the language of the Maharal, Moses' nature, fully removed from the physical world, is nearly pure form (*tzurah*), as opposed to the material world, which is substance (*chomer*). Moses was pulled totally from the water, from the world of potential.

In this light, we can understand why Moses could not bring himself to kill the Egyptian until he had determined there were no potential converts among his descendants. Moses' very essence was to extract the maximum potential of everything; he could not end a life which had the potential to bring added value to the world, even generations later. He could not cause the waste of any divinely endowed potential.

Perhaps this also explains why he buried the Egyptian in *chol,* sand. The word *chol* derives from the root meaning empty, *chalal;* the word *chol* also means profane, since such things are empty of holiness. Sand is called *chol,* because it supports no plant growth; it is empty. Its granular and disparate nature further reflects its emptiness, since no grain naturally connects with another. By describing Moses as placing the Egyptian's body in *chol,* the Torah reveals that Moses had assessed his situation and decided he had not prevented any potential from emerging. Moses had acted true to his nature.

viii. *Pharaoh's Surprise Reaction*

OSES, RAISED IN THE PALACE AS A ROYAL PRINCE, KILLED an Egyptian overseer in order to save a Jewish life. He buried the body in the sand and thought that was the end of it. The next day, however, he intervened in a dispute between two Jews, and one of them taunted him for having killed the Egyptian. The Torah tells us (2:14-15), "And Moses was frightened, and he said, 'Behold, the matter is known,' and Pharaoh heard about the matter and sought to kill Moses, and Moses fled from Pharaoh."

Apparently, despite being frightened by the discovery of his deed, Moses did not feel compelled to flee immediately. Though Moses likely did not expect a Jew to inform on him, he must have suspected that perhaps others also saw him kill the Egyptian. Despite this, however, he did not flee. Moses must have thought that Pharaoh might let it pass without consequence — and certainly not kill him. He took a wait-and-see attitude. Once Pharaoh decided to kill him, of course, Moses had no choice but to flee for his life.

Why did Moses not think his life was in danger? Why did he entertain the possibility that Pharaoh would let him go unpunished for taking the life of an Egyptian?

Two factors might have caused Moses to feel safe. Moses had been raised in the royal palace as Pharaoh's grandson for all intents and purposes, and there must have been a close personal relationship between the two of them. It would be natural for Moses to presume that Pharaoh would instinctively protect him if it were at all possible, especially since he believed his action completely just. Moreover, he had just saved an innocent life, albeit a Jewish one. Would a virtual prince of the realm be punished for a morally justifiable deed? Moses thought he was safe.

But why indeed did Pharaoh react so harshly? Why did he seek to kill Moses instead of just allowing the whole sordid incident to be swept under the proverbial rug?

Perhaps it was the very intimacy between Pharaoh and Moses that triggered this harsh reaction. When Pharaoh saw how profoundly Moses identified with the plight of the Jewish people, he felt personally rejected. In this new frame of mind, Pharaoh reconsidered the wisdom of his entire relationship with Moses. His astrologers had already told him that a Jewish redeemer was soon to be born. Could Moses be that redeemer? After all, who would be better equipped to lead a Jewish rebellion against Egypt than a favored prince in the royal palace? And so, Pharaoh's wounded pride guided his thoughts to the conclusion that Moses posed too great a threat to be allowed to live.

Moses, however, had not acted with any kind of ulterior motives, not to reject Pharaoh personally nor to undermine him politically. He simply could not tolerate injustice. He did not anticipate Pharaoh's extreme response and fled only when Pharaoh sought to kill him.

The Midrash (*Tanchuma* 10, *Shemos Rabbah* 130), quoted by Rashi, takes this approach one step further. According to the Midrash, Moses was not frightened personally when he learned his deed had been discovered. He feared only that the wickedness of some of his Jewish brethren might make his people unredeemable. The basis of this Midrash can be found in a close reading of the verse, "And Moses was frightened, and he said, 'Behold, the matter is known.' " It would have been enough to say, "And Moses was frightened, because the matter was known." The extra words "and he said" divide the verse into two independent clauses, the first relating his fear for the spiritual condition of his people and the second acknowledging that there would be ramifications for his discovered act. In other words, he feared for his people, and while he was concerned for himself, he felt no immediate need to flee. He fully expected that Pharaoh would not respond as harshly as he did.

ix. *Soul Mates*

IPPORAH, THE TORAH INFORMS US, WAS ONE OF JETHRO'S seven daughters (2:16). Why does the Torah include this seemingly insignificant historical fact? Did her having six sisters somehow make her a more appropriate mate for Moses?

It is a tenet of Jewish belief that divine providence is manifest in finding an appropriate mate. Jewish thought considers the spousal relationship almost indispensable to maximizing an individual's relationship with God; a special providence governs this aspect of life.

Zipporah must have been a woman of extraordinary qualities in order to be a matched soul mate for Moses, the greatest of all men. We find some indication of Zipporah's qualities in her name. Moses often describes himself as restricted in communication skills (*kvad peh, kvad lashon* and *aral s'fasaim*). The name Zipporah (צִפֹּרָה) means bird, which chirps and twitters effortlessly. The name itself is etymologically related to the word *sippur* (סִפּוּר), which means to speak or relate. Thus, Zipporah complements that area in which Moses is most renowned for being deficient. On a deeper level, we can understand these complementary roles according to the Maharal who explains that Moses' communications deficiencies reflected his singularly elevated soul that transcended words. Language and speech represent a limitation and diminution of a more sublime understanding. Zipporah complemented that practical area in which Moses was deficient (albeit due to his very perfection).

Just as Zipporah's name suggests an appropriateness for Moses, so too does her selection from among seven sisters. Numerous sources connect Moses' life mission to the concept of the Sabbath. Like one of the central themes of the Sabbath, Moses' life work was to return people to their Source (see the *Sfas Emes* in numerous places). The Sabbath morning liturgy describes the Sabbath as a prized gift bestowed on Moses. It is another fitting facet of Moses' soul mate that she be elevated from among seven sisters, as the Sabbath is elevated from among the days of the week.

x. *Prelude to Prophecy*

OR PURE MYSTICAL IMAGERY, FEW SCENES COMPARE WITH Moses' encounter with a burning bush in the desert. Moses saw the bush awash in fire on the mountain, but to his utter astonishment, it was not being consumed. He drew closer to investigate, and then God spoke to him from the flames on the bush.

Our Sages find great symbolism in the indestructible burning bush. They see in it the ultimate survival of the Jewish people despite all the tribulations and persecution. The bush may be engulfed in flames, but it will never be consumed.

All the mystical beauty notwithstanding, what purpose did this vision really serve? What message did it convey to Moses that he did not and could not receive from God through direct prophecy? For instance, when God speaks to Moses from the bush he tells him explicitly that He has not allowed nor will he ever allow the Jewish people to be consumed by the Egyptian cauldron. Why then did God's revelation to Moses require the initial aberration of a burning bush?

There is another oddity in the narrative of the burning bush (3:2-4). "[Moses] saw that, behold, the bush was aflame with fire, but the bush was not consumed. And Moses said, 'I will turn aside now and look at this magnificent sight; why is the bush not being burnt up?' And God saw that he had turned aside to investigate, and He called to him from the bush." Why state that "God saw that he had turned aside to investigate"? Why wasn't it enough that God called out to him from the bush?

The Rambam in his commentary to the tenth chapter of Tractate *Sanhedrin* discusses the thirteen foundations of the Jewish religion. In this discussion, he devotes the most space to the seventh principle, which concerns the singular nature of Moses' prophecy, in contrast to all the other prophets in Jewish history. Moses attained a level of prophecy called *aspaklaria meirah*, a crystal clear light, whereas other prophets only attained *aspaklaria she'einah meirah*, a prophecy absorbed through the translucent lenses of their own personalities.

The Rambam considers this a fundamental principle of faith because Jewish allegiance to the Torah rests on our awareness that it was received directly from God without any filter of human personality; it is the perfect conveyance of God's will. Moses wrote the Torah, but doing so through *aspaklaria meirah*, his prophecy came across with absolute perfection. The Torah is, therefore, the pure word of God. Rejection of this principle has been at the core of most of the Jewish schismatic movements from Korach on, and they have all fallen by the wayside. The prophecy of Moses is the solid pillar upon which Judaism rests.

On the day Moses encountered the burning bush in the desert, he had his first prophetic experience. Of course, being nursed and raised by his mother in early childhood, he already knew of God's existence. He already knew that he was a Jew and that the Jewish people were to be redeemed in fulfillment of God's promise to Abraham. Moses also had advanced spiritual and intellectual virtues. He was already a person of high moral

standards, as we see from his coming to the defense of a persecuted Jew at great risk to himself. But he had never experienced
prophecy.

Furthermore, he was about to receive prophecy of the very
highest order, far superior to any ever received by other
prophets before or after. It was critical that he achieve the highest state of spiritual elevation possible, so that the prophecy
would be perfectly clear and pure, without the slightest intervention of his own personality. That was the function of the
burning bush.

When Moses saw a bush that defied the laws of nature, he
understood that this was a supernatural event caused by the One
Who controls the laws of nature. As he stood there, alone in the
desert, and contemplated the burning bush, he realized that this
miraculous phenomenon could only be for his exclusive enlight-
enment. The analogy to the seemingly forsaken Jewish people
was not lost on Moses. Why was this symbol being shown to him?
Surely, this was a message that he had an important role to play
in the manifest expression of God's protection and redemption of
the Jewish people. Moses was about to receive a prophecy. He was
about to hear the voice of God.

God saw that the burning bush had the intended effect on
Moses. He saw that Moses had "turned aside to investigate"; he
had redirected and focused his thinking and achieved a state of
spiritual elevation. By "turning aside to investigate," Moses prepared himself to encounter God's will and thereby became the
vessel for the highest form of prophecy a human ever
achieved.

Let us listen to the first words God says to Moses as he
approaches the burning bush (3:4), "And [God] called to him from
the bush, and He said, 'Moses! Moses!' "

This sort of greeting, whereby God summons a person to
prophecy by repeating his name, occurs in only two other places
in the Torah. When God commands Abraham to refrain from

slaughtering Isaac, He begins (*Genesis* 22:11), "Abraham! Abraham!" Two generations later, Joseph sends for his father Jacob to join him in Egypt. Jacob is fearful of leaving Canaan, and God speaks to him (*Genesis* 46:2), "Jacob! Jacob!"

What is the significance of the double mention of Abraham's name? The Midrash sees it as an indication that at the moment, when Abraham was prepared to slaughter his beloved son to fulfill the will of God without question, אַבְרָהָם דְעֵילָאֵי שָׁוֶה לְאַבְרָהָם דְתַתָּאֵי, the Abraham of above was equal to the Abraham below.

What does this mean? Rabbi Gedaliah Schorr, in *Ohr Gedaliah*, explains that, having passed all ten tests, all the potential of Abraham's soul had been achieved by his earthly personality. Abraham had reached *sh'leimus* (perfection) of his original human potential.

This concept may be applied to Jacob as well. At the point in his life when Joseph invites him to come to Egypt, Jacob has already overcome numerous adversities and has successfully raised his twelve children to the point where they were able to become the patriarchs of the twelve tribes of Israel. "Jacob! Jacob!" God called out to him. You have fulfilled all your earthly potential and reached a level of *sh'leimus*. Your family is now ready to be planted in the potentially corrupting environment of Egypt, where it will become the nation of God.

In contrast to Abraham and Jacob, whose names were called twice after a lifetime of divine service, Moses hears his name called twice at the very beginning of his service. As the receiver and transmitter of the Torah, Moses would have had to experience prophecy with an *aspaklaria meirah*; he therefore had to achieve, from the very beginning, a level of perfection so sublime that his personality would in no way alter God's communication. The burning bush was the final step. Moses' deductions upon seeing it led to the inspiration that helped him achieve that supernal spiritual state.

xi. *Remove Your Shoes*

S MOSES APPROACHED THE BURNING BUSH, GOD COMmanded (3:5) to "remove your shoes from your feet, for the place upon which you stand is holy soil." As there are no superfluous words in the Torah, we cannot help but wonder why Moses was to remove his shoes "from your feet." Where else would he be wearing shoes if not on his feet?

Perhaps there was a dual message in this command. If God had told Moses simply to "remove your shoes," the message would have been that it is disrespectful to enter a holy place wearing shoes, which often come into contact with filth and excrement.

The addition of the phrase "from your feet" conveys a second message. The emphasis is on "your feet." God instructs Moses that there should be no barrier between his feet and the holy place where he is standing. Shoes provide a barrier between the wearer and the potentially noxious surface of the earth. On holy ground, however, the thought that a person needs any protector other than God is an affront. Indeed, the Torah requires all Kohanim to serve barefoot in the Mishkan and afterward in the Temple. "Remove your shoes from your feet" conveys both messages, the removal of the offending shoes and the submission of one's vulnerability to the protection of God.

xii. *Why Moses Took Liberties*

DURING HIS PROPHETIC ENCOUNTER AT THE BURNING BUSH, Moses received instructions from God regarding his first confrontation with Pharaoh (3:18). "And you shall say to [Pharaoh], 'God the Lord of the Hebrews happened upon us, and now, please let us go on a three-day journey into the wilderness, and we shall bring offerings to God our Lord.'"

Later on, when Moses actually confronts Pharaoh and challenges him to release the Jewish people, he does not repeat God's words verbatim (5:3). "And [Moses and Aaron] said to Pharaoh, 'The God of the Hebrews happened upon us, and now, please let us go for a three-day journey in the wilderness and we shall bring offerings to God our Lord, lest He strike [you] dead with pestilence or the sword.'" The literal translation is "lest he strike us." Rashi explains, based on the Midrash, that Moses spoke euphemistically to Pharaoh out of deference to his royal position.

We notice immediately that God makes no mention of pestilence and swords, while Moses does. But there is also an important difference in the spelling of the Hebrew words "happened upon us." The first time, when God tells Moses what to say to Pharaoh, the words for "happened upon us" are *nikrah aleinu* (נִקְרָה עָלֵינוּ), with the letter *hei* at the end of *nikrah*. When Moses speaks to Pharaoh, however, he says "*nikra aleinu*" (נִקְרָא עָלֵינוּ), with a silent *aleph* at the end of the word instead of the guttural *hei*.

What is conveyed by this slight but significant difference? How does it affect the meaning of the verses? Furthermore, wasn't it presumptuous of Moses to modify the language that God had formulated for him? Did he think his version was an improvement?

In order to clarify the difference between *nikrah* and *nikra*, let us consider the first word in Leviticus, which is *vayikra* (וַיִּקְרָא), and

God "called" to Moses. As written, the final letter of the word, *aleph*, is much smaller than the other letters. The Midrash (*Vayikra Rabbah* 1) comments that its smallness reflects a compromise between God and Moses. God wanted it spelled with a full-sized *aleph*, because *vayikra* is a word of endearment and closeness. Moses, in his modesty, wanted the final *aleph* omitted (or replaced by a *hei*) to indicate that God's communication with him was by happenstance. They compromised on the undersized *aleph*.

According to the Midrash, then, God told Moses to say *nikrah aleinu* (נִקְרָה עָלֵינוּ) in order to give the impression that His relationship with the Jewish people was somewhat distant, that He appeared to them as a happenstance. Moses, however, revealed a closer relationship with the words *nikra aleinu* (נִקְרָא עָלֵינוּ).

The question remains: If there was indeed a more intimate relationship between God and the Jewish people, as Moses indicated to Pharaoh, why didn't God instruct Moses to speak of it in the first place?

Elsewhere, the Midrash tells us (*Shemos Rabbah* 42:6) that Moses wanted to include in the Exodus those Egyptians wishing to convert (the *erev rav*). God advised against it, but He did not explicitly forbid it. Moses, on his own initiative, took them. Here again, we are faced with a difficult question. How could Moses do other than as God suggested? Moreover, if God considered it inadvisable, why didn't He forbid the Egyptians to join the Jewish people?

Moses' desire to include as many Egyptians as possible with the Jewish people was consistent with God's ultimate goal that all mankind form "a united group" (*agudah achas*) to worship Him. In God's infinite wisdom, He advised Moses that this goal would be best accomplished, given human limitations, in gradual stages. However, since God's ultimate will is to include all peoples in knowledge of Him, He did not bar entry to the prospective Egyptian converts; nor would he forbid Moses to make heroic efforts to accomplish this goal in an accelerated fashion despite the inherent risks involved. And this is what Moses, overflowing with boundless love of God and love of His creatures, attempted by taking along the *erev rav*. In retrospect, in view of all the trouble they caused, the Jewish people would have been better off had they not come; but at the time, Moses felt compelled to make the attempt.

In this first confrontation with Pharaoh, God advised Moses to say *nikrah aleinu* (נִקְרָה עָלֵינוּ), that the relationship was based on happenstance. He chose to conceal the intimacy of the relationship, because He did not want the Egyptians to feel drawn to inclusion, although this remained the ultimate goal for mankind. But Moses, driven by his love for God, strove to inspire Pharaoh to seek the divine embrace. It was a heroic enterprise that God had not sanctioned, but had also not forbidden. Therefore, Moses chose the words *nikra aleinu* (נִקְרָא עָלֵינוּ) to reveal to Pharaoh the true and attractive nature of God's intimate relationship with the Jewish people.

In this light, we can also understand another puzzling fact. Moses suggested that Pharaoh should send along animals as well to be sacrificed to God (10:25). Never do we find God instructing Moses to say this. Here, too, Moses revealed a desire that Egypt participate in the coming revelation.

In the same breath that Moses offers Pharaoh the carrot of a close relationship with God, he judiciously adds the stick; he warns Pharaoh of "pestilence and the sword." It is unlikely that these are references to the ten plagues. There was no reason for him to single out pestilence for special mention, and as for the sword, it does not figure at all in the ten plagues. Rather, it would seem that pestilence and the sword are metaphors for the two kinds of catastrophe that can befall mankind. Pestilence represents natural, seemingly capricious catastrophes such as floods, earthquakes and infestation; the sword evokes willful human harm in any of its myriad forms. Moses informed Pharaoh both of the possibility of a closer relationship with God, and of the fact that the consequence of intransigence was the unleashing of the malevolent forces of nature and man that are under the divine purview.

We find another reference to pestilence and the sword in the Passover Haggadah with regard to Moses' exhortation to the nation just prior to his death (*Deuteronomy* 26:8), "And he took us out of Egypt with a strong hand, with an outstretched arm, with great awe-inspiring feats, with signs and with wonders." What do these expressions signify?

The Haggadah offers two interpretations. In the first, "a strong hand" refers to pestilence, "an outstretched arm" refers to the sword, "great awe-inspiring feats" refers to the revelation of the Divine Presence, "signs" refers to Moses' staff and "wonders" refers to the blood. The second interpretation offered in the Haggadah suggests that each term hints at two plagues, for a total of ten.

Let us take a closer look at the first interpretation. How are we to understand these references to "pestilence and sword"? If they refer to the fifth and final plagues, the sword being equated with the death of the firstborn, the sequence of plagues is out of order. The first plague, blood, is not mentioned until the very end.

If, however, pestilence and the sword are metaphors for the disasters that can befall mankind, natural and manmade, we gain new insight into the verse. In effect, Moses was describing the historical process of the redemption. God took us out of Egypt through his providence over nature and the affairs of men; through the revelation of His Divine Presence at the burning bush where He appointed Moses the redeemer of the Jewish people; through the introductory signs Moses performed with his staff; and, finally, through the ten plagues, which are represented by the first of them, the plague of blood.

With this understanding of Moses' ardent desire to draw Egypt into the divine embrace, we can explain yet another small anomaly in the story. In all his meetings with Pharaoh, Moses never shows a flash of anger save once. When Pharaoh rebuffs his final ultimatum (11:8), Moses leaves with "burning anger."

Why only now does Moses become angry? On the contrary, with the Jewish people on the threshold of freedom and Pharaoh's recalcitrance becoming increasingly irrelevant, he should have looked at Pharaoh with pity or indifference. Why anger? Rashi explains that he took issue with Pharaoh's brazen banishment, "You shall never see my face again!" Perhaps we can offer an additional insight.

In this moment of Pharaoh's final refusal, Moses knew that his ambition to draw Egypt into a closer relationship with God would remain unfulfilled. Although his kingdom lay shattered at his feet, Pharaoh persisted in his obstinate refusal to recognize God. This kindled Moses' burning anger.

There is an echo of Moses' carrot-and-stick approach in the ninth plague, which plunged Egypt into three days of paralytic darkness. This is the only plague the Torah describes as lasting for three days. What was so unusual about this plague that it lasted this odd number of days?

The only other mention of a three-day period in the Exodus story is when Moses asked Pharaoh for permission to travel three days to worship God. At that time, he also asked Pharaoh to send sacrifices. Perhaps we can discern a connection between that request and the plague of darkness.

According to our Sages, the plague of darkness caused the Egyptians far more than mere visual impairment. In fact, it was so dense and palpable that it completely immobilized the Egyptians. For all practical purposes, it was as if they had ceased to exist for three days. The message was clear. If the Egyptians refused to participate or at least permit the Jewish people a three-day worship of God they would be defying the whole purpose of creation and thereby forfeit their own place in it.

xiii. *First Ask Permission*

OR SEVEN DAYS, MOSES PROTESTED HIS INADEQUACY AS A potential leader of the Jewish people, then he succumbed. The Torah tells us (4:18-19), "And Moses went and he returned to Jethro, his father-in-law, and he said to him, 'I would go now and return to my brethren, and I will see if they are still alive.' And Jethro said to Moses, 'Go in peace.' And God said to Moses in Midian, 'Go, return to Egypt.' "

There are a number of peculiarities with these verses. Why did Moses find it necessary to ask his father-in-law Jethro permission to leave? Hadn't God just sent him to lead the Jews out of Egypt? Apparently, God had never actually given him the go-ahead to start his mission. He had only designated him as the future leader of the Jewish people, but the practical initiation of his mission only began after he returned to Jethro, when God told him, "Go, return to Egypt." Why was this so?

The issue here was *hakaras hatov*, gratitude. It would have been a display of ingratitude for Moses to return to Egypt without taking leave of Jethro, his father-in-law and benefactor, who had shielded him for almost thirty-nine years and given him his daughter in marriage.

How did Moses know he was obliged to ask Jethro's permission to leave even though God had appointed him the leader of the Jewish people?

He realized that God had never given him a specific command to return to Egypt, and from this he surmised that there was something holding it back. After he thought about it, he understood that he had to take proper leave of his father-in-law. When God immediately afterward commanded Moses to return to Egypt, it confirmed the thoughts that Moses may have had earlier on his own.

Moses thus learned two important lessons. First, he could not be wholly passive in his relationship with God; in many instances, it would be up to him to interpret the divine will according to his best understanding. Second, Moses learned the importance of gratitude; the redemption of the Jewish people would wait until he expressed his appreciation properly.

The primacy of *hakaras hatov* is displayed weekly in the Jewish home. There is an ancient custom to sing *Eishes Chayil*, the last chapter of Proverbs, on Friday night before *Kiddush*. There are many allegorical interpretations of these verses that connect them to the Sabbath, but their plain meaning is a description of the many virtues of a Jewish woman of valor. At that moment, with the candles lit, the table set and the house fragrant with the smells of Shabbos, it is appropriate that the husband express gratitude to his wife for her endless daily kindnesses to him and the entire family. The woman of the house, feeling appreciated, in turn fosters harmony between herself and her husband (*shalom bayis*) in the home, an essential concept in Sabbath observance.

xiv. *The Uncircumcised Firstborn*

AT THE BURNING BUSH, GOD GAVE MOSES GENERAL INSTRUCtions about his mission to Egypt, and later on in Egypt, He reviewed them, adding specific instructions regarding the plagues. Between these times, just after Moses left the home of his father-in-law Jethro, there is yet a third divine communication on the subject (4:20-23). "And Moses took his wife and sons, and he mounted them onto the donkey, and set out for the land of

Egypt. And God said to Moses, 'When you go return to Egypt … Then you shall say to Pharaoh, "My firstborn son is Israel. So I said to you, 'Send out My son that he may serve Me' — but you have refused to send him out; behold, I shall kill your firstborn son." ' "

The question arises: Why did God bring up the issue of the plague of the firstborn at this particular juncture? Why not include it in one of the other divine dialogues with Moses?

Immediately after Moses sets out for Egypt with his family, we read about the mysterious incident of his near death. While stopping at a roadside inn, an angel attempts to kill him for failing to circumcise his son. At this point, Moses had two sons, the older Gershom and the newborn Eliezer. It is logical to assume it was the younger Eliezer who was yet uncircumcised, and Rashi identifies him as such. *Targum Yonasan*, however, states that the incident revolved around the older Gershom who was still uncircumcised at the time. This seems puzzling.

Earlier, the Torah tells us (2:21), "And Moses desired to dwell with [Jethro]." The word used here for desired is *vayoel* (וַיּוֹאֶל). The Midrash (*Mechilta*) comments that the word can also mean "swore." When Moses married Zipporah, Jethro's daughter, he swore to his father-in-law, who was the high priest of an idolatrous cult, to dedicate his firstborn son to idolatrous practice. Accordingly, we can understand why Gershom, Moses' firstborn, was still uncircumcised. This bears out *Targum Yonasan's* interpretation that it was Gershom whose uncircumcised status had endangered Moses.

Difficult as Moses' arrangement with Jethro may seem, it exceeded the bounds of toleration when Moses actually began his divinely ordained mission. From that point on, it became intolerable for the redeemer of Israel to allow his eldest son Gershom to remain outside the covenant of circumcision.

We can understand the need for a third, seemingly superfluous communication. In the passage preceding Moses' near death, God hints to Moses that there is an overriding obligation to which Pharaoh and, by implication, Jethro are obliged. Just as the Jewish people are God's firstborn, and barring them from their divine service would lead to the death of every firstborn in Egypt, so should Moses consider his own firstborn son and realize that the covenant of circumcision superseded his oath to Jethro. All of mankind, including Jethro, are obliged to acknowledge God and his firstborn nation Israel.

xv. *Zipporah's Sharp Insight*

STRANGE THINGS HAPPENED TO MOSES WHEN HE RETURNED to Egypt with his wife Zipporah and their two sons (4:24-26). "And it was along the way, in the hostel, that God encountered [Moses] and sought to kill him. And Zipporah took a sharpened flint and cut off her son's foreskin, and threw it at his feet, and she said, 'Because you are a groom of blood to me.' And He released him, then she said, 'A groom of blood with regard to circumcision.' "

Why does God seek to kill Moses after just giving him the command to return to Egypt? According to the Talmud (*Nedarim* 32a; *Rashi*), Moses delayed circumcising his son Eliezer and attended to the arrangements for their lodging. But why should this have been a cause for punishment by death? Failure to circumcise one's child is not a capital offense. Why then was Moses almost killed for his delay?

Another striking detail is that Zipporah emerges as the protagonist of this episode. Is there a deeper significance to this? Why does she refer to her husband as her "groom" when they have already been married for a number of years? And what does that have to do with circumcision?

Moses was being judged by a different standard. Under normal circumstances, a brief delay of a circumcision would not result in a divine decree of death. Moses, however, was to be the divine messenger for the redemption of the Jewish people. His new role called for him to be pure and untainted. Any slight blemish would disqualify him, especially in the area of circumcision, which is vitally bound up with the very identity of the Jewish people. Moses could not lead the Jewish people into a nationhood dependent on Torah observance even if it only appeared his commitment was lacking.

Zipporah accurately identified the cause of her husband's mortal danger. Moreover, she anticipated yet another threat that might emerge in the not too distant future, that he might have to contend with yet a second blemish. Moses would have to explain the seeming impropriety of being married to a non-Jew, intermarried so to speak. How non-Jews joined the Jewish nation in pre-Sinaitic times is the subject of extensive rabbinic discussion. But Zipporah, having been born to an idolater and living her entire life away from the Jewish community, could easily have been perceived as outside the fold.

Zipporah understood that in one fell swoop she could not only save her husband's life but also solve the problem of his seeming intermarriage. By her bold action of circumcising her son in that moment of extreme danger, she demonstrated her identification with the covenant of Abraham — and thereby her commitment — to anyone who doubted that she was a righteous convert. By her act, she convinced the Jewish people that she was a fitting partner in marriage for her "groom" Moses.

פרשת וארא
Parashas Va'eira

i. Look at the Brother

HOM DID AARON MARRY? THE TORAH TELLS US (6:23), "AND Aaron took for a wife Elisheva, the daughter of Aminadav, the sister of Nachshon, and she bore him Nadav and Avihu, Elazar and Isamar." Nachshon ben Aminadav was a great leader, the prince of the tribe of Judah. According to the Midrash (*Shemos Rabbah* 29), the sea did not split until Nachshon courageously plunged into the water. Nonetheless, the Torah does not ordinarily identify a wife's brother when it outlines genealogies. Why was an exception made in this case?

According to the Talmud (*Baba Basra* 101a), it teaches us that when a man considers a woman for marriage he should take a long look at the character traits of her brothers. This gives him insight into the home in which the prospective bride was raised. Since a woman usually follows her mother's example in many subtle ways, a look at her brother provides a good indication of how she will raise her own children.

But why does the Torah choose to teach us this lesson at this particular point? Perhaps it is because the marriage of Aaron and Elisheva was an extraordinarily important match in Jewish history. Every one of Aaron's male descendants for all generations is invested at birth with the awesome responsibility and privilege of being a Kohen, a member of the priesthood designated for divine service in the Temple. The Kohanim did not share in the land. They were supported by the tithes of the people so that they could be free to serve in the Temple and be the teachers and sages of the Jewish people. All Jews were, of course, free to become scholars and sages, but the Kohanim were designated for that role by birth. Aaron and his wife had to be perfectly matched in order to bring forth children suited to such a role.

The subtle pedagogy of the Torah is evident here. The Torah uses this singularly important marriage to set a paradigm. It informs us that Aaron's marriage to Elisheva was indeed suitable because her brother was a virtuous prince.

ii. *Just a Snake*

GOD INSTRUCTED MOSES IN HIS INITIAL MEETING WITH Pharaoh to cast his staff to the ground where it would turn into a snake (7:10). In this encounter, the Torah refers to the snake as a *tanin* (תַּנִּין) rather than using the more common word, *nachash* (נָחָשׁ).

Everywhere else a snake is discussed in the Torah we find the word *nachash*. Earlier, when Moses expressed reservations about being accepted by the Jewish people, God commanded him about this same staff (4:3), "And He said, 'Cast [your staff] to the ground,' and [Moses] cast it to the ground, and it became a snake (*nachash*)."

Later, when God tells Moses to afflict Egypt with the plague of blood, the Torah quotes God as saying (7:15), "Go to Pharaoh in the morning … and take in your hand the staff that was turned into a snake (*nachash*)." The reference is to the very sign the Torah earlier describes as the staff turning into a *tanin*, yet here the Torah refers to the snake as a *nachash*.

Why then does the Torah in this particular case use the unusual word *tanin* to describe the snake?

In the *Haftarah*, which is a reading from Ezekiel, the prophet describes a divine retribution, which will again be visited on the arrogant Pharaoh, king of Egypt. The prophet (*Ezekiel* 29:3) considers Pharaoh arrogant because he claims to be a "God, ruler of the Nile, and of the great snake (*tanim*) that lurks beneath it." Apparently, a snake called *tanim*, a variation of the word *tanin*, lived underwater in the Nile and served as a symbol of Egyptian power and the divine status of its kings. At the outset of the Ten Plagues the Torah specifies that the staffs all turned into *taninim*, and that Moses' staff swallowed the Egyptian *taninim*. The symbolism was clear. Pharaoh's claim to divine status was empty and specious.

iii. A False Sense of Security

FTER MOSES TURNED ALL WATERS IN EGYPT TO BLOOD, Pharaoh's magicians demonstrated that they too could duplicate the feat with their sorcery. The Torah tells us (7:23), "And Pharaoh turned about and entered his house, and he did not turn his heart to this either."

Why is it necessary to mention that Pharaoh "entered his house"? It would have been sufficient that he turned away and paid no attention to the plague. What is added by his "entering his house"?

The saying "a man's home is his castle" expresses the security and ease a person feels in his home. This was all the more true for Pharaoh, whose house was a fort and palace. The Torah tells us that Pharaoh, threatened by a Higher Power he did not know or control, retreated to the safety of his home.

But it didn't help him. Immediately afterwards, in the warning of the second plague, Moses tells Pharaoh (7:28), "[The frogs] shall come into your palace and your bedroom and your bed." Our Sages divide the first nine plagues into three groups of three, and the warning before the second plague in each series occurs at Pharaoh's home. God chases Pharaoh into his place of refuge to teach him that there is no escaping Him, not in a house, not in a palace, not in a fort. With hail, the first of the final set of plagues, God forces people to bring their livestock into their homes, turning their homes into stables and depriving them of their last place of refuge.

The Torah addresses the concentric circles of security with which we naturally surround ourselves by giving us mitzvos that tag each respective circle. We affix *mezuzos* to the doors of our homes. We tie *tzitzis* (fringes) to the corners of our garments. We place *tefillin* on our bodies, and finally, we circumcise our very flesh. When our poor behavior demands reproof, the physical lesions of *tzaraas* first afflict our homes, then our garments, then our bodies. In total, these instruct us that relying on physical security may obscure the only genuine security, which is forging an eternal relationship with our Creator.

iv. *The Sorcerers Succumb*

 LEVEN TIMES, MOSES CONFRONTED PHARAOH WITH demonstrations to secure the release of the Jewish people, the first time to establish that he was God's messenger and the next ten times to visit plagues upon Egypt. During five of these confrontations, the Egyptian sorcerers played a significant role.

At the first meeting in the royal palace, Moses cast his staff to the ground. It turned into a snake, but the Egyptians were not impressed (7:11-12). "And the Egyptian sorcerers also did so with their magic, and each man cast down his staff and it became a snake." The sorcerers also put in an appearance during the confrontations preceding the first, second and third plagues. They were able again to duplicate the first two plagues by transforming water into blood and multiplying frogs. They are unable, however, to duplicate the third plague of lice with their magical powers, declaring (8:15) that "the finger of God" was at work in this plague.

Why, we may ask, did God first send plagues that the sorcerers could imitate? Wouldn't it have been more effective for these two plagues to reflect their Author unambiguously?

If we look closely at the words used for the magic of the sorcerers, we find a slight difference between the first time and the next three times. When they used magic to transform their staffs into snakes, the Torah describes their magic as *lahateihem* (לְהֲטֵיהֶם), but the next three times, during the plagues of blood, frogs and lice, their magic is described as *lateihem* (לְטֵיהֶם), without the letter *hei*. What is the significance of the slight differences in spelling?

The Talmud tells us (*Sanhedrin* 67b) that *lahat* refers to magic (*kishuf*), while *lat* refers to the use of demons (*shedim*). Magic creates an illusion that is not dependent on anything supernatural. The word *lahat* (לַהַט) is also used to describe the spinning, flashing sword that blocked Adam and Eve from returning to the Garden of Eden (*Genesis* 4:24); the flashing blade created the appearance of a solid obstruction. This type of illusory magic would have been effective for the sorcerers to transform a staff into a snake. Even today, there are snake charmers in the East that can cause a snake to appear stiff as a staff. These can then be "transformed" into writhing snakes.

Legerdemain, however, would not work with the first two plagues. Duplicating the blood and the frogs called for real supernatural powers. Did the Egyptian sorcerers have such powers?

This issue is the subject of a dispute among the Rishonim. According to the view that people can have occult powers, the sorcerers may have had some sort of power that enabled them to tap into the recently created divine force and duplicate the blood and the frogs. According to those, including the Rambam, who are of the opinion that supernatural forces such as black magic or the occult do not exist, they must have resorted to another form of subterfuge. They actually exploited the miracle of the plague itself to give the appearance that they had genuine mystical powers. For instance, the Midrash tells us that when an Egyptian took a glass of water from a Jew it immediately turned into blood. The sorcerers might have taken possession of water belonging to a Jew while uttering an incantation and claiming they had also turned water into blood. The Midrash also relates that whenever someone struck a frog it replicated itself. Again, the sorcerers could have manipulated the phenomenon to give the impression that they produced it with their supernatural powers (lateihem). However, by the third plague, lice, they could no longer find a way to replicate the miracle and were forced to acknowledge "the finger of God."

How did they explain their inability to duplicate lice after they claimed credit for matching the first two plagues? Undoubtedly, they had to admit that they had been dissembling and resorting to trickery and lies. The net effect was to discredit the sorcerers completely in the eyes of the royal palace and the public at large. The first two plagues, by allowing imitation, served a very important purpose. They contributed to the collapse of the hierarchy of the occult in Egyptian society.

The sorcerers put in a final appearance after the sixth plague (9:11). "And the sorcerers were unable to stand in front of Moses because of the boils, because the boils had beset the sorcerers and all of Egypt." Not only couldn't they imitate the plague, they couldn't even protect themselves. And thus the sorcerers step off the stage and never return. Why were they driven away as the pressure of the plagues escalated?

Most probably, the sorcerers represented the best and brightest of the Egyptian intelligentsia. It stands to reason that as the hopelessness of Pharaoh's position became increasingly manifest, some of the sorcerers would have advised him to capitulate and salvage that which had not yet been destroyed. But once they were driven away by the plague of boils, Pharaoh was left with slavish servants and sycophants who told him what they thought he wanted to hear. In this fashion, God made sure that Pharaoh would "harden" his heart, as He had promised Moses from the sixth plague on.

v. *Five Steps to Personal Redemption*

O N THE SEDER NIGHT, WE DRINK THE FOUR CUPS OF WINE to recall the four expressions of redemption delineated in the Torah (6:26-27), "And I shall take you out (*vehotzeisi*) from under the burdens of Egypt, and I shall rescue you (*vehitzalti*) from their oppression, and I shall redeem you (*vega'alti*) with an outstretched arm and with great judgments, and I will take you (*velakachti*) to Me for a nation." There is yet a fifth expression in the next verse, "And I will bring you (*veheiveisi*) into the land." Our Sages connect it to the unfulfilled promise of the Messianic era. Elijah's Cup at the Seder recalls this expression.

These expressions relate to the Jewish people as a whole from a national perspective. It is also possible to relate these five stages of redemption to each individual on a personal level.

The *Nefesh HaChaim* and numerous other Kabbalistic works describe the five levels of the soul as *nefesh, ruach, neshamah, chayah* and *yechidah*. The *nefesh* is associated with the animalistic aspect of human existence, with its biological drives and desires, such as food and base impulses; it relates to the liver, the organ to which food is first transported from the intestines. The *ruach* is related to emotional states, such as pride, joy, fear and hope; it relates to the heart, the next organ to which nutrient-enriched blood travels after leaving the liver. The *neshamah* is the soul related to the mind or intellect; it relates to the brain, the most important organ serviced by blood exported from the heart.

The highest two levels of the soul have a more "religious" character and do not correspond to any anatomic structure of the body. They represent successively elevated levels of spiritual existence. The *yechidah*, the most sublime, has the capacity for the most intimate relationship with God. It is associated with the idea of the soul being "a portion of God from above," *chelek Eloka mimaal*, capable of clinging to the Creator. (This term is not literal, since God is perfect in His indivisible Oneness, rather it refers to the capacity of the highest aspect of the soul to intensly desire knowledge of God.)

It is possible to discern a correspondence between the five expressions of redemption and the five successive levels of the soul. Being taken out of the physical burdens of Egypt corresponds to the animalistic considerations of the *nefesh*. Delivery from the degradations of slavery corresponds to the emotional needs of the *ruach*. The Torah does not present the third redemption as being "from" anything. It represents a concept and relates to the intellectual level of the *neshamah*. The fourth redemption speaks of God bringing us to Him as a nation. This suggests a more sublime aspect of the soul, the *chayah*, which relates more directly to God. The final redemption in the Messianic era, which relates to the highest level of the soul, the *yechidah,* awaits the time when God and His Name are one.

The concept of dual redemption, national and personal, is echoed in many ways in Jewish thought and practice. While prayer is a private act, it is far more valuable when performed in the community of a *minyan*. Yom Kippur offers forgiveness to a penitent when he considers himself part of the Jewish people. On the high holidays, we pray that all mankind "form a single group" in unified worship of God. Our obligation as individuals is to become a willing cog in the vast clockwork of humanity so that the entire world will resonate harmoniously with the will of its Creator.

The Maharal, among others, discusses the conceptual significance of various numbers. For example, he associates the number three with potential and the number four with the development of that potential. Thus, there are the three patriarchs who implant the potential of the Jewish people and the four matriarchs who develop it.

There are numerous instances of a noteworthy four or forty (a tenfold four signifies the expansion of the concept) in the Torah and even in nature. There are the forty days of the Flood, the forty years the Jewish people spent in the desert, the forty lashes (less one) administered to a willful transgressor of the Law, the forty *se'ah* measures of water in a *mikveh*, the forty days until the human fetus is considered a life, the forty weeks of fetal gestation and the four ribonucleotide codes that express all human life. All of these involve, in one form or another, development of or transformation from potential.

The number five, the Maharal explains, connotes the uniting and relating back of "developed" things towards God, the ultimate fulfillment. As discussed previously, there are five levels of the soul, the highest being the *yechidah*, which is most able to relate to God. There are also five levels of creation, the highest being Adam HaKadmon, the realm "closest" to God. In both cases, the fifth level is the link that relates the other four most intimately back to God. Even in the physical realm, this pattern is expressed in the appositional thumb, which binds the fingers to form the functional hand.

If we examine the division of the *Chumash* into Books and *parshios*, we can perhaps discern this numeric significance in operation as well. For instance, the fifth Book, Deuteronomy, is both a summary and an exhortation focused on the relationship between the Jewish people and God.

Another example of this pattern may occur in the five final *parshios* of Genesis and the first five of Exodus. The last part of Genesis describes the development of Jacob's offspring into the embryonic nation that is planted in Egypt. *Vayeitzei*, the first of the last five *parshios*, tells the story of the birth of all but one of Jacob's children. The fifth of the series, the last of Genesis, is *Vayechi*, which brings the story to a successful conclusion. The family conflict that threatened to create a schism is resolved, harmony reigns, and the brothers receive prophetic blessings from their father. The fifth *parashah* brings resolution.

This structure is duplicated in Exodus. The first four *parshios* detail the redemption of the Jewish people from Egypt. The fifth *parashah*, *Yisro*, crowns that process with the receiving of the Torah, concluding the redemption and the formation of the Jewish nation.

We may further suggest that there is a rough correlation between these five *parshios* and the five levels of the soul. One of the main themes of the first *parashah* in Exodus is the physical afflictions suffered by the Jewish people, relating to the *nefesh*. In the second *parashah*, Pharaoh increases the torment in order to break the Jewish people's spirit, relating to the *ruach*. The third *parashah*, *Bo*, begins the *geulah*, redemption, which is an intellectual concept, relating to the *neshamah*. The fourth *parashah*, *Beshalach*, includes both the salvation at Sea of Reeds, the commandments given at Marah and the actual Exodus from Egypt, relating to the intergrative and more spiritual *chayah*. The fifth *parashah*, *Yisro*, binds the people eternally to God with the receiving of the Torah, relating to the *yechidah*, the supernal aspect of the human soul.

In a similar speculative vein, we may see the same five levels of the soul corresponding to the last five *parshios* of Genesis, which begin with the physical birth of Jacob's children, corresponding to the *nefesh*, and conclude with the prophetic blessings to the future tribes of Israel, corresponding to the supernal *yechidah*.

Underlying this exposition is a glimpse at the harmony of creation and the elements that mirror and resonate with each other. The five-digited hand, the five levels of the soul, the five levels of creation,[1] the five languages of redemption in Egypt and, if the above is correct, the five *parshios* of Genesis and Exodus that describe Israel's descent to and emergence from Egypt may correspond to each other. If so, they would reflect that which we know to be true, that there is in creation a fundamental harmony that reflects the infinite knowledge of the Creator.

---

1. According to the Kabbalah, God's creation proceeded in five stages, from the supernal Adam HaKadmon (man who proceeds) to the fifth stage, *asiah* (action), the realm of man's creation. The goal of creation, which is to realize the potential for perfect harmony in the universe, awaits the Messianic era. At history's conclusion, man, who is descended from Adam HaRishon (the first man), will be in harmony with the Adam HaKadmon, the most supernal aspect of creation. A harmony born of the knowledge of God will be expressed in actuality, as we now express our hope for it in the conclusion of our prayers (*Zechariah* 14:9), "On that day, God will be One and His Name will be One." This capacity for the harmonic conclusion of history may be part of the intent of the expression, "*Istakel b'Oraisa u'bara alma*, [God] looked into the Torah and created the world."

i. Unprecedented Hail and Locusts

OTH THE PLAGUE OF HAIL AND THE PLAGUE OF LOCUSTS shared one salient feature. According to the Torah, both were unprecedented in Egyptian history. The Torah does, however, present their unusual character with subtle differences.

With regard to the hail, we learn (9:18), "There will be very heavy hail, such as has never been in Egypt since it was established until now." Later, the Torah describes the actual plague (9:24), "And there was a hail, and a fire raged within the hail, it was very heavy, such as there had never been in all the land of Egypt from the time it became a nation."

In predicting the locusts, Moses uses slightly different language (10:6), "And they will fill your homes, and the homes of all your servants and the homes of all Egypt, such as your fathers and ancestors have never seen from the day they appeared on the land until this day." Later, the Torah describes the actual plague (10:14), "[The locusts] spread throughout the boundaries of Egypt, very heavy, never before had there been such a locust plague, nor will there ever be another like it."

In both cases, the Torah stresses that the plagues were unprecedented. In the case of the hail, the Torah states it had never happened since the "establishment" of Egypt as a "nation." The reference is to the national and political entity called Egypt. In the case of the locusts, however, the reference is the "land" of Egypt, not the political entity. Why is this so? Moreover, only in the case of locusts does the Torah predict "there will never be another like it." Why is there no similar prediction with regard to hail?

A political government has only a few essential tasks. It must protect society from external threats, it must protect individual members of society from each other, and it must initiate and coordinate collective efforts to improve the public weal. Most critical of these functions is protection from external threat. Without it, no nation can survive over a period of time.

The plague of hail, fire sheathed in ice, was not a natural phenomenon. It was an external attack on Egypt, descended from the heavens themselves. It terrorized the people with its incredible noisiness. Pharaoh, the demigod charged with protecting Egypt from external threats, pleaded primarily for the removal of the thunderous sounds (9:28). The Torah, therefore, emphasizes that the stream of unnatural "hail" attacked the Egyptian nation in a singular way.

The plague of locusts, however, was a grossly exaggerated natural phenomenon that primarily blighted the land rather than the nation-state. In this sense, it was apolitical and internal, and the people did not reflexively look to the government for protection against it. The Torah speaks about it being a singular experience for the land but not for the nation.

The absence of a prediction about hail in the future is

understandable. Nation-states are ephemeral; they come and go. A prediction concerning the state of Egypt would lack significance. The plague of locusts, however, assaulted the geography of Egypt. Here the Torah prophesies that there will never be another like it in the land.

A few decades ago, scientists released their findings about locust swarming. To their bewilderment, locusts migrating eastward across North Africa inexplicably stopped at the Egyptian border, as did locusts migrating southward from Asia Minor. We, of course, understand why: God's promise still holds true.

ii. *How to Stop a Plague*

ROM THE SECOND PLAGUE ON, WE FIND PHARAOH BEGGING for relief. A pattern develops. Pharaoh calls upon Moses to intercede with God on his behalf and remove the plague. Moses accedes to his wishes and gets him relief, but Pharaoh reverts to his intransigent ways.

A close reading of the verses reveals a curious distinction among the plagues of frogs, wild animals and hail. In all three cases, Pharaoh tells Moses and Aaron, "*Hatiru* (הַעְתִּירוּ), plead with God." Yet in each case, Moses responds differently.

In the case of the frogs, we find (8:8), "And Moses and Aaron left Pharaoh's presence, and Moses cried out (וַיִּצְעַק) to God." Later, in the case of the wild animals, Moses responds even more emphatically (8:26), "And Moses left Pharaoh's presence and pleaded with (וַיֶּעְתַּר) God." Finally, in the case of the hail, Moses falls silent (9:33), "And Moses went out from Pharaoh from the city, and he stretched out his hands to God, and the thunder ceased, and the hail and rain no longer struck the ground."

It would appear that Moses did the least to terminate the hail.

He just lifted his hands in supplication, and the plague instantly halted. Of the other two, it took him more effort to stop the wild animals; it was not enough for him to "cry out," he had to "plead with God." How do we explain these differences?

First, let us note a basic distinction between hail and the other plagues. Most of the plagues only required a miracle to activate them, an efficient cause in the language of logics. From that point on, their sustained existence required no special miracles. Once God brought the frogs into existence miraculously and they swarmed over Egypt, there was no need for a constant miracle to keep the frogs alive. They lived and behaved as all frogs do. The same applies to the wild animals.

The plague of hail was different. Its very nature, a blend of fire and ice, was miraculous. It was not enough for God to create the hail through a single miraculous act. Each moment that the hail existed required an additional and continuous miraculous intervention, a substantial or conditional cause in the language of logics.

All that was required to stop the plague of hail was a cessation of the ongoing miracle that sustained it. It did not require an active reversal but a passive cessation of action. As soon as Moses lifted his hands towards the heavens to indicate he no longer wanted the miracle, the hail ceased. But this was not enough to stop the frogs and the wild animals. Once they were running rampant, a new divine miracle was required to remove them. Only Moses' articulated prayer could bring them to an abrupt end. Outstretched hands were not enough.

As for the difference between the frogs and the wild animals, perhaps the answer lies in the additional purpose that only the wild beasts served. The plague of wild animals did not strike Goshen, where the Jewish people lived, in order to distinguish the Jewish people from the nation of Egypt. Perhaps because the plague served this higher purpose in God's overall design, Moses required additional prayers for its removal.

iii. *Pharaoh's Silence*

PHARAOH ASKED MOSES TO PRAY FOR RELIEF FROM ONLY four plagues out of the ten — frogs, wild animals, hail and locusts. During the remaining six plagues — blood, lice, pestilence, boils, darkness and the death of the first-born — Pharaoh does not ask Moses to pray on his behalf. How do we account for the limited number of Pharaoh's pleas?

We can easily understand Pharaoh's silence with regard to two of the plagues — pestilence and the death of the firstborn. They initiated no request because there simply was no purpose or opportunity for one. Both of these plagues did their damage in one fell swoop. They were over in an instant, their terrible damage irreversible. But the question remains, why didn't Pharaoh request relief during the other four plagues?

Our Sages have divided the plagues into three groups, with the third of each group coming without warning. This will explain why the plagues of lice, boils and darkness did not engender a request from Pharaoh. Moses never warned Pharaoh about their pending occurrence and thereby give him the opportunity to avoid them by agreeing to let the Jewish people go. Since Pharaoh had not been responsible for initiating these plagues, he correctly assumed he would not be a party to their conclusion either.

Only the plague of blood remains with unexplained silence. When Moses warns Pharaoh of the impending disaster he does not use the phrase "if you will not let the people go." He only informs him that Egypt's waters will turn to blood. Apparently, Pharaoh was not to have the choice of averting a blood-ravaged land by letting the Jewish people go. This plague was to be a mandatory demonstration, just as the staff turning into a snake had been previously. The sign of the snake rebutted Egypt's false metaphysical beliefs. Turning the water of the Nile into blood demonstrated that Egypt's belief in physical idols was vacuous. This was the indispensable prologue to all of the other plagues. Once again, Pharaoh played no part in the onset of the plague and did not participate in its conclusion.

iv. *Pharaoh's Hard-Hearted Servants*

HE PRESSURE WAS MOUNTING. MOSES WAS ABOUT TO administer the eighth plague — locusts — and God said to him (10:1), "Go to Pharaoh, for I have hardened his heart and the hearts of his servants in order to place these signs of mine in their midst." Clearly, God promises to harden not only Pharaoh's heart but also the hearts of his servants against releasing the Jewish people.

What actually happened? The response is unexpected (10:7), "And Pharaoh's servants said to him, 'How long shall these be a snare for us? Send away the men so that they may worship God, their Lord; don't you yet realize that Egypt is lost?' " This does not sound like the words of people whose hearts God had just hardened. On the contrary, they seem to have come around to Moses' point of view. What happened to God's promise?

Upon further consideration, we cannot help but wonder why it was necessary to harden the hearts of the servants. Pharaoh was an absolute autocrat. He did as he pleased, and his servants had no say. At most, they offered advice. The decision as to whether or not the Jews should be set free rested solely with Pharaoh. What difference did it make if the hearts of the servants were hardened?

The commentators discuss at length the issue of God's hardening of Pharaoh's heart. What happened to free will? The Ramban, among others, explains that in hardening Pharaoh's heart God was, in effect, giving him the emotional fortitude to resist the coercive effect of the overwhelming plagues. The net effect of God's hardening was not to remove Pharaoh's free will but actually to sustain it. Pharaoh became fearless, and, thereby, his decision regarding the release of the Jews remained voluntary. He did not have to set them free until he intellectually recognized that God was Master of the Universe and that he had no right to prevent the Jews from worshiping Him.

Several question remain. If God intended to perform numerous spectacular miracles, why was it important that Pharaoh retain his free will? Why give him the opportunity to abort the miracles by giving in to Moses' demands?

Furthermore, why should Pharaoh's free-willed decision be so critical? Why should the fate of an entire nation, including little children, depend on one man's decision? If the earlier plagues had already convinced the entire nation that the Jews should be freed, why should Pharaoh's obstinacy or mental imbalance bring down suffering on their heads?

Let us consider the structure of Egyptian society and its belief systems. One of the most powerful appeals of Egyptian society was that its king was a man-god. By elevating one of their own to the status of a god, the Egyptians believed they gained a powerful ally in the metaphysical world. Faced with the vicissitudes of life, they could venerate a man with whom they identified and who identified with them. A culture which elevates a man to the status of a god has created (imagined) a potential powerful ally. The success of Christianity rests on this anthropomorphic appeal.

The man-god who occupied the throne by accident of birth merely acted out the ideology spawned by the entire society. The king himself, who became intoxicated by his own powers and prerogatives, represented the ultimate corruption in thought and being to which the human soul may fall prey. But in concept, his position and role were embraced by all the

Egyptians, who identified with their god-king. Under the onslaught of the plagues, the Egyptians as individuals may have been ready to capitulate, but each of them, had he been in the position of god-king, would have been no less obstinate; he would have persisted in his own self-worship. They, too, would have refused to acknowledge their subservience to God.

In this light, we can understand the overriding importance of Pharaoh recognizing God as a result of the plagues. It was necessary for the utter destruction of the Egyptian god-king cult. Any obstacle to his free-willed acknowledgment of God's supremacy would have to be removed.

When God hardened the hearts of Pharaoh's servants, he did not compel them to resist the emancipation of the Jewish people. On the contrary, just as with Pharaoh, He inured them to the emotionally overwhelming impact of the plagues to allow them to deal with the question on an intellectual level. Pharaoh, steeped in his self-worship, chose of his own free will to resist. His servants, however, came of their own free will to the rational decision that Moses was right and that the Jews should be allowed to worship God.

Why was it necessary to have the servants come to this epiphany when the decision lay in the hand of Pharaoh? Because if their hearts had not been hardened and they had caved in out of personal fear, it would have been an erosion of the hierarchical societal base upon which the monarchy of the god-king stood. They would have framed their statement to indicate they feared God more than Pharaoh. Such a development would have been emotionally jolting to Pharaoh, and his free will might have been impaired. But since his servants' hearts were hardened and their opinion was merely intellectual advice rather than a rebellion, Pharaoh felt comfortable, as always, to reject the advice of his advisors if he so chose, leaving his free will intact.

v. Blood on the Lintel

O N THEIR LAST NIGHT IN EGYPT, MOSES TOLD THE JEWISH people to place the blood of the paschal lamb on both doorposts and the overhead lintel (22:23) so that God "will see the blood that is on the lintel and the two doorposts, and God will pass over the entrance."

According to Rashi, each placement of the blood required a separate dipping of the hyssop into the basin, thereby emphasizing the importance of all three placements for protection. With regard to the mitzvah of *mezuzah*, however, the Torah requires only a placement on one doorpost. Why then did God oblige the Jewish people to place blood on the lintel as well?

Let us consider a house from an abstract perspective. Its two basic structural components are the horizontal roof and the vertical walls, each of which has a different conceptual function. The walls are barriers against people and moving objects; they give us privacy and security. The roof protects mainly against the elements — blocking out rain, snow and sun. In some areas, such as heat retention, both are, of course, needed. In essence, the roof or horizontal component of the house can be conceived as protecting against forces of nature, while the walls or vertical component function in the social arena. The lintel and post represent these two realms of utility.

By placing blood on the doorposts and the lintel, the Jewish people expressed their separation both from the social environment of Egyptian culture and from the belief that the Egyptian deities controlled the forces of nature. They expressed their total connection to God.

vi. *The Silence of the Dogs*

N THE LAST NIGHT OF THE JEWISH CAPTIVITY IN EGYPT, the tenth and most appalling plague devastated Egyptian society. At the stroke of midnight, every firstborn perished. The Torah observes (11:7), "But no dog barked among the children of Israel, whether for a man or an animal, in order that you should know that God distinguished wondrously between Egypt and Israel." What is so significant about the silence of the dogs that it warrants mention here?

In Kabbalistic literature, the dog is described as having a lesser soul than other animals, and consequently, it is more distant from the Creator. As such, it has the compensating grace of attaching itself to its human master. Since it cannot relate to the Creator, it worships mankind. For this reason, the nation of Amalek, the implacable enemy of God and the Jewish people, is compared to a dog. By denying the supremacy of God, Amalek resembles the dog that worships mankind.

The dog, because of its devotion, is by nature singularly attuned to the welfare of his human master. Nonetheless, no dogs of Jews barked on the night when the firstborn died. God's protective presence was so clear that the dogs knew their Jewish masters were not at risk. And so the silence of dogs became a medium through which God manifested the distinction between Jews and Egyptians.

An animal that suffers from a mortal ailment is *treifeh* and its meat may not be eaten, even if the animal is slaughtered properly. The Torah tells us (22:30), "You shall be a holy people to Me, and you shall not eat ravaged (*treifeh*) meat from the field, throw it to the dogs."

The Midrash (*Mechilta*) relates the only two mentions of dogs in the *Chumash* to each other and points out that God never withholds well-earned reward. Since the dogs did not bark in Egypt, they were rewarded with *treifeh* meat.

In actuality, *treifeh* meat can be sold to non-Jews who are not required to eat kosher. Only eating it is forbidden. Throwing the meat to the dogs is apparently only a figure of speech, because the owner would first sell it if he could. Why then does the Torah express the permission to derive monetary benefit from *treifeh* meat in terms of throwing it to the dogs?

Other questions present themselves. The dogs in Egypt were not exercising free will; why then did they deserve to be rewarded? Furthermore, what do the dogs of future generations have to do with the dogs that were silent in Egypt? Are contemporary dogs considered their descendants? Are our dogs, perhaps, reincarnated canines?

Before telling us that *treifeh* meat is forbidden, the Torah calls on us to be holy. What is the connection between holiness and refraining from *treifeh* meat? The word *kadosh*, holy, means separate. By withdrawing from our physical impulses, we sanctify ourselves. This comes into particular play with regard to *treifeh* meat. Once a person has slaughtered an animal properly, he feels he has fulfilled his religious obligations, and now he can eat. But the Torah restricts him. First, he must inspect the slaughtered animal to make sure it had no prior life-threatening blemishes or defects that rendered it *treifeh*. In so doing, we are called upon to make the distinction between an animal that was dying and an animal that was fully alive at the moment it was slaughtered. If it was defective, we must withdraw, and thereby, we are sanctified.

Here we find the deep parallel between our refraining from *treifeh* meat and the silence of the dogs. In Egypt, the dogs instinctively distinguished between those who would die and those who would not. We, too, are required to make this distinction, between which animals were moribund and which were not, before we sit down to eat a piece of meat. The Torah's reward for the dogs serves as a model for us. By distinguishing and then restraining our aroused instinctual desires, we inject holiness into our lives.

vii. *A Significant Sign*

MOSES INSTRUCTED THE JEWISH PEOPLE TO TAKE BLOOD from the slaughtered paschal lamb and place it on their doorposts as a sign for God to pass over them when he killed the firstborn of Egypt (12:7,13). Rashi explains that the people placed the blood on the inside of the doorposts, where it was visible only to them; it was a "sign for them." The language indicates that the blood would somehow be significant to them in itself, not only as a sign for God to pass over them. How?

Furthermore, the Midrash quotes the words of the prophet (*Yechezchel* 16:6), "And I said to you, 'In your blood, live!' And I said to you, 'In your blood, live!' " This repeated statement, the Midrash explains, indicates that the Jewish people were deemed worthy of redemption in the merit of the blood-related mitzvos of circumcision and of the paschal lamb, which included placing the blood on the doorposts. We can easily understand why both the Jewish mark of circumcision and the slaughter of animals the Egyptians worshiped as deities earned them redemption. These two mitzvos, the only two positive commandments whose neglect is a capital offense, express the minimal level of Jewish identification required to be considered within its folds. But why was the merit of placing the blood of the sacrifice on the inside of the doorpost so important?

Let us consider the "organic" development of the Jewish nation. Frequently, the Midrash and rabbinic writings view the extraction of the Jewish people as a birth. As long as the Jewish people were in Egypt, they were enmeshed in its culture emotionally, intellectually and spiritually; their identity as a nation was not complete. The Exodus extracted them from Egypt and fashioned their singular spiritual identity.

Prior to his death, Moses tells the Jewish people (*Deuteronomy* 4:34), "And has God ever done such a thing to extract one nation from amidst another?" Moses was not only referring to the miracle of physically separating them from Egypt; he was referring even more significantly to their extraction from the fabric of Egyptian society and their formation into a new nation, which culminated at Mount Sinai. Many of the circumstances that led up to Sinai are reminiscent of birth and development. The most obvious example occurs when the sea splits and the Jewish people emerge from a narrow place, like a newborn child emerges with the waters of the amniotic sac. Moreover, the word Mitzraim, Egypt, can be translated as "from the narrows."

For an infant in the womb, everything around him is an extension of himself. Food is always available, and he never experiences the frustration of an unfulfilled need. The newborn begins life in this psychological state; all it knows or cares about is itself. In psychological terms, this is called primary narcissism. The earliest processes of differentiation and individuation begin with the oral stage. The infant satisfies its biological need for food with its mouth. Unlike the time spent *in utero*, delay of gratification and frustration inevitably occur. The child begins to be aware of his separateness from his mother and the world at large.

This concept of an initial oral stage is echoed in the Jewish people's development — their first mitzvos were oral. God forbade them to eat *chametz* and commanded them to eat matzah and the meat of the Pesach sacrifice. He also commanded them to retell the story of the Exodus. These mitzvos steered them away from instinctuality and prepared them to receive the Torah. The channeling of instinctual drives by using the intellect is a prerequisite for keeping the Torah without distortion. For this reason, the mitzvah of *milah*, circumcision, was also reintroduced prior to the Exodus.

Later on, we find an unexpected law among the laws of Passover. The Torah tells us (34:26), "Do not cook a kid in its mother's milk," which is the prohibition against eating meat and milk cooked together. Rabbi Shamshon Raphael Hirsch comments on both the language and location of this command. The language of the law is a symbolic reference to the Jewish people who are likened to a young goat whose emergence from its mother Egypt is celebrated on Passover. We must not allow the kid to become intermixed again with the mother that gave birth to it. The prohibition against milk and meat is one more element in the total severance of our identification with the instinctually driven Egyptians.

That is also why the Torah forbids us to return to Egypt, even thousands of years later. Egypt represents the place from which we were extracted and distinguished as a nation that bears God's ideas and laws. The mitzvah of not returning to Egypt is a constant representation of our obligation never to reject our divine mission by trying to merge again with the other nations. This is further codified in the Rambam's *Mishneh Torah*, which states that Egypt is the one land that can never be annexed to Israel.

In this light, we can better understand the importance of the blood on the inside of the doorposts.

It is a well-known psychological phenomenon that we are more sympathetic to people with whose suffering we easily identify. We are often more moved by the plight of a single child lost in the forest than by the anguish of millions of people starving to death on a distant continent. By placing the blood on their doorposts, the Jewish people demonstrated confidently that the disaster about to befall Egypt's firstborn children did not relate to them. Despite being intermixed with the Egyptians, they no longer identified with them. The process of individuation and separation had begun. They were ready for redemption.

King David declares (*Psalms* 119:162), "I rejoice over your words like one who discovers a great treasure." What does this mean? The Talmud (*Menachos* 43b) interprets this as referring to the mitzvah of *milah*, circumcision. Elsewhere, the Talmud (*Shabbos* 130a) explains the circumstances that led David to compose these words. While disrobed in the bath, David was saddened that he couldn't study or pray. But then he contemplated his *milah*, and he realized that he was never bereft of mitzvos. This gave him cause for great joy.

Still, the verse seems to imply that the joy of the mitzvah of *milah* is unexpectedly great, like the discovery of a great treasure. How is this so?

The foundation stone of God's covenant with Abraham was the mitzvah of *milah*; it represents a subordination of the physical desires to higher spiritual goals. At first glance, *milah* appears to trade off anticipated physical pleasure for the increased spirituality of a closer relationship with God.

In reality, however, the Torah's mitzvos provide unexpected benefits in the physical domain as well. Unbridled physical impulses, directed solely for self-gratification, pall after a while. They lose their ability to satisfy, and other fleeting pleasures must be sought. But when physical pleasure is restricted and channeled toward higher spiritual fulfillment, the pleasures remain strong and renewable. For example, modern psychology has discovered that the laws of *niddah* enhance the pleasures of marriage.

This then may have been one unexpected aspect of the mitzvah of *milah* over which David rejoiced. Unable to pray or study in the bath, David was saddened that he had no means at that moment of drawing close to God. But as he contemplated the mitzvah of *milah*, he was reassured. When man is stripped of his higher intellectual capacity as a human being, he is left with his animalistic self. He feels debased. But the mitzvah of *milah* elevates the Jew and brings him closer to God. By demonstrating that he can restrain the animalistic side of his nature out of his own free will, the mitzvah is instructive. Even by his appropriate forbearance, man elevates his existence and binds himself to God.

The mitzvah of *milah* was one of the mitzvos the Jewish people performed in Egypt to facilitate their redemption. In its observance, they expressed Judaism's highest values and aspirations for each individual Jew and for the Jewish people as a whole.

viii. *Worthy of Redemption*

OUR DAYS BEFORE THE REDEMPTION, GOD COMMANDED the Jewish people to take lambs and prepare them for the paschal sacrifice. The Talmud tells us (*Kiddushin* 40b), "When the time of the Exodus arrived, the Jewish people had no divine commandments by which to earn redemption. Therefore, God gave them the commandments of the blood of the paschal lamb and the blood of circumcision." Why did God choose specifically these two commandments?

In his commentary on Proverbs, the Vilna Gaon states repeatedly that there are two *yitzrei hara*, literally evil inclinations, embedded in man from birth — *taavah*, desire, and its matched pair *kaas* or *kinah*, anger or jealousy. *Taavah* is a combination of man's appetitive and base drives. *Kaas* or *kinah* may be identified as the aggressive drive. These two forces in man are inborn and instinctual.

A third *yetzer hara*, the Vilna Gaon explains, develops later. In the language of our Sages, this force is *gaavah* or *kavod*, arrogance or the pursuit of honor. In the language of modern psychology, this *yetzer hara* is the ego and its cravings, which develops as a person's self-awareness emerges; an infant, which has not yet developed a sense of self-awareness, does not yet have an ego. For the same reason, this *yetzer* is not found in the animal world, where there is no true self-awareness.

Our Sages tell us (*Pirkei Avos* 4:28) that these three inclinations can "remove a person from the world." In other words, they threaten the eternal existence of the soul. Interestingly, these desires appear at the root of the three cardinal sins which may not be transgressed even on pain of death. *Taavah* motivates illicit relations (*gilui arayos*), rage motivates murder (*shefichas damim*), and *gaavah* motivates idolatry (*avodah zarah*). Idolatry arises when man, burdened by egocentricity, projects his own needs and desires onto idols formed in his own image.

Our Sages understood the mitzvah of circumcision as a commitment to minimize the pursuit of earthy desires as an end in themselves.

The other mitzvah performed prior to redemption was the paschal sacrifice. The lamb was an object of worship in Egypt. By slaughtering the god of their masters, the Jewish people rejected the idolatrous culture under which they had lived for over two hundred years. At the same time, they struck a blow against the inclination to *gaavah*, which lies behind idolatry.

Having differentiated themselves from the Egyptians and mankind in general by their commitment to curb and control the inclinations of the *yetzer hara*, the Jewish people became worthy of redemption.

ix. *Why the Rush?*

THE STORY OF THE EXODUS MAKES IT CRYSTAL CLEAR THAT the Jewish people left in a hurry, but no reason is given for it. Why indeed? The Torah provides the answer in Deuteronomy (16:3), "For you went hastily from the land of Egypt in order that you should remember the day you went out from the land of Egypt all the days of your life."

Why are we not told this reason immediately in the context of the Exodus story? Why wait until Deuteronomy? Furthermore, how would leaving in haste assure that they would "remember the day ... all the days of your life"?

Modern psychiatry has identified an illness called posttraumatic stress disorder (PTSD). Sometimes, people experience an overwhelming shock or trauma, and subsequently, they have recurrent flashbacks, intrusive thoughts and repeated dreams related to the event, among other symptoms. They will then keep returning, in their conscious and unconscious thoughts, to the sudden and unexpected event that they find so difficult to assess and incorporate. For instance, most people age five or older will always remember where they were during a great blackout or what they were doing when they heard about a sensational assassination.

The same holds true in the reverse as well. A shocking positive development can also cause the mind to try again and again to process the event "all the days of your life."

This then is one benefit to God taking the Jewish people out of Egypt in haste. The shock of their sudden miraculous emancipation imprinted the memory of that event on the minds of those leaving in a way that they could never forget it. But revealing the cause of the haste to the people immediately would have diminished the shock and astonishment and thereby the effectiveness.

Forty years later, when Moses gave the reason for the haste (in the Book of Deuteronomy), the event had imprinted itself deeply on the collective memory of the Jewish people — never to be forgotten. At that point, revealing the reason no longer diminished the impact.

Another psychological aspect of a sudden shocking experience also finds expression in the laws of Passover night. We know that recurrent reminders of a traumatic event reawaken its jolting effect. On Passover night we are obligated to see ourselves as if we went forth from Egypt. The yearly recollection of the shocking events of the Exodus revive the vivid memories and associated feelings. As we experience for our families and ourselves the shock of our ancestors yearly, the redemption from Egypt remains a living legacy for the Jewish people.

פרשת בשלח
Parashas Beshalach

i. They Left With Wealth

HE TORAH TELLS US (13:18) THAT WHEN THE JEWS LEFT Egypt they were *chamushim*, a rather unusual word. According to our Sages, it means either armed or wealthy. Our Sages also find an allusion in this word to the number five (*chamesh*), and thereby a subtle reference to the Midrashic statement that only one in five Jews left Egypt. The other four fifths, being reluctant to leave, died during the plague of darkness.

Perhaps we can discern an association between the word *chamushim* as wealthy and its etymological connection to the number five. Joseph had greatly enriched Egypt by his foresight and leadership during the great famine. As a result of his economic policies, all Egyptians became sharecroppers on the estates of the king. However, they were allowed to keep fully four fifths of their produce, paying the king only a fifth (*chomesh*). In other words, they had a flat 20 percent income tax.

Joseph understood that a progressive tax structure (higher rates of taxation at higher income levels), with tax rates above 20 percent in the higher tax brackets, would produce less revenue. Interestingly, scientific economic research consistently demonstrates that both government and individual revenues maximize at a 20 percent flat income-tax rate. Joseph realized that higher tax rates actually cause royal revenues to fall. Oppressive taxes decrease the incentive of people to take risks and produce more, and increase the incentive to hide wealth or income.

By enslaving the Jewish people, the Egyptians showed their ingratitude to Joseph who had enriched their country through his prescient *chomesh* tax policies. The Almighty's justice dictated, measure for measure, that the Jewish people left Egypt *chamushim*, carrying off their wealth.

ii. *Stone, Straw and Lead*

HEN THE JEWISH PEOPLE EMERGED FROM THE SEABED, the waters converged on their Egyptian pursuers and drowned them. But the Egyptians did not all meet an identical death. The Torah uses three different metaphors to describe the demise of the Egyptians. First we learn (16:5) that "they went down into the depths like a stone." Then (16:7), "You sent forth your wrath, it would consume them like straw." And finally (16:10), "The sea enveloped them, the mighty sank like lead in the water."

Rashi, quoting the Midrash (*Mechilta*), explains that each Egyptian pursuer met a death suited to his degree of iniquity. The worst among them were tossed about in the waves like straw, suffering a prolonged and painful death. The middling ones went down like stones, while the least iniquitous sank like heavy lead and perished right away. Along the same lines, *Targum Yonasan* states (14:27) that the Egyptians were given the strength to bear extended punishment before they died.

Although God ultimately repays the wicked measure for measure, the retribution is usually delivered in a hidden fashion. Moreover, throughout history we do not find the wicked perishing in an especially gruesome fashion. Why here, according to the Midrash, was it necessary that the punishment be so painfully precise?

The ten plagues and the splitting of the sea were the greatest revelations of God's providential justice in the history of the world. These would stand for all time as the proofs of God's perfect judgment in His providential guidance of the world. Therefore, all the fine nuances of His justice had to become manifest to the observer. At that unique time in history, unseen subtleties would not suffice; God meted out death miraculously to fit the crime precisely.

Careful scrutiny of the verses gives us a hint as to how the three categories of Egyptians were demarcated. The brazenly contemptuous that "stand up against [God]" were obviously the worst; they drowned like straw, slowly and painfully. Those who were "the strength and the pick of his army," the warriors who proudly carried Pharaoh's banner, ever loyal to their god-king, drowned like stones. Those who were motivated by greed, who said, "I will divide the plunder; I will satisfy my lust with them," sank like lead and were quickly put out of their misery. They were the least iniquitous; they acted out of self-interest, not out of commitment to a philosophy antithetical to God nor a commitment to its leader.

One anomaly remains. The order in which they appear is stone, straw, lead, progressing from the middle to the most severe to the least severe death. Shouldn't the sequence have been progressive, either from most severe to least severe or the reverse?

Perhaps God delayed the punishment of the least iniquitous Egyptians in order to give them the opportunity to repent. The sequence, then, is chronological. First, He punished the worst two categories simultaneously. Those who sank like stones died first and are, therefore, mentioned first. Then those who thrashed about like straw finally perished. The least iniquitous still did not repent. Condemned to death, they sank most quickly, like lead.

iii. *Aaron's Sister*

AFTER THE JEWISH PEOPLE'S TRIUMPHAL MARCH THROUGH the parted sea, Moses leads the grateful nation in a tribute to God. And then (15:20-21), "Miriam, the prophetess, Aaron's sister, took her drum in her hand, and all the women followed her with drums and dancing. And Miriam spoke to them, 'Sing to God for He is exalted above the arrogant; he hurled horse and rider into the sea.' "

Why is Miriam identified here as Aaron's sister? Since she was emulating what Moses had just done, singing the exact same votive praise, wouldn't it have been more appropriate to identify her as Moses' sister?

Rashi offers an explanation, derived from the Midrash (*Mechilta*), that connects her to Aaron, because he extended himself on her behalf after she was stricken with *tzaraas* for speaking ill of Moses (*Numbers* 12:1-12). This is somewhat puzzling. Why would the Torah record a connection based on an event that had not yet occurred and would not be mentioned in the Torah for another two Books?

We can pinpoint a special connection between Miriam and Aaron in a character trait they shared. Aaron was the older of Amram's sons, a man of incredible brilliance, piety and charisma.

It would have been possible for a lesser person to feel resentment that his younger brother had usurped his rightful position as leader. In fact, the opposite was true. Aaron welcomed his brother's arrival in Egypt as the divinely appointed leader with joy (4:14), not only on his face but also "in his heart." This selfless deference existed in Miriam as well. She too gladly subjugated herself to her younger brother Moses' leadership; at the splitting of the sea, she, like Aaron, deferentially sang her brother's song.

This may explain the Midrash's reference to Aaron's exertions on Miriam's behalf. Aaron came to her defense because he knew that she did not have any personal resentment to the primacy of Moses. He knew they shared this important character trait, and that any complaints she expressed were for the higher good. The Torah reveals Aaron's perception, which becomes manifest when Miriam, "Aaron's sister," leads the women in song right after Moses leads the men.

iv. *Two Laws and a Stick*

THREE DAYS AFTER THE SPLITTING OF THE SEA, THE JEWISH people arrived at Marah. The people complained to Moses about the bitter water. The Torah continues (15:25), "And [Moses] cried out to God, and God showed him a stick, and he threw it into the water, and the water became sweet. There He established for [the Jewish people] an edict and a law, and there He tested [them]."

What were the edict and law established at Marah? According to the Midrash and the Talmud (*Sanhedrin* 56b), these were Sabbath observance and honoring parents, the fourth and fifth of the Ten Commandments. How did these two particular commandments relate to the events at Marah?

The Maharal in *Netzach Yisrael* offers a profound analysis of the Ten Commandments. He points out that they can be divided into two groups. The first five are sins against God, while the second five are sins against other people. They are ordered in decreasing severity.

The first law pertains to a denial of God's existence, the most grievous and gravest sin against God. The second command concerns a rejection of His most fundamental trait, His oneness or uniqueness. The third involves abusing God, so to speak, in the only way possible, which is to misuse His Name by swearing falsely. Sabbath observance, the fourth commandment, is a testimony to God's general providence in creating the world, as well as His providence in guiding the world to redemption, through the vehicle of the Jewish people. Honoring parents, the fifth and last of the first set of commandments, requires individuals to acknowledge the specific divine providence which resulted in one's own existence. Each individual's parents were the necessary means God used to introduce each soul into its corresponding body. Acknowledging and honoring parents is also an appreciation of God's providence in one's very existence.

The Jewish people had witnessed the greatest manifestation of God's providence in history. They had seen the simultaneous death of every Egyptian firstborn and the splitting of the sea. Providence couldn't have been clearer. God was looking after them. Faith, however, requires us to trust in the divine guidance even when things do not seem to be going well. At Marah, the people's faith was tested.

The Torah does not state, as it does in other places, that they were thirsty or parched. Presumably, they had brought along water for their journey in the desert. They had also been expecting, after their glorious salvation, to find abundant potable water in Marah to replenish their partially depleted supply. But they were bitterly disappointed. Yes, there was water, but it was bitter!

By complaining they were in effect questioning whether God was looking out for them. They lacked faith that there was a divine purpose in their temporary insecurity. The commandments of Sabbath observance and honoring parents directly addressed their wavering faith in God when they did not get what they wanted and expected. These commandments specifically instruct about God's general and individual providence, which operates in good times as well as seemingly bad times.

Careful scrutiny of the verse supports this view. Why did God wish to have the water turn sweet by means of a stick (*etz*)? Why was Moses' praying for the waters to become drinkable not sufficient? Moreover, why does the Torah say, "God showed [Moses] a stick"? Would it not have been simpler to write that "God commanded Moses to take the stick"?

By giving such prominence to the stick (*etz*), God alluded to the other famous *etz* in history, namely the *Etz HaDaas* (Tree of Knowledge). There, too, God had instructed Adam and Eve for their own good not to eat its fruit. Regardless of their motivation, Adam and Eve also had a failure of faith. They failed to trust that God's command not to eat the fruit was for their good. When God "showed him a stick," He was directing Moses' attention, and the nation's, to the primeval tree. Thus, in addition to the commandments of Sabbath observance and honoring parents, the casting of the stick into the water at Marah also reinforced concepts about God's consistently benevolent providence.

After the events at Marah, God assures the Jews that if they follow His laws diligently they will avoid the illnesses of Egypt. He concludes (15:26), "I am God, your healer."

Illness is generally something unseen and pernicious to the body. Conversely, adhering to God's will leads to an unseen providence in accordance with our desire for good health. If we have faith in God's providence, the Torah states, His unseen providence will protect us from unseen threats — insidious illness. Egypt, in its stubborn refusal to release the Jewish people, was the ultimate denier of God's providence; in their denial, they represent the ultimate recipients of seemingly capricious sickness.

This idea, that there will be a providential provision of our needs if we have faith in God and live in accordance with His will, is God's message in Elim, the next stopping place in the desert. There, the Jewish people found twelve wells and seventy date trees. Right around the corner from where the people had questioned whether God's presence was in their midst, Providence had supplied the needs of the nation. There was a well for each tribe and a date tree for each elder who would one day serve on the high court, and in the comfort of its shade he could instruct the people.

v. *Beyond the Self*

MOSES WAS THE EPITOME OF SELF-EFFACEMENT. WHEN THE Jewish people besieged him and Aaron with complaints, he responded with genuine puzzlement (16:7), "And what are we that you should complain against us?" In fact, the Torah tells us (*Numbers* 12:3) that Moses was "more humble than any man on the face of the earth."

The Talmud (*Shabbos* 87b) describes ascending levels of humility. King David declared, "I am a worm and not a man." Abraham went beyond equating himself with lowly animal forms; next to God, he was inanimate "dust and ashes." Moses, however, considered himself absolutely nothing, as he said, "What are we?"

At first glance, we are impressed by this extreme self-effacement on the part of the towering figures of Jewish history, but was it accurate? Didn't these great men know their own worth? Moses, for instance, attained the highest level of prophecy ever. It would be naïve to think he considered himself inferior to other people. How then do we define his extraordinary humility?

The Talmud (*Berachos* 63b) quotes the verse in Proverbs (30:33), "The extract of anger yields blood, and the extract of twofold anger yields dispute." What does this mean? The Talmud explains, "'The extract of anger yields blood' refers to a student who remains silent when his teacher rebukes him. He will be able to distinguish between ritually impure and ritually pure blood. 'The extract of twofold anger yields dispute' refers to a student who remains silent even when his teacher rebukes him a second time. He will be able to judge even capital cases and civil suits."

What quality may be ascribed to the first student who doesn't respond to rebuke? How is one who remains silent in the face of a second censure superior?

There is a type of personality that may be described as having a healthy ego. Such a person is not burdened with an underlying sense of low self-esteem. He does not feel compelled to boast, put down other people or seek fame in order to feel better about himself. In other words, he does not need to prove he is great in order to feel worthwhile. He is at ease with himself. If such a person is upbraided once, he does not feel threatened by the criticism, and consequently, he feels no need to defend himself. Such a person is qualified to judge a case regarding the status of blood, which will determine whether marital relations are permitted. The questioner may have strong emotions concerning the outcome, but the person with a "healthy ego" will not feel swayed by the possible reaction his response will trigger in his questioner.

Nonetheless, the person with a "healthy ego" does value himself. If he encounters persistent criticism (the twofold anger metaphor), he may consider it a sign of his own inadequacy. His sense of self may be threatened, causing him to react defensively. Such a person does not have the higher level of objectivity needed to rule on capital cases or civil suits, which involve abstract principles and are difficult to adjudicate.

There is, however, a different kind of personality whose mental energies are so far removed from himself that he assigns no importance to personal concerns. Unlike the person with the healthy ego, who finds a happy medium between inflated and diminished self-worth, this person has removed himself from the entire issue. Such a person has risen above subjectivity and is qualified to rule on capital cases or civil suits.

This was the humility that Moses exhibited. Keenly aware of the all-pervasive presence of God and drawn towards Him, Moses' interest in himself evaporated. His humility did not stem from the paradoxically extreme self-absorption present in a person with low self-esteem. Like Abraham and David, but even more so, Moses had no sense of self; his mental energies flowed only toward God.

vi. *The Importance of Empty Pockets*

ANNA FELL FROM THE HEAVENS FOR SIX DAYS OF THE week. On the sixth day, a double portion descended, enough for Friday and for the Sabbath as well. God had demonstrated the proper acts and attitude with regard to the advent of the Sabbath. Everything that entailed forbidden labors on the Sabbath was prepared beforehand.

The Talmud and the rabbinic writings assign an importance to Sabbath preparations that goes beyond mere expedience. There is an intrinsic value in these preparations that imbues them with religious significance.

Let us take a closer look at one particular passage in the Talmud (*Shabbos* 12a): "Rabbi Chananiah said, 'A person must make sure the pockets of his clothing are empty at nightfall on the eve of the Sabbath, for he may inadvertently go out [into the street while carrying].' Rav Yosef commented, '*Hilchasa rabsa leshabata*, This is a great law regarding the Sabbath.' "

There are myriad rabbinic regulations governing the observance of the Sabbath. Why does Rav Yosef single out this particular one, which actually applies to the eve of the Sabbath, as a "great law regarding the Sabbath"?

The Rambam states that our Sages frequently issued edicts to serve several purposes, although they often chose not to reveal all of them. Perhaps on a deeper level the requirement to check one's clothing encapsulates the spiritually elevating disposition to which one should aspire as the Sabbath approaches. The removal of all objects from one's clothing serves as a metaphor for the obligation to strip away our mundane concerns and accept upon ourselves the spiritually uplifting focus of the Sabbath. This is what prompted Rav Yosef to remark on the greatness of this regulation.

There is a tradition that the prophet Elijah will appear one day before the Messiah to herald his arrival. From this, the Talmud deduces that the Messiah cannot come on the Sabbath, since this would entail the disruption of the Sabbath preparations by Elijah's arrival. Apparently, the disruption of the Sabbath preparations are of greater concern than preparing for the Messiah. Why?

The Sabbath preparations strip the Jewish soul of its mundane entanglements and bring it to a level of transcendence that allows it to form an eternal relationship with God. This is a fitting metaphor for our purpose in life. God would not send the Messiah when we are already engaged in the Messiah's work of establishing God's kingdom on earth.

We may further suggest that the disruption of the Sabbath preparations is only the first chronological reason why the Messiah cannot come on the Sabbath. A deeper one may be that on the Sabbath we experience a verisimilitude of the ideal potential of our souls for an eternal relationship with God. Any longing expressed on the Sabbath, even for the Messianic era, would impugn the relationship as flawed. It would also contradict part of the task of the Sabbath, which is to show that the perfect relationship with God of Messianic times can be realized in the here and now.

Another multifaceted rabbinic regulation is the prohibition for anyone who is not bedridden to take medicine on the Sabbath. Our Sages state that doing so may lead to grinding the pharmaceutical components. A further benefit underlying this injunction is that it encourages us to be dismissive of the minor distractions of our physical existence and focus on the spiritual uplift that derives from Sabbath observance.

For the same reason, we are instructed not to mention our physical needs in our Sabbath prayers. We even alter the greeting with which we address an ailing person. During the week, we would say, "May you have a complete recovery." On the Sabbath, we say, "It is improper to cry out on the Sabbath. Recovery is at hand." On the Sabbath, prayers and blessings focus on the world of spirituality.

vii. *Rephidim Spells Trouble*

REPHIDIM SPELLED TROUBLE, EVEN THOUGH THE JEWISH people only stopped there briefly during their journey from Egypt to Mount Sinai (17:1-8). As soon as they arrived in this waterless spot, even before they were thirsty, they beleaguered Moses for water. Moses called them argumentative, and he accused them of putting God to the test. Soon thereafter, the nation of Amalek, the archenemy of God and the nemesis of the Jewish people, launched a sneak attack against them.

Why was this place called Rephidim?

There is a difference of opinion among our Sages (*Sanhedrin* 106b). Rabbi Yehoshua states that the name implies that here the Jewish people were weakened (*rafah yedeihem*) in their observance of the Torah. Rabbi Eliezer disagrees. Rephidim, he states, was the name of the place even before the Jewish people arrived there. According to Rabbi Yehoshua, however, the Jewish people did not refer to the place as Rephidim when they arrived. It is rather the divine Author who does so in light of later events.

How are we to understand this argument? What is the deeper underlying issue about which these two sages disagree?

It would seem that Rabbi Eliezer believes that it was not a coincidence; there was something about that place which predisposed the Jews to sin there. The implication is that the sin would not have occurred without the particular external influence associated with that place. Rabbi Yehoshua, on the other hand, believes that the sin would have occurred in any case, and that the place earned its name only after the fact.

Understood this way, the argument is akin to what our Sages say about Adam before and after sin. Prior to eating from the Tree of Knowledge, Adam's *yetzer hara* — evil inclination — was external, driven by environmental cues. After he sinned, it was internalized. At that time, his very nature, even without outside temptation, became internally drawn towards corruption.

In perhaps a similar way, Rabbi Eliezer and Rabbi Yehoshua debated the status of the Jewish people as they left Egypt. Rabbi Eliezer considered the nation like a pristine newborn, similar to Adam before the sin. Only a place like Rephidim, or the presence of the *erev rav* on other occasions, could provoke the Jewish people to sin. The Jewish people sinned at Rephidim only because they were affected by the malignant environment. Rabbi Yehoshua, however, considered them like Adam after the sin, with the *yetzer hara* entrenched within, prodding them to sin irrespective of special environmental cues.

viii. *Travel Restrictions*

HE JEWISH PEOPLE ARRIVED AT MOUNT SINAI ON A Sunday. Does that mean that they traveled on the Sabbath? This is a point of contention in the Talmud (*Shabbos* 87a). Rava says that they did, while Rav Acha bar Yaakov maintains that they had to wait until the Sabbath was over to break camp.

At the core of their dispute is the law of *techum*, the restriction of travel beyond a specified radius from one's Sabbath domicile. This restriction is separate from the prohibition of constructive labors (*melachos*), which both rabbis agree was already given to the Jewish people at Marah, weeks before they reached Sinai. God accelerated the requirement for Sabbath observance and other laws as a sort of antidote to the nation's recidivism. It is not clear, however, if God gave the *techum* restriction then as well. Rava contends that it was peeled off from the Sabbath laws prior to Sinai, allowing the people to travel on the Sabbath. Rav Acha argues that the people kept all the Sabbath laws and must have broken camp after nightfall.

At first glance, Rava's view is difficult. Since it was possible to arrive at Sinai on Sunday even with a Saturday night departure, why wouldn't they have waited? Why hold back the *techum* restriction if it didn't interfere with their timely arrival at Sinai?

Considered more deeply, Rava is of the opinion that the *techum* restriction could not have been given prior to the Jewish people's receiving the Torah at Mount Sinai. Since the entire purpose of creation was fulfilled at Sinai, God would not have given the Jewish people any law that might impede or delay their arrival there; even if practically it wouldn't have hindered their arrival, it remained a theoretical and theological impossibility. Hence, the *techum* restriction could not have been given at Marah along with the rest of the Sabbath laws.

Rav Acha, on the other hand, considers the Sabbath laws, as well as each of the remainder of the 613 commandments, one integrated and indivisible unit. Any law that God found expedient to give ahead of schedule would have to be given in its entirety.

ix. *Moses, Perennial Stranger*

OSES FATHERED TWO SONS IN MIDIAN. HE NAMED THE first Gershom (2:22), because "I have been a stranger (*ger*) in a foreign land," and the second Eliezer (18:4), because "my father's God came to my aid and saved me from Pharaoh's sword."

In which "foreign land" was Moses a stranger? Some commentators understand this as a reference to his exile in Midian, while others interpret it as his clandestine existence as a Jew in Egypt. Moses was "saved from Pharaoh's sword" when he killed the Egyptian overseer in order to save a fellow Jew. He found refuge in Midian and lived there as a fugitive from Pharaoh's wrath until returning to Egypt forty years after taking flight. From a chronological perspective, this is puzzling. Moses should have named his firstborn Eliezer, commemorating his miraculous escape, and his second son Gershom as a wistful reflection of his exilic condition.[1] Why did he do the opposite?

Moses undoubtedly had an intense sense of being a stranger long before he reached Midian. In fact, this state in a way defined his existence from birth. All Jews were "strangers" in Egypt, oppressed and persecuted, exploited foreigners stripped of their

---

1. There is also a subtle hint of appreciation in the name Gershom. It is a play on words alluding to Moses saving Zipporah from the ruffians at the well, where he "chased them away (*girshom*)." This virtuous act led to his marriage and the birth of his son.

rights. Moses' mother who nursed him had made him aware of his Jewish identity; surely, he shared the Jewish sense of disenfranchisement. Moreover, growing up in the royal palace in the guise of an Egyptian prince forced to conceal his profound allegiance to the Jewish people, his feelings of strangeness were intensified. Alienation was the dominant feature of the first part of his life, and even after he left Egypt, his fugitive existence in Midian perpetuated his sense of otherness.

As Moses became a father for the first time, as he began to build a family and a future, he reflected on his personal history. His thoughts ranged back across the landscape of his life and observed the consistent alienation, and he commemorated it in the name of his firstborn. Only later, after the birth of his second son, as he prepared to face the tyrannical Pharaoh again,[2] did he commemorate his escape from Pharaoh's sword as a prayer for God's continued protection.

But the question remains. Why indeed did providence contrive that Moses should experience so much alienation in his life?

The answer can be found hundreds of years earlier, when God introduced the concept of alienation with regard to the Jewish people. After God informed Abraham that his offspring would one day be as numerous as the stars and would be given the land of Israel, Abraham asked (*Genesis* 15:8), "How can I know they will inherit it?" Our Sages interpret Abraham's question as, "How can I know they will deserve to inherit it?" And God replied (15:13), "Know full well that they will be strangers in a land not their own ... for four hundred years." Apparently, their status as strangers would give them sufficient merit to receive the land.

Why did Abraham sense that the Jewish people would need additional merit to inherit the land? After all, God had already promised it to Abraham. The Talmud (*Nedarim* 32a) finds the answer in Abraham's own question. When he expressed concern about the faith (*emunah*) of his offspring and their right to the

2. Eliezer was born after God commanded Moses to return to Egypt. We know this because Eliezer reached his eighth day while the family was en route to Egypt.

land, he revealed a minuscule deficiency in his own faith. Over the years and generations, this infinitesimally imperfect faith would deteriorate further and develop into a flawed faith in his descendants.

God, however, reassured Abraham that He would prescribe an antidote to their flawed faith. They would become strangers in a strange land, ill at ease in their surroundings, exposed and unprotected. Redemption by God from such a prolonged experience would restore their faith, since they would recognize that God had never been absent. That is the essence of faith, the conviction that God is there even when His presence is not manifest in the way we would prefer.

All of Moses' life, he was being providentially directed toward becoming the leader who would bring the Jewish people from Egypt to Sinai to receive the Torah. In order to accomplish this, he had to become a man of perfect faith. Therefore, God caused him to experience alienation and otherness at every turn, because this would engender that ultimate level of faith. Even to his last breath, Moses remained a stranger, not allowed to enter the land of Israel. Appropriately, one of the accolades God bestowed upon Moses (*Numbers* 12:7) is that *bechol beisi neeman hu* (בֵּיתִי נֶאֱמָן הוּא בְּכָל), "he is trusted in My entire house." The word *neeman* is derived from the root word *emunah*, faith. This was his salient quality

In this light, we can perhaps clarify a rather elliptical expression in the Sabbath liturgy. The central portion of the morning prayer begins, "Moses rejoiced in the gift of his portion for You considered him a trustworthy servant." His portion is the Sabbath, and the prayer connects his delight with the Sabbath to his being a faithful servant (*eved neeman*). How are these two connected?

A basic concept concerning the Sabbath is that it attests to God's general providence (*hashgachah klalis*) as it was revealed in creation and the Exodus. We must have faith in God's providence, which is guiding history towards its destiny when mankind will realize the potential for harmony underlying creation. The

Sabbath, which our Sages consider a taste of the next world, gives us the opportunity to encounter the hidden harmony and providence that surrounds us. Moses, the ultimate stranger, was more keenly aware of this harmony and providence than anyone else who ever lived. It earned him the honor of being called God's faithful servant and the privilege of rejoicing in his Sabbath portion.

פרשת יתרו
Parashas Yisro

i. *Jethro Heard Everything*

HAT EVENT IS MORE CENTRAL TO JEWISH HISTORY THAN the stand at Mount Sinai when the people heard God pronounce the Ten Commandments? None, of course. Isn't it incongruous then that the *parashah* that describes these transcendent events should be named after Moses' father-in-law, Jethro, a non-Jew albeit an eventual convert?

The *parashah* begins as Jethro comes with Moses' wife and children to join the Jewish people in the desert after the Exodus. Why did he come? The Torah reveals his motivation (18:1), "And Jethro, the priest of Midian, father-in-law of Moses, heard everything (*kol*) God had done for Moses and His people Israel."

Let us consider the word "everything." Isn't it superfluous? Why is it important for us to know that Jethro hear everything? Suffice it to say that he heard.

In psychology, the response to another's good fortune varies widely. At one extreme, there are people so desperately dissatisfied with their lot that they feel jealous and resentful when they hear good news about a friend or relative; they cannot bear that someone else enjoyed the good fortune they crave for themselves. On the other extreme, psychologically healthy people are happy when their friends and relatives enjoy good fortune, even if they do not share it themselves. Nonetheless, even a healthy personality may feel twinges of jealousy when the sheer volume of good fortune befalling another is overwhelming. He may say he is busy and has to break off the conversation, but resentment lurks underneath.

Notwithstanding these human tendencies, the Torah teaches us that Jethro was able to hear "everything" God did for the Jewish people without any ill feeling toward their fortune (see also 18:8). The more he heard the more he sought to know. This reflects the great virtue of his character. Appropriately, the initial portion of the narrative of Jethro's reunion with Moses concludes, "And Jethro rejoiced over all (*kol*) the good that God had done for Israel (18:9)."

Although the Ten Commandments represent a special covenant between God and the Jewish people, they also represent an unparalleled blessing for all mankind, a moral beacon that illuminates all civilization. It is God's ultimate will that through the Jewish people their teachings will radiate to all humanity. This is the message of the name of the *parashah*. If non-Jews want to tap into the benefit of Torah, they have to embrace without reservation the good of the Jewish nation.

Just as Jethro did.

ii. A Bit of Persuasion

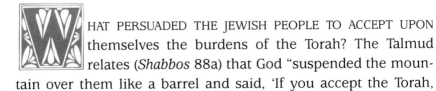 HAT PERSUADED THE JEWISH PEOPLE TO ACCEPT UPON themselves the burdens of the Torah? The Talmud relates (*Shabbos* 88a) that God "suspended the mountain over them like a barrel and said, 'If you accept the Torah,

good, but if not, your graves will be there!' " The Talmud finds an allusion to this bit of persuasion in the verse (19:17), "And the people stood below the mountain." They were not merely at the foot of the mountain but literally beneath it.

Superficially, the Talmud seems to be saying that had the Jewish people not accepted the Torah God would have dropped the mountain and buried them right on the spot. A closer reading, however, reveals a slight problem with the language. According to the Talmud, God told them that if they did not accept the Torah, "your graves will be there." Had He dropped the mountain on them, their graves would have been "here," where they stood.

As a practical manner, the people would not have been able to survive in the desert without God's special protection. And even if they somehow reached habitable land and established themselves "there," they would eventually perish as a nation, as even the great Greek and Roman empires were eventually buried by history. This was, in fact, an element of coercion the Jewish people faced in choosing to accept the Torah.

Without Torah, there would be no national eternity (*nitzchius*). But with Torah, nothing would stand in their way. According to the Midrash, just as God had uprooted a mountain, the epitome of an immovable object, He would sweep away all impediments to their national survival until the end of history. By specifying that they would be interred "there," the Midrash suggests that the coercion of the dangling mountain was not so strong that it completely took away their free will. It was rather an act of persuasion, reminding them that if they rejected the Torah in the desert they forfeited their chance to be an eternal people.

iii. An Unforgivable Sin

MONG ALL THE TEN COMMANDMENTS, THE TORAH SIN-
gles out taking God's Name in vain as unforgivable
(20:7). "You shall not take the Name of God your Lord
in vain, for God will not cleanse those who take His Name in
vain." Why is this sin so unforgivably heinous? Why does the
Torah here employ the unusual language of "uncleansable"?

The Maharal divided the Ten Commandments into two parallel sets of five that are interrelated on each level. The prohibition
against taking God's Name in vain is the third of the first set of
five. Its counterpart, the third of the second set of five, is the prohibition against kidnaping. It would seem that their commonality is exploitation. The kidnaper subjugates and exploits another
person for his own benefit. With regard to the intangible living
God, only His Name is within reach, and the one who takes it in
vain is, so to speak, exploiting Him.

When a person makes a false oath, he uses God's Name to
lend credence to his own deceit. In so doing, he construes God as
existing to serve his needs; he binds God's Name to a falsehood,
an affront to God's will for truth. He considers himself the center
of all things to the extent that he sees even God as an object to
serve his needs.

In a certain way, the prohibition against taking God's Name in
vain is more serious than the first two Commandments, which call
for monotheistic belief. Frequently, the transgression of these commandments reflect an intellectual error, which can be corrected.
Taking God's Name in vain, however, reflects an abiding corruption
that has seeped into the sinner's personality and very soul. He is so
egocentric that he believes everything outside of himself exists
only to serve him, including God. Such a corruption is not only
unforgivable, it is uncorrectable. No soap can cleanse him.

iv. Ordinary Stones

BEFORE REVEALING HIMSELF ON MOUNT SINAI, GOD TOLD Moses to warn the Jewish people (19:12-13), "You shall set boundaries for the people around [Mount Sinai], saying, 'Beware of going up onto the mountain or touching its edge.' … after the long extended blast of the shofar, they may go up onto the mountain."

Why does the Torah point out that God allowed them to go up on the mountain after the revelation was over? At first glance, it seems the Torah is informing us that the revelation of the Divine Presence did not imbue the mountain with an eternal holiness that proscribed anyone other than Moses from ever setting foot on it. Even if one would consider that a reasonable alternative, we may still wonder why we need to know if the mountain's holiness was temporary or permanent. Upon reflection, however, another insight emerges.

The words *yaalu vahar* are ordinarily translated as "they may go up onto the mountain." A more common and accurate translation of this grammatical form would be "they shall go up onto the mountain." It is a commandment, not just permission. Why would it be required to "go up onto the mountain"?

During the revelation, the mountain was not docile and passive. On the contrary (19:18), "The entire Mount Sinai was smoking, because God had descended upon it in the fire; the smoke ascended like the smoke of the furnace, and the entire mountain shuddered exceedingly."

As the people gazed awestruck at the trembling, smoking mountain, it might have occurred to some of them that the mountain itself was somehow miraculous; it too had powers. In order to dispel this erroneous belief, God instructed the people to go onto the mountain after the revelation and examine it carefully. They would find only ordinary dirt and ordinary stones. The source of all they had experienced was the metaphysical Source of all existence, God who had revealed Himself to them.

v. *Four Intermediate Commandments*

BETWEEN THE REVELATION ON MOUNT SINAI AND THE exposition of the vast corpus of halachah that begins in *Parashas Mishpatim*, the Torah introduces four commandments. What is so significant about these laws that they needed to be presented right away?

Briefly summarized, the commandments are as follows:

• the prohibition against using idols in the worship of God;

• the obligation to make an earthen or stone altar for the sacrifices;

• the prohibition against using hewn stones for the altar;

• the prohibition against having stairs leading up to the altar.

The Midrash relates that after the Jewish people heard the first two commandments directly from God at Mount Sinai the experience was so powerful and overwhelming that their souls separated from their bodies; they survived only because the angels reconnected them. Realizing they could not tolerate the ecstatic experience of prophecy that Moses experienced daily, the people asked him to serve as their intermediary for the rest of the Commandments.

Yet the memory of that exquisite experience lingered. There was a danger that people might attempt to recapture some of its supernal rapture by making tangible icons through which to cling to the living God. Thus, the first prohibition after the Ten Commandments proscribed icons.

But if it was forbidden to bring God into the physical world, so to speak, how could mankind connect with Him? It can be accomplished by elevating the physical world, oneself included, toward God by offering sacrifices on an earthen altar, earth (*adamah*) being cognate with man (*adam*). This is the second of the four intermediate commandments.

Even as the mundane is sanctified toward the holy, danger remains. Man is a composite creature of animalistic instinctual drives of the body and spiritual imperatives of the soul. This dichotomy gives him free will. The most basic of the animal drives are aggression and lust. The last two commandments place restraints on these two drives. One may not use metal implements, the instruments of aggressive destruction, to build the altar. Furthermore, man must ascend the altar on a ramp, which allows him to remain perfectly modest, rather then on stairs, which cause him to extend his legs and cause his garment to ride up immodestly. Here we find a limitation of man's other base drive, his lust. Together, these two laws convey the concept that in elevating the world we must not let our earthly passions interweave themselves and distort our divine service.

The pressing need for these laws became manifest a mere forty days later when the Jews made the *Eigel*, the Golden Calf, to serve as a physical representation of God. They succumbed to the widespread desire to relate to God in a tangible way, a desire manifested by all idol worship. Apparently, they had mistakenly related to Moses himself as a physical vehicle to gain access to God, a sort of representative of God. Once Moses was gone, they demanded a replacement. According to the Talmud (*Shabbos* 87a), God commended Moses for breaking the first set of Tablets when he saw the Golden Calf. He understood that the divinely crafted Tablets could have been corrupted into another icon of the Almighty. The Torah's clairvoyant admonition against sword and steps is borne out; the frenzy that led to the Golden Calf resulted in aggressive violence, threatening Aaron's life and causing the death of his nephew Chur, while the celebration expressed itself in lewdness and license. Unfortunately, despite the warning of the intermediate commandments, the people sinned with the Golden Calf.

The first of the four intermediate commandments prohibiting icons is addressed to the second person plural, the other three commandments to the second person singular. Why this discrepancy in syntax?

People had different emotional responses to what they "saw" at Sinai. Similarly, different emotions draw different people toward idolatry. The use of the second person plural indicates a lack of unified purpose among those who seek icons. In the commands concerning the proper construction of the altar, however, the Torah uses the second person singular to indicate that all the people should unite to build the altar with a single shared purpose and dedication.

vi. *Seventy-Two Verses*

HIS *PARASHAH*, WHICH DESCRIBES GOD'S REVELATION AT Sinai, has seventy-two verses. Traditionally, the ultimate ineffable Name of God is composed of seventy-two letters; according to one opinion, the Kohen Gadol uttered this Name on Yom Kippur. Perhaps the entire *parashah* can be seen as an expanded revelation of God's Name, the seventy-two verses representing the seventy-two letters.

פרשת משפטים
Parashas Mishpatim

i. Judicious Juxtaposition

ERSES OFTEN APPEAR NEXT TO EACH OTHER IN THE TORAH in almost bizarre juxtaposition; the stranger the juxta-position the greater the pleasure and reward when we decipher the Torah's hidden meaning. In these instances, the Torah's very obscurity is often part of the message itself.

The Torah outlines three prohibitions in consecutive order (21:15-17), "Whoever strikes his father or mother shall surely be put to death. Whoever kidnaps a man and sells him, and he was found to have been in his possession, shall surely be put to death. Whoever curses his father or mother shall surely be put to death."

One would have expected that the prohibitions against hit-ting a parent and against cursing a parent would appear right next to each other. Yet the Torah interposes between them the prohibition against kidnaping. This startling arrangement of verses demands an explanation. Why?

The essential evil in kidnaping is that the offender has the arrogance, self-importance and self-absorption to take possession of another human and exploit him; from the perspective of the kidnaper, no one exists other than himself. If he then sells his captive like a mere piece of chattel, his corruption is complete, and he deserves the death penalty.

Let us now consider the prohibitions against striking and cursing parents. It is a rare child who will be inclined to do so. Parents naturally love their children and provide for them, generating a natural reciprocal love. There are, however, unfortunate exceptions.

Occasionally, parents use their children to satisfy their own ambitions or resolve their own inner conflicts; they live vicariously through their children. A parent may push his son to excel in academic subjects or sports in which he himself was deficient. Or else, a parent may feel that a certain personality flaw has always held him back in life, and he tries to eradicate that flaw from his child, even though the child shows no signs of having it or being bothered by it. In essence, the parent who presses a child in these matters is using him to satisfy his own psychological needs.

In such cases, the child, although wanting to love his parent, feels trapped and used; he feels kidnaped. It is no wonder that if he becomes so rebellious and angry toward his parents he might even go so far as to strike or curse them.

The placement of the prohibition against kidnaping between the prohibitions against striking and cursing parents is yet another example of God's infinite pedagogical wisdom. The strange juxtaposition calls out for investigation and explanation. This reinforces the concept that we must examine ourselves fully and honestly to see to what degree, however small, kidnaping may lie within our own child-rearing practices.

Let us consider three more consecutive verses that occur further along in the *parashah* (23:3-5). "Do not favor an unfortunate person in his litigation. When you happen across your enemy's stray ox or donkey, you shall surely return it to him. When you see your enemy's donkey squatting under his burden, would you refrain from helping him? You shall surely help him!"

At first glance, the prohibition against misplaced compassion in a court of law seems weakly connected to the next commandment that calls for helping an enemy. The Torah encourages us to make a connection by placing these two commandments together without any break. Upon deeper reflection, we find their connection in the conflict between emotions and justice. Although our hearts rightfully go out to the unfortunate, we may not subvert justice in his favor. Conversely, although we may hate our enemy, we may not allow him to suffer an avoidable loss through our inaction. This, too, is injustice.

The third prohibition would appear to be an extension of the second; help your enemy not only by returning his lost animal but also by lending a shoulder when he is struggling with a heavy load. Oddly, the Torah here separates these two prohibitions by a *stumah*, a mandatory gap of at least several spaces, the Torah's equivalent of a paragraph break; the *stumah* encourages us to discover how these two seemingly similar laws are actually more different from each other than we might first imagine. What is the distinction between returning an enemy's lost animal and helping him balance a heavy load?

The difference lies in the degree of the loss. In the first case, the enemy stands to suffer the loss of his stray animal, and understandably, justice demands that if we are in a position to prevent the loss we should do so. In the second case, the enemy will suffer no loss even if he receives no assistance. Helping him alleviates his stress and weariness is an act that goes beyond justice all the way to friendship. This law directs us to change our relationship with him, to go beyond basic justice.

In the third verse, the Torah chooses the unusual words *azov taazov imo* to express "you shall surely help him." These words ordinarily mean to abandon rather than to help. *Targum Onkelos* weaves a very illuminating comment into his translation. "Abandon the grudge you bear against him in your heart," he writes, "and help him unload his animal." The Torah is calling for more than justice. It is calling for the necessary underpinnings of a cohesive just society. It is calling for friendship.

Another interesting juxtaposition occurs with the following two verses (22:27-28), "Do not curse a judge nor malign a prince amongst your people. Do not be late with your first fruit and priestly tithes; give Me your firstborn sons." The verses seem unrelated. How are cursing a leader and donations to the Kohen connected? Furthermore, the Torah doesn't even place a *stumah* gap between the verses, suggesting a rather close connection.

Let us consider. Why would someone curse a judge or a prince? More often than not, it is because they are insecure in themselves and resentful of people in positions of power and privilege. Because of their own low self-esteem, they resent others whose status they covet. The Torah commands that one should not react to these feelings with verbal aggression; one should rather try to correct them as they arise.

Failure to deliver Temple donations and tithes may reflect mere indifference or indolence. But it may also reflect a deeper resentment against the Kohen, the privileged recipient of the donations and tithes. In this case, the resentment is expressed by inaction. In modern psychology, this is called passive aggression.

By its juxtaposition to the prohibition against cursing a prince, the Torah is signaling that this delay may be related to that prohibition, a kindred expression of resentment of another's position. By doing so, the Torah not only forbids the aggression, it also encourages the violator to ferret out and correct the true feelings that may lead him to delay his tithe.

ii. Taunting as a Capital Offense

AUNTING IS ALWAYS FORBIDDEN, BUT IF THE VICTIM IS A widow or an orphan, it can have terrible consequences (22:21-3). "Do not taunt any widow or orphan. If you will indeed taunt him, then should he cry out to Me, I will surely hear his cry. And My anger will flare, and I will kill you by the sword; your wives will be widows, your children orphans."

There are some intriguing textual and grammatical anomalies in the verse. In the Torah, the order of their mention is ordinarily "orphans and widows," yet here it is "widows and orphans." Also, when speaking about "orphans and widows" or "orphans or widows," the Torah ordinarily refers to "them" in the third person plural. Here, the verse concludes, "if you will indeed taunt him, then should he cry out to Me," referring to "him," the third person singular. Even more puzzling, when speaking about the retribution, "I will kill you by the sword," the Torah uses the plural form of the pronoun even though it has spoken until now to a lone tormentor. Finally, we cannot help but wonder why taunting, albeit an unpleasant act, elicits such harsh consequences.

It may be that the Torah reverses the regular order and mentions the orphan second in order to show that the focus of the severe retribution of the next verse is more related to the case of the orphan than the widow. Although the pain and suffering which taunts inflict on a widow are great, they do not compare to the irreparable harm they inflict on an orphan. Modern psychology finds, not unexpectedly, that the basic structure of our personalities, emotional predispositions and our attitudes to our surroundings are determined in childhood. It follows that the taunt inflicted on an orphan is singularly injurious.

By permanently skewing the orphan's perceptions and causing him to become wary and suspicious, the tormentor impedes the ability of the orphan to form a meaningful and trusting relationship with God. In essence, then, he is depriving the orphan of this most important aspect of life, and the Torah predicts that the tormentor will pay for this heinous crime with his own life. Although this may hold true with a widow to a lesser extent, the Torah juxtaposes the consequences to the orphan and expresses them in the singular, to emphasize that the more severe damage and hence the harsher divine consequences are with the orphan.

Although the Torah uses the singular in referring to the tormentor of the orphan, the Torah returns to the plural in the description of the punishment. This is a common grammatical device employed by the Torah to indicate that the community bears collective responsibility for certain types of egregious crimes committed by and against individuals, that silence and inaction in the presence of injustice and cruelty are also crimes. This is particularly true with crimes committed against the widow and the orphan, people whom we know to be particularly vulnerable and defenseless, and whose welfare we must proactively ensure.

iii. *The Fourth Festival*

HE TORAH OBLIGES US TO CELEBRATE THREE FESTIVALS each year (23:14) in commemoration of historical events during the Exodus and its aftermath. Passover commemorates the Exodus itself, Shavuos the giving of the Torah and Succos the providential existence in the desert. These occasions are celebrated with feasting and joy, and labor is forbidden.

Is there a possibility for a fourth?

Megillas Esther records (9:22) that Mordechai sought to designate the days of Purim as "days of feasting, joy and festivity." The Talmud states (*Megillah* 5b) that the Jewish people accepted the requirements of feasting and joy but they did not accept the obligation to treat the day celebrating their salvation as a festival (*yom tov*).

Was there a deeper significance to Mordechai's request?

Mordechai had wanted to establish Purim as an added festival commemorating the historical events that had just taken place in Shushan. Why did he think he could institute a new festival with the stature of a Passover or a Succos?

In *Netzach Yisrael*, the Maharal states that the prohibition against forbidden labors on the festivals, allowing only those necessary for the celebration of the day, foreshadows and mirrors the Messianic era. At that time, the awareness and knowledge of God will be so great and clear that people will not engage in activities extraneous to furthering their relationship with God.

In light of this thought, perhaps we can understand Mordechai's rationale in proposing that Purim be instituted as a fourth festival. Purim represented the defeat of Amalek, the implacable enemy of God and the Jewish people. Furthermore, the nation had become reinvigorated in their commitment to keep the Torah (*kiyemu vekiblu*). It is possible that Mordechai expected that the deliverance of the Jewish people would now lead speedily to the completed building of the Second Temple, whose construction had been abruptly halted several years earlier. Most importantly, it would signal the advent of the Messiah. As a harbinger of the Messianic era (*ikvesa d'Meshicha*), Purim would join the other festivals as days on which forbidden labors are proscribed, days restricted to festivity and joy, days that celebrate the pivotal historic moments of God's providence for the Jewish people.

For whatever reason, Mordechai's request was not agreed to. The *Havdalah* ritual, which distinguishes the Sabbath from the weekday, the holy from the mundane, retains a vestige of Mordechai's vision: It features a quote from Megillas Esther as part of its liturgy. "For the Jews there was light and joy, gladness and glory," and we add, "so should there be for us." In this statement, we express our hope and expectation that the complete redemption Mordechai envisioned awaits us as we return to the toils of our workweek.

פרשת תרומה
Parashas Terumah

i. *Testimony to Truth*

HE TABLETS UPON WHICH THE TEN COMMANDMENTS were engraved were placed in the *Aron Kodesh*, the Holy Ark (25:16). "And you shall put testimonies I give you into the Ark." In what way are the Ten Commandments considered testimonies?

As understood by many of the great medieval rabbis, the revelation at Sinai, as it was before an entire nation of some three million people, serves as proof of the Torah's veracity. The following quick and necessarily superficial exposition of this proof is based on the *Kuzari* and as further elaborated by Rabbi Israel Chait.

All knowledge falls into two categories, firsthand information, which is observed or deduced directly, and secondhand information, which is received from others in oral, written or any other form. Although firsthand information is the most credible, our lives depend to a great degree on secondhand information that we cannot verify from our own experience. For example, if we go to a doctor, how do we know he attended medical school? And how do we know that what he was taught there is accurate? If we board an aircraft, how do we know the pilot is qualified to fly it? We must rely on secondhand knowledge at every turn, but how do we know it is reliable? How can we believe anything we read in a history book, a textbook or a newspaper? The answer is that we can know by logical deduction. Something is either true or false. If we can determine that it cannot be false, we know it is true.

Secondhand information may be false for only one of two reasons. Either there has been a deliberate lie, or there has been a mistake. If we know that neither of these two factors could be present, we can correctly deduce that the information is true. The events at Sinai were unmistakably miraculous; there was no possibility of error. Furthermore, it occurred before millions of people; it would have been impossible to get them all to share a lie. Since it was impossible to create the record of such an event through error or deceit, the Torah must be true. Was it possible that the Torah was introduced at a later time? It could not happen; the people would never have accepted as true a document containing onerous obligations and describing a critically important event in their own history of which no one had ever heard or spoken.

Let us now focus on the Ten Commandments? Why were they even necessary? The halachah makes no differentiation among the 613 commandments of the Torah. In fact, the Rambam contends that the congregation should not stand up for the reading of the Ten Commandments to avoid any implication of preference.

Rav Hai Gaon and the Maharal, among others, addressed this question by giving a universal significance to the Ten Commandments. According to Rav Hai Gaon, they encapsulate the general principles of all the Torah; any of the other 603 commandments can be traced to a concept they represent. According to the Maharal, the Ten Commandments represent successive layers or levels of infractions, the first five against God, the last five against people.

According to both opinions, we can understand how the Ten Commandments are a testimony to the entire Torah. The revelation at Sinai served as proof of the Torah's veracity for all generations. Since every new commandment Moses would introduce related in some way to the Ten Commandments that everyone had already heard, they would be accepted as the truth.

The "proof of Sinai" supports the conviction that the Torah is true through rational proofs or at least persuasive evidence. Judaism does not demand that we accept the truth of the Torah on faith alone. It would seem that any true religion of God would have to include some rational proof of its veracity. Otherwise, how could a just God hold anyone responsible for that which they cannot know.

It follows that a seeker of truth can determine that the only logical place to investigate is Judaism. Presuming someone has concluded there is a God for whatever reason — cosmological, teleological, ontological, the big bang or several others — he will limit his investigation to those religions which profess the existence of the one God and claim to be demonstrably true. Christianity and Islam, the other two major religions of monotheism, do not claim they can prove Jesus or Mohammed received an instruction from God. When it comes right down to it, they claim it must be accepted on faith. Since these religions do not make claim to be demonstrably true, they must be false. They are in contradiction. They maintain that a just God holds people responsible to believe that which cannot be known. This last logical wrinkle does not prove the truth of Judaism, but it establishes it as the only place for an earnest monotheist to seek the true way to worship God.

פרשת תצוה

Parashas Tetzaveh

i. Bells on the Way Out

AMONG THE EIGHT GARMENTS THE KOHEN GADOL (HIGH Priest) wore throughout the year was a turquoise robe called a *me'il*. This garment had a very elaborate hem (28:33-35). "You shall make on its hem pomegranates and gold bells between them, all around them, a gold bell and a pomegranate on the hem of the robe all around. It must be on Aaron in order to minister. Its sounds shall be heard when he enters the sanctuary before God and when he leaves so that he shall not die."

One phrase in the last verse calls for our attention. The bells announced the arrival of the Kohen Gadol in the Holy of Holies, and we may understand that if the bells are missing when he enters, he deserves to die. But why should he die if the bells are missing and he makes no sound "when he leaves"? He has already completed his service, and he is leaving. Why is it so critical that he should be heard?

Let us reflect. Why was the Kohen Gadol required to announce his arrival in the Holy of Holies with the sound of the bells on his hem? Obviously, the purpose wasn't to let God know he was coming. Rather, we must say it was for the benefit of the Kohen Gadol, to impress upon him that his presence was known before God. While he was inside the Inner Sanctum, the constant noise generated by his garment reminded him that he was before God.

In this light, we can understand why it was important that he also wear the bells as he was leaving. People have a way of deluding themselves that they can step before God and step away from Him. But it is no more than a delusion. In actuality, the entire Universe is filled with His glory (מְלֹא כָל הָאָרֶץ כְּבוֹדוֹ); and there is nothing besides Him (אֵין עוֹד מִלְבַדּוֹ). The sound of the bells as he walked out reinforced this concept; it reminded the Kohen Gadol that a person never departs God's awareness or presence. The Kohen Gadol's activities represented the idealized divine service, and it was a capital offense in this instance for him to act as if it were possible to leave God's presence.

ii. *The Missing Conduit*

NTIL THE DESTRUCTION OF THE FIRST TEMPLE, THE JEWISH people had a hotline to God. Called the *Urim VeTumim*, it was God's written ineffable Name placed in the Kohen Gadol's bejeweled breastplate. When specific questions were posed to the Kohen Gadol, the *Urim VeTumim* illuminated a succession of letters on the breastplate, delivering the answers directly in a prophetic communication from God.

The Talmud relates (*Yoma* 21b) that there were no *Urim VeTumim* during the Second Temple era. In view of the law of *mechusar begadim*, the disqualification of a Kohen not wearing any part of his priestly attire, the Tosaphists conclude that the Kohen Gadol wore the physical *Urim VeTumim* in the Second Temple as well. They were only missing in the sense that they no longer functioned as a conduit of prophecy. The Rambam, however, contends that the *Urim VeTumim* were indeed missing. Nonetheless, this did not disqualify the Kohen Gadol from service as a *mechusar begadim*.

The crux of this dispute is the status of the *Urim VeTumim*. The Tosaphists consider them part of the priestly attire, which would render the Kohen Gadol a *mechusar begadim* if they were missing. The Rambam, however, considers them an independent instrument; the priestly attire is complete without them.

In Leviticus, when Moses dresses Aaron to inaugurate him into the priestly service, he places the *Urim VeTumim* into the breastplate. Here, however, where the garments of the Kohen Gadol are described, there is no mention of the *Urim VeTumim*. We find here support for the Rambam's view that the *Urim VeTumim* were not part of the Kohen Gadol's attire. They let him communicate with God, but did not invest him in his sacred office.

iii. *Covered Nakedness*

THE KOHEN WORE FOUR PRIESTLY GARMENTS WHEN HE performed the Temple service — shirt, trousers, hat and sash. The Talmud specifies (*Yoma* 23b; *Rashi*) the order of donning the garments, with the trousers going on first. The Talmud derives this rule from a verse in Leviticus (16:4) describing the Kohen Gadol's service on Yom Kippur.

Curiously, here in Exodus where the garments are first introduced (28:40ff), the trousers are not initially mentioned. Moreover, we learn shortly afterward (29:6) that Moses was to inaugurate Aaron and his sons into their priestly service with the hat, shirt and sash — but there is no mention of the trousers. If we can surmise that the trousers are of lesser importance, why did they take precedence in the process of donning the priestly garments?

The Torah declares that the purpose of the Kohen's trousers was to cover his nakedness. The requirement for this covering metaphorically expresses the thought that the animalistic aspect of man must be fully covered and subordinated to the higher element of man, his intelligence in the divine image. Unlike the other garments, the trousers do not express the positive goal of the Kohen's service of God and hence were not mentioned as part of the inauguration. Rather they represent the base at which the Kohen starts. Consequently, the Torah mentions them only after the clothes that invest the priest with his high duties and devotion. Nonetheless, the trousers must be donned first, since there can be no ascension without first controlling the earthly passions.

פרשת כי תשא
Parashas Ki Sisa

i. *The Order of Repentance*

NE OF THE HIGH POINTS OF THE YOM KIPPUR SERVICE IN
the Temple was the Kohen Gadol's confession (*vidui*)
on behalf of the entire Jewish nation. His confession
acknowledged and expressed regret over inadvertent infractions
(*chet*), willful transgressions (*avon*) and rebellious sin (*pesha*).

There is a dispute recorded in the Talmud (*Yoma* 36b) as to the
order of the Kohen Gadol's confession. The Rabbis maintain (as is
our practice today in the Yom Kippur liturgy) that the Kohen
Gadol declared, "*Chatasi avisi pashati*, I have sinned inadvertently, willingly and rebelliously." Rabbi Meir states that the Kohen
Gadol said, "*Avisi pashati chatasi,* I sinned willingly, rebelliously
and inadvertently."

Rabbi Meir brings two sources that list the hierarchy of sins
in the order he advocates. In the description of the Yom Kippur
service in Leviticus (16:21), the Torah tells us, "Aaron shall ... confess upon [the goat] all the willful sins (*avonos*) of the children of

Israel and all their rebellious sins (*pisheihem*) according to their inadvertent sin (*chatasam*)." In the aftermath of the sin of the Golden Calf in Exodus (34:7), God conveys to Moses that He is a "*nosei avon va' pesha v'chataah*, a forgiver of willful, rebellious and inadvertent sins." In both cases, the order supports Rabbi Meir's position.

The Rabbis offer alternate interpretations of the inverted order in the verses quoted by Rabbi Meir, and they argue against his position on a basic point of logic. It does not seem reasonable, they contend, to confess and request forgiveness for a more severe sin and then afterwards to beseech God for expiation of a less severe one. It is more reasonable to plead for forgiveness in ascending order of severity. Their argument is powerful, and Rabbi Meir's position, for all its seeming proofs, is left seemingly incomprehensible. The great Rogatchover Gaon addresses this issue without finding a resolution.

Perhaps we can suggest that Rabbi Meir has a different perspective on the Kohen Gadol's confession. It may be understood as a demonstration of the process of repentance. When a person repents, he goes through successive stages of introspection. He must come to grips with himself as the author of his sin. This is not a simple matter. Human nature tends to deny or at least minimize responsibility for one's unpleasant deeds.

It is least difficult to come to grips with sins committed willingly when the sinner's desire overcame his reluctance to sin. Even at the time of sin, he was of two minds. Later, it is relatively easy to tap back into one's correct inclination when released from the clutches of the anticipated pleasure of the moment — and repent. It is more difficult to repent for rebellious sins that include an insubordinate rejection of God's supremacy. The good impulse, so to speak, had not been present in the struggle against sin.

Most difficult of all is repentance for inadvertent sins. This does not mean sins committed by total accident, for which a person is not responsible. Rather, it refers to sins resulting from neglect or heedlessness. Such neglect is an indication of a subconscious or unconscious indifference to the sin. It is easy to deny that an underlying indifference exists and conveniently shirk responsibility. Indeed, the inadvertent nature of the transgression itself reflects the sinner's desire to hide from himself his inclination toward the misdeed.

Accordingly, the dispute between the Rabbis and Rabbi Meir relates to the essential form of the Kohen Gadol's confession. The Rabbis maintain that its structure reflects its primary purpose — to effect forgiveness for the Jewish people collectively. It proceeded as would any individual seeking pardon, advancing toward increasing severity. According to Rabbi Meir, the form of the Kohen Gadol's confession demonstrates the methodology of repentance, authentic to the natural patterns of introspection and change. The penitent must delve into successively deeper levels of the heart.

Ensconced in the Kohen Gadol's confession, according to either opinion, is an important demonstration of the dual aspect of the Torah's laws. On a manifest level, they direct our correct normative behavior. On a deeper level, they recognize a person's actions and attitudes as the direct outgrowths of the deepest state of his mind, or state of his soul. In requiring confession and penitence for inadvertent sin, the Torah seeks to change not just our behavior but also the state of mind and being that gave rise to these "inadvertent" sins.

ii. *The Center of the Universe*

ORTY SHORT DAYS AFTER GOD REVEALED HIMSELF TO THE Jewish people on Mount Sinai and gave them the Ten Commandments, they made a Golden Calf. True, only some of the people were guilty of the actual deed, with the rest only guilty of silent acquiescence. True, the people were disoriented by the prolonged absence of Moses on the mountain. Still, their precipitous fall in such a short time shocks us.

Just a short while earlier, there is already a harbinger of this Jewish fickleness. With the spectacular images of the splitting of the sea still vivid in their memories, they walk through the waterless desert and ask (17:7), "Is God among us or not?"

We see in these events that people can experience God intimately and then quickly "lose sight" of Him. Such is the nature of the free will with which the Creator endows mankind. He creates an area where His presence is sufficiently "distant" or "hidden" to allow what our Sages refer to as the *milchemes hachaim*, the battle of life.

The ambivalence of God's perceived presence, alternating between proximity and transcendence, is singularly manifest in the first blessing of the daily *Shemoneh Esrei* prayer. "Blessed are You, O God, Lord of our forefathers, Lord of Abraham, Lord of Isaac, Lord of Jacob, the Power, the Great One, the Mighty One and the Awesome One, the Supreme Power who bestows true kindnesses as Possessor of everything, Who recalls the kindnesses of the patriarchs and brings a redeemer to their descendants for the sake of His Name with love. O King, Helper, Savior and Shield, blessed are You, God, the Shield of Abraham."

Let us look carefully at the progression. We begin with God's intimate relationship with us through our patriarchs. The next term, the Power, refers to God as the exalted power, followed by expressions of three logical categories that arise when considering any subject — the nature of the entity in itself, in this case, the Great One; His relationship to us, in this case the Mighty One, might being an expression of comparative power; and finally, our reaction to Him, in this case, the Awesome One.

Immediately afterwards, however, we refer to Him as the Supreme Power, stating in effect that our perception of Him is inadequate, that He is transcendent. But this is immediately balanced by the next statement, that He "bestows true kindnesses," a manifestation of His proximity. We then anticipate the misconception that His giving diminishes Him and declare that He is "the Possessor of everything," beyond needs and limitations. In other words, transcendent.

The blessing again returns to God's intimate relationship with us through His providence in history; He is with us from our beginnings with our patriarchs to our ultimate destination in the Messianic era. But this proximity is immediately tempered by the next words, "for the sake of His Name." He does it as a result of His own transcendent perfection. And then we swing right back to proximity by declaring that He does it "with love."

In its conclusion, the blessing identifies God as King, more accessible than the remote Power. The three measures are again identified, this time for the King. Helper delineates His essence, Savior his relationship with us and Shield our resulting state of being protected. Applied to God as King, these attributes express a more intimate relationship than those applied to God as Power.

This constant flux between proximity and transcendence, visibility and invisibility, is the dynamic which makes free will possible and gives meaning to our lives.

Scientists have observed that man is uniquely positioned in the universe. He can perceive and understand the microscopic world, estimated as 10^{-25} of his size. At the same time, he can relate to the cosmic realms of the universe, estimated at 10^{25} times his size. If he were only a factor of 10 smaller or larger, it is thought he would be unable to fathom the opposite extreme of the universe.

This positioning corresponds to the moral spiritual universe as well, where God's revelation is balanced between being distant and proximate, creating the optimal environment in which man can exercise his free will. Man has the freedom to oscillate between accepting the Torah and forty days later worshiping a Golden Calf.

The structure of the first blessing addresses another issue as well. Our Sages were wary of our forming false conceptions of God. The Rambam devotes much of his *Guide for the Perplexed*, his major philosophical treatise, to demonstrate that we can only gain true knowledge by stripping away false conceptions. We may say that in the first blessing, which we say as we stand before God, our Sages repeatedly and carefully jarred us from thinking we fully know Him.

iii. Let Us Count the Words

VERYTHING IN THE TORAH AND THE LITURGY IS SO PRECISE that even the number of words in a verse or prayer reveals hidden layers of meaning. Let us count the words in the first three blessings (all praises) of the *Shemoneh Esrei*, the nineteen-blessing mainstay of daily prayer otherwise known as the *Amidah*. The first blessing, called *Magen Avos* (Protector of the Forefathers), contains 39 words; the second, called *Mechayeh HaMeisim* (Reviver of the Dead), contains 49; the third, called *Atah Kadosh* (You Are Holy), contains 14.

Is there any significance to these word counts?

At first glance, we may sense concealed meaning in the numbers 39 and 49, which are associated with various Torah concepts, but the number 14 does not ring any Judaic bells. Upon closer scrutiny, however, a profound pattern emerges.

Let us begin with the third blessing. Although the number of words in the Hebrew version is 14, the translation into the more verbose English is considerably longer. "You are holy, Your Name is holy, and the holy praise You daily, *selah*. Blessed are You, O God, the holy powerful One."

The ninth Hebrew word in the blessing is *selah*, a word without a definitional meaning. It is rather a sound, like "aha," expressing an emotional state or feeling. Accordingly, there are only 13 bona-fide words in the blessing. Instead of the number 14, we now contemplate 13, a very significant Jewish number, whose deeper meaning lies in its being the *gematria*, the numerical value, of the word *echad*, one (*aleph* [1] + *ches* [8] + *dalet* [4] = 13).

In this *parashah*, we encounter the 13 divine attributes (*shalosh esrei middos*) God reveals to Moses as a means of effecting reconciliation between Him and the people. Spread over two verses, they begin (34:6), "O God, O God, powerful, merciful, compassionate, slow to anger, abundant in kindness and truth." It continues (34:7), "Preserving kindness for thousands, forgiving sin, transgression and guilt, He absolves ..."

There are eight attributes in the first verse and five in the second. The first set is more abstract, while the second reveals aspects of His nature directly related to His creatures, such as forgiving the sinful. This subdivision into two sets is paralleled in the *Atah Kadosh* blessing, which is also subdivided into sets of eight and then five words separated by the intervening particle *selah*. Thus, this blessing, in which man comes closest to praising God's essence, is comprised of 13 words structured and patterned after the 13 divine attributes enumerated in the Torah. The count of 13 emphasizes God's oneness — the 13 attributes of the one God, the 13 words of transcendent praise.

We find other examples where 13 appears as an elliptical reflection of God's oneness. Rabbi Yishmael's 13 Rules of Biblical Exegesis are the means of discovering God's further revelation and His oneness. The central part of the *Shemoneh Esrei* contains

13 blessings of supplication (*bakashos*); we pray for those things which aid us in the goal of our existence — to reveal God's oneness. There are also the 13 tribes of the Jewish people, whose aim is to reveal God's oneness. (In both cases, the thirteenth element was subsequently added and is somewhat veiled; the prayer is called the Eighteen Blessings, and we commonly refer to the twelve tribes of Israel. The idea of a mystical thirteenth element is already suggested in *echad*, whose first letter, *aleph*, is silent with a numerical value of one.)

With 13 identified as an expression of oneness, let us reexamine the first blessing of the *Shemoneh Esrei*, comprised of 39 words. If we consider it closely, we see it subdivided into three sets of 13 words each. The first set addresses God's relationship to the *Avos*, our forefathers, in the past.

The second set addresses God's continual present guidance; the verbs in this set are in the present tense — *gomel* (bestows), *koneh* (acquires), *zocher* (remembers).

The final set of 13 begins with "He brings a redeemer to [the Jewish people]"; it expresses confidence in God's future providence. Past, present and future are, of course, only distinct from each other in human perception, which is linear within the confines of time. To God, who is beyond and above time, past, present and future are one. The expression of God's continuous providence included in a threefold 13-word prayer reinforces the fundamental truth that God's providence through history reflects His oneness.

The numerical significance of the 49 words in the second blessing, *Mechayeh HaMeisim* (Reviver of the Dead), is more readily apparent. According to different customs and at different times of the year, additional words are inserted, but the core number of words is 49. The Jubilee year (*Yovel*) occurs after seven cycles of seven years, or a total of 49 years. At that time, all land lies fallow and returns to its original owner, and Jewish slaves gain their freedom. The Maharal sees the reversion of property and the emancipation of slaves in the Jubilee year as a metaphor for the resurrection of the dead, which will reunite bodies and souls. This provides the connection to the 49 words of the blessing, whose theme is revival of the dead.

The assigning of significance to the number of words in the respective blessings raises a question. Would the Sages who formulated these blessings have sacrificed even the smallest amount of content for an elegant numerological pattern?

Furthermore, the Talmud relates that the text of the *Shemoneh Esrei* was formulated by the Anshei Knesses HaGedolah, the Men of the Great Assembly, which had one hundred and twenty members, including many prophets, such as Ezra, Daniel and others. If the Talmud mentions the presence of prophets, it suggests there was an element of prophecy in the formulation of the prayers. If so, why did the entire Assembly have to deliberate? Why didn't they just follow what the prophets told them? The maxim "that the Torah is not in heaven" applies to matters of law, which people must determine for themselves, but this would not preclude prophetic guidance in coining the prayers with perfect precision.

Perhaps we can suggest that prophecy was only available to them for the formulation of the first three blessings, which are exclusively in praise of God. For people even to attempt to utter God's praise is presumptuous; as King David states (*Psalms* 106:2), "Who can articulate God's might, make all His praise heard." Prayer is a divine dispensation. Here, in the first three blessings that enunciate God's praise, prophetic inspiration was necessary. The central set of 13 supplication blessings may, then, have been entrusted to the Sages for formulation without the benefit of prophetic guidance. Man, who partners with God in effecting His kingship on earth, must formulate his requests specifically in these blessings. By a count of 13 — which is the numerical value of the word (אֶחָד) *one* — our Sages fixed the prayers whose ultimate goal is to make God's oneness manifest so that He and His Name will be one.

Perhaps we can also surmise that the thirteenth blessing (and nineteenth overall), which was composed centuries later and inserted into the central section of *Shemoneh Esrei*, was placed in ninth position with an eye to the numerological significance. Thus, the blessings were subdivided into eight and then five, reminiscent of the subdivisions in the divine attributes and the third praise blessing, *Atah Kadosh*.

Having established that the number 39 reflects God's oneness as reflected in His providence through history — past, present, and future — other Torah concepts that feature the number 39 may be more deeply understood.

There are 39 categories of forbidden labor (*melachah*) on the Sabbath. The Talmud derives them from the creative activities used in the *Mishkan* (Tabernacle) in the desert. Rabbeinu Bachya among others states that these creative activities mirror the very activities God used, so to speak, to create the universe. Creation brings time, history and the realm of providence into existence. Thus, the perfect unity of God that permeates history, as reflected by the number 39, is also expressed in the 39 activities of creation.

The number 39 also occurs in a somewhat odd fashion with regard to the punishment of lashes administered by the courts. The Torah seems to set the maximum number at 40 (*Deuteronomy* 25:3), but the Sages of the Talmud determine (*Makkos* 22b) that it is really 39. Why did the Torah mention the number 40, we may ask, if God wanted only 39?

The number 40 is frequently associated with regeneration. For example, 40 days after its inception a fetus is considered a life; human gestation lasts 40 weeks; the Flood lasted 40 days; the Jewish people spent 40 years in the desert; a kosher *mikveh* must have a minimum of 40 *se'ah* measures of water. All of these instances have a regenerative aspect to them. Here, too, it would seem that 40 lashes are necessary to regenerate and rehabilitate the sinner so that he is no longer wicked before God. Why then is the actual maximum number of lashes reduced to 39?

Penalties in Jewish jurisprudence are primarily for rehabilitation of the sinner rather than for retribution, vengeance and deterrence. If the sinner harbors ill feeling against the judges, the purpose of the punishment would be compromised. The administration of 39 lashes invokes the concept of divine providence through history. It reminds both the judges and the condemned that the courts are God's agents. The merciful reduction to 39 lashes minimizes the resentment of the punished and facilitates his rehabilitation. In God's infinite wisdom, He expresses the duality of the court's role as His agents and the sinner's rehabilitation by a simultaneous expression of 39 and 40.

iv. *A Time to Smash*

HEN MOSES WAS STILL ON MOUNT SINAI, GOD INFORMED him that the Jewish people were worshiping the Golden Calf. Moses hurried down from the mountain (32:19), "And when he neared the camp and saw the calf and the dancing, Moses became angry and he cast the Tablets from his hands." Our Sages find an allusion later in the Torah commending Moses for smashing the Tablets of the Ten Commandments. Although God had not instructed him to do so, he did the right thing.

The question arises, if God had already informed Moses of the idolatry, why did Moses wait until he arrived at the camp before smashing the Tablets? His anger should have flared right there on the mountain, and he should have smashed the Tablets immediately.

A careful examination of the verse draws our attention to the word "dancing." God had told Moses only about the idolatry, not about the dancing. Apparently, Moses did not feel compelled to smash the Tablets on the basis of their idolatry alone. However, once he saw them dancing around the idol, he realized he had no choice but to smash them. What was the significance of the dancing?

According to most commentators, the sin of the Golden Calf lay in the people seeking a tangible artifact by which to relate to the true God. People find it difficult to conduct a relationship with an abstract deity, and consequently, they seek tangible connections. A representative idol, by virtue of a physical presence which a person can control, allows a person to delude himself that he has assured his future security. Once he creates the idol, even if for intellectual and spiritual reasons, the next tendency is to project his base physical desires onto it. That is why ancient pagan cults featured defecation and other instinctual physical acts. At a result, a person becomes even further removed from God, since his instinctual nature overwhelms his intellectual faculty.

When God told Moses on the mountain that the people had made a Golden Calf, Moses had hoped the corruption was only intellectual and that he might be able to effect their repentance through a more profound attachment to the Torah. The divinely crafted Tablets would spark an awakened involvement. But when he saw the dancing and the orgiastic revelry, he knew the corruption was deeper than the misguided search for security. The Tablets themselves stood to become another physical icon, and Moses had no choice but to shatter them.

v. *The Semblance of Evil*

AVING FOUND FAVOR WITH GOD, MOSES NOW ASKS (33:13), "Please make Your ways known to me." And God replies (33:23), "And I will remove My hand, and you will see My back, but My countenance will not be seen."

What ways did Moses want to be taught? The Talmud explains (*Berachos* 7a) that he wanted to understand how divine justice and providence interfaced with free will. In the language of our Sages, why do the wicked sometimes prosper while the righteous suffer?

Explaining God's justice, one of the thorniest issues in religious philosophy, is a topic discussed extensively in the Bible, Talmud and rabbinic writings.

A related passage in the Talmud (*Berachos* 60b) provides a useful framework in which to view this issue. The Talmud seeks Scriptural support for the requirement to bless God when bad things happen, just as we must bless Him when good things happen. Four opinions are given.

Rabbi Levi quotes (*Psalms* 101:1), "Kindness and justice, I will sing to God." In other words, I will sing not only when I receive kindness but even when facing judgment.

Rabbi Shmuel bar Nachmani quotes (*Psalms* 56:11), "With God I will praise [with the] word; with the Lord, I will praise [with the] word." I will praise God (the Tetragrammaton, the Name signifying the Attribute of Mercy), provider of benevolence. I will even praise the Lord (Elo-him, the Name signifying the Attribute of Strict Justice), sender of tribulation.

Rabbi Tanchum quotes (*Psalms* 116:13), "I will raise a cup of salvation and invoke God's Name. Although I encounter affliction and grief, I will call out God's Name."

The Rabbis quote (*Job* 1:21), "God has given, God has taken away, may the Name of God be blessed."

It is quite possible that there is no fundamental dispute among these Sages of the Talmud, that each is addressing a different aspect of the same phenomenon (*mar amar chada u'mar amar chada velo p'ligi*). With respect to God's providence, we can categorize unfortunate life-events in three ways — how we view God's actions, how we view God's relationship to us as a result of those actions and how we react to them. The first three views cited in the Talmud correspond to these three perspectives.

Rabbi Levi states we must bless God regardless of whether we see His actions as kindness or justice. Rabbi Shmuel bar

Nachmani states we must bless Him regardless of whether we perceive Him as a compassionate or a strict judge. Finally, Rabbi Tanchum's verse proves we must bless Him regardless of whether our responsive emotional state is joyous or sad and grief-stricken. The Rabbis, based on the Book of Job, transcend the principles of the first three. They endorse a type of surrender to the Omniscient One, for man is incapable of forming any judgment other than that God is the source of all "giving and taking."

The Talmud concludes the discussion with an anecdote. Encamped for the night outside a town where he could find no lodging, Rabbi Akiva has the seeming misfortune of successively losing his candle, rooster and donkey. *"Kol mah de'avid Rachmana letava avid,"* he reassures himself. "Everything God does is for the good." The following morning, he discovers that raiders had ransacked the town; his life was saved by the loss of his light, rooster and donkey, any of which might have betrayed his presence nearby.

Upon consideration, we can find allusions to the basic realms of human activity — physical, emotional and intellectual — in Rabbi Akiva's three losses. The donkey represents the physical world; the word for donkey, *chamor*, is cognate with *chomer*, material substance. The candle represents the intellect. The rooster, a winged creature of the heavens tethered to the earth, represents the emotional heart; it is there, our Sages say, that the lifelong battle between the intellect and the earthly instincts rages.

Although Rabbi Akiva could have initially perceived these occurrences as misfortunes, he remained confident despite the veil that obscured the "good" in the inconvenient events while they were occurring.

Appropriately, after the story of Rabbi Akiva, his disciple Rabbi Meir comments, "Man should limit his words before God." The interpretation of this may be that man should not excessively complain or petition God, since he may unwittingly be asking to change a providence already perfectly tailored for his ultimate good.

This then is the philosophical answer to the puzzle of our suffering when introspection reveals no immediate explanation. Since we do not have the Creator's infinite knowledge, we are not qualified to draw final conclusions about difficult times.

God's final response to Job's suffering underscores this point (*Job* 38:4,12; 40:8). "Where were you when I laid the Earth's foundation? Tell Me if you know understanding ... Did you ever in your life command the morning or teach dawn its place, to grasp the edges of the Earth and shake the wicked from it? ... Will you discredit My judgment? Will you declare Me wrong in order to make yourself right?"

We, in our ignorance, are only left to bless God for the bad as well as the good, secure only in our faith that all God does is for the good.

Rabbi Akiva's attitude toward suffering is further evident in a famous passage in the Talmud (*Makkos* 24a). While walking in Jerusalem, the Rabbis and Rabbi Akiva heard the rumble of Roman legions and saw the ruins of the Temple Mount. The Rabbis wept bitterly, but Rabbi Akiva laughed. As the ensuing conversation reveals, the Rabbis were focused on the present calamity, while Rabbi Akiva saw the tragic events as another step in the fulfillment of the prophecies that promised to bring the Jewish people from their present nadir to the zenith of triumphant redemption.

These different perspectives are actually manifest in the different words they use for "why" in their questions. Rabbi Akiva asked the Rabbis, "Why (*mipnei mah*) do you cry?" But the Rabbis asked Rabbi Akiva, "Why (*lamah*) do you laugh?" Rabbi Akiva used the words *mipnei mah*, literally "in the face of what," because he knew their reaction was related to the awful present they faced. The Rabbis, on the other hand, used the word *lamah*, literally "toward what," because they understood that Rabbi

Akiva's laughter could only be caused by his vision of the future.

Incidentally, the appearance of this story in Tractate *Makkos* is illuminating. According to Rav Tzadok HaKohen, our Sages judiciously placed the Aggadic passages in tractates appropriate to their themes. The theme of *Makkos* is rehabilitation through punishment. The story about the punishment that has befallen the Jewish people also bears the implicit promise that it would result in their rehabilitation and redemption through exile and suffering.

פָּרָשַׁת וַיַּקְהֵל
Parashas Vayakhel

i. *The Paradox of Fire*

FTER MOSES STERNLY WARNS THE JEWISH PEOPLE TO refrain from forbidden labors on the Sabbath, he singles out one of these labors for special mention (35:3). "Do not light a fire in all your dwelling places on the Sabbath day."

Why is the prohibition against lighting a fire (*hav'arah*) extracted from the collective mention of the 39 forbidden labors?

The Talmud (*Shabbos* 70a) cites two views. According to one it is paradigmatic, to show that each individual labor is a distinct violation (*hav'arah lechalek yatza*). According to the other view, the differentiation of labors is derived elsewhere. The prohibition against lighting a fire sets it apart from the other labors and downgrades it from being a capital offense (*hav'arah lelav yatza*).

What are the underlying principles of this dispute?

Let us first consider the view that *hav'arah lechalek yatza*. Why would ignition be singled out as the paradigm for a self-standing forbidden labor? Is it because ignition is the archetypal labor? If this is so, then it would be diametrically opposed to the view that *lelav yatza* that sees ignition as less severe and hence somehow inferior to other labors. This is highly unlikely, since the Talmud eschews *sevaros hafuchos*, diametrically opposed views; a dispute is more likely to center over shades of gray than black and white.

According to Rabbeinu Bachya and other commentators, the forbidden labors mirror the creative activities by which God created the universe, so to speak. Accordingly, our cessation from labor on the Sabbath is a potent reminder that God rested from creation on the seventh day. Elsewhere, however, the Midrash states that fire was first created by Adam at the conclusion of the first Sabbath, one day after he himself was created. Ignition, then, is the one forbidden labor representing an activity specific to mankind that does not reflect any of God's acts in creation.

At the conclusion of creation, the Torah records (*Genesis* 2:3), "And He sanctified [the Sabbath], because He ceased from all His labors that God created to do." Our Sages comment that the verb "to do" (*laasos*) refers to the work God left unfinished for mankind to complete. Man, through his moral choices, may become a partner in creation by causing it to resonate with the knowledge of God; it is within his power to unleash or actualize the potential of creation. Ignition, which is essentially the release of the potential energy locked in the chemical bonds of matter, is the labor most closely associated with the specific purpose and creative power of mankind.

We can now discern the dual nature of the forbidden labor of ignition. On the one hand, it represents the teleological aim of all the acts of creation. As such, it is the archetypal labor; the first view sees it as representative of all the other labors (*lechalek yatza*). On the other hand, it is the one labor that, according to the Midrash, does not reflect God's handiwork; it is rather man's specific labor. From this perspective, it is inferior to the other labors; the second view considers its particular mention as an indication that it alone is not a capital offense (*lelav yatza*).

ii. God's Dual Kingship

SHACHARIS, OUR DAILY MORNING PRAYER, CONCLUDES each day with a different chapter from Psalms that reflects an aspect of creation associated with that particular day of the week. On Friday, we recite Psalm 93 (*Hashem Malach*), which describes the glory of God's kingship. According to the Talmud (*Rosh Hashanah* 31a), it implies that man, a creature singularly equipped to laud God's handiwork and sovereignty, came into existence at the end of the sixth day.

On the Sabbath, in the evening and in the morning, we recite Psalm 92 (*Mizmor Shir L'Yom HaShabbos*), which anticipates the revelation of the ultimate justice of God's guiding hand in history; by analogy, we experience salvation from weekly toil when we observe the Sabbath faithfully. Then we again read Psalm 93.

We may wonder why the order of these two psalms is reversed. If Psalm 93 reflects the theme of the sixth day, shouldn't it have been placed before Psalm 92, which reflects the theme of the Sabbath?

Man encounters God's sovereignty on two levels, theoretical and experiential. He may contemplate and theorize intellectually that God wants man to recognize His sovereignty; this is man of the sixth day. He may also experience His sovereignty within the framework of Sabbath observance; he recognizes that God's providential guidance, although often unseen, accompanies us throughout the six days of the week or by extension the six millennia of history. Both in the Messianic era and to a degree on the Sabbath, we recognize His dominion increasingly as we become partners in its revelation. In this sense, the psalm of God's sovereignty is an outgrowth of the Sabbath psalm.

פרשת פקודי
Parashas Pekudei

i. The Message of
Monotonous Repetition

EIGHTEEN TIMES IN THIS *PARASHAH*, THE TORAH ASSURES us that "the people of Israel did everything God commanded Moses, so did they do." What is the purpose of this repetitive emphasis on obedience? Would we have thought otherwise?

This *parashah* also raises questions about the divine "literary style" of the Author. *Parashas Terumah* and *Parashas Vayakhel* already describe the plan of the construction of the Mishkan in painstaking detail. Why then was it necessary to repeat all the details with regard to the actual construction and installation in *Parashas Pikudei*? Why wasn't it enough to write that everything was done according to plan?

The same questions arise in *Parashas Nasso* (Numbers 7:11ff) regarding the sacrifices of the tribal princes following the construction of the *Mishkan*. On twelve successive days, one after the other of the tribal princes brought their offerings, all of which were identical, yet the Torah expends seventy-eight verses to describe them twelve times. Why the monotonous repetition? Why didn't the Torah simply describe the first day's offering and then tell us that all the rest were identical?

It is the nature of a human being to want to feel special and outstanding, especially in an enterprise of eternal significance. It would have been natural for anyone bringing an offering or donation to the *Mishkan* to seek some individual expression, to do something that distinctly identified him as the donor and set him apart.

Nonetheless, as the eighteen repetitive verses demonstrated, the Jewish people disregarded their own inclinations and followed God's command faithfully. They were not trying to mold their religious worship to their own desires and personalities, but rather, they were clinging to the divine instruction. The tribal princes as well sought no expression of their own individuality in their offerings, as the seventy-eight repetitive verses demonstrated.

The Torah, in its inimitable style, allows us to experience a bit of the greatness of these people. If we are already impatient with the repetitiveness after a few minutes of reading these verses, we can well imagine the feelings of those whose obedient acts allowed for no creativity or expression of their individuality. And they still complied wholeheartedly and joyously with the divine will.

ii. *A Chariot in the Wings*

HE BOOK OF EXODUS, TO WHICH THE RAMBAN REFERS AS the Book of Redemption, concludes with the construction of the *Mishkan*, the fitting culmination of the Exodus redemption. It is the dwelling place of the Divine

Presence, the consecrated conduit for greater awareness and knowledge of God.

Redemption is also a theme that appears in the first blessing of the *Shemoneh Esrei*, "[God] remembers the kindness of the forefathers and brings a redeemer." Why is this idea expressed in the present tense? In view of the as yet unfulfilled promise of redemption, wouldn't it have been more appropriate to say, "He will bring a redeemer"?

The language of the blessing seems to teach that God "brings a redeemer" in every generation. He prepares the savior, but our own behavior impedes his revelation. The chariot of our redemption is already waiting in the wings, so to speak, until we are deemed worthy.

Just as we await the Messiah, he also awaits us.